China's Housing Reform and Outcomes

CHINA'S HOUSING REFORM AND OUTCOMES

Edited by

Joyce Yanyun Man

LINCOLN INSTITUTE OF LAND POLICY

CAMBRIDGE, MASSACHUSETTS

Library of Congress Cataloging-in-Publication Data

China's housing reform and outcomes / edited by Joyce Yanyun Man.
     p. cm.
  Includes index.
  ISBN 978-1-55844-211-5
  1. Housing policy—China. 2. Housing—China. I. Yanyun Man, Joyce.
  HD7368.A3.D563 2011
  363.5'5610951—dc22   2010041127

Designed by Westchester Book Services

Composed in Minion Pro by Westchester Book Services in Danbury, Connecticut. Printed and bound by Puritan Press, Inc., in Hollis, New Hampshire.

♻ The paper is Rolland Enviro 100, an acid-free, 100 percent recycled sheet.

MANUFACTURED IN THE UNITED STATES OF AMERICA

Contents

Comparative Studies of Housing Policy and Implications for China

Illustrations

FIGURES

BOX

Foreword

Many observers and analysts are familiar with the remarkable growth of China's economy, its market-oriented reforms, and the large investments from both domestic and foreign sources that have taken place in the past 30 years. Less known, however, is how these economic changes have profoundly affected China's housing market. For example, China now represents the world's largest construction market in terms of built space, adding over 2 billion square meters of floor area annually—nearly half the global total. About half of China's annual constructed space is residential, which is divided about evenly between urban and rural housing.

This volume provides background and explanations about the causes and consequences of China's boom in residential construction, and it reviews how some well-established and ongoing trends are likely to impact China's housing sector in coming years. The expected demographic shifts and growth in urban populations suggest that the high rate of change in the housing sector will continue.

Since China's population has increased by about a third in the last three decades—from 1.0 billion in 1982 to an estimated 1.33 billion today—some of the growth in housing construction obviously results from this population growth. However, the more significant factor driving residential construction has been the dramatic rise in housing standards in terms of residential space per capita. From 1978 to 2007, residential space per capita quadrupled in urban areas (from 6.7 square meters to 28.3 square meters), and tripled in rural areas (from 9.4 square meters to about 29 square meters). China's per capita floor area now exceeds the averages in Japan and Europe, but this is unlikely to expand much beyond current levels.

Two major housing reforms in the past three decades have transformed China's housing market. The 1988 reforms fostered the privatization of housing, and much of the stock of rental housing was sold to employees of public enterprises at low prices. The 1998 reforms ended enterprise-supplied housing and moved to comprehensive market-based housing provision.

In recent years housing prices have risen much faster than incomes, making housing unaffordable for many. The government has taken steps to moderate housing prices by raising mortgage interest rates, increasing down payment requirements, taxing short-term capital gains from real estate, and constraining household purchases of multiple dwellings. The rapid rise in housing prices indicates that some recent housing demand has been speculative, resulting in urban vacancy rates that may be well above those required for a healthy housing market. However, documenting this is difficult because little data on urban vacancy rates are available.

Looking ahead, at least two major challenges face China's housing market. The first is the continuing high rates of migration from rural to urban areas; it is projected that 15 million migrants annually will move from the countryside to the cities. This flow will maintain demand for urban housing in the next decade or two and will moderate demand for rural housing. The second challenge is the aging of the population; the share of China's population over 65—7.7 percent in 2009—is projected to rise to 11.8 percent in 2020 and 24 percent in 2050. Currently, 70 percent of the elderly live in rural areas, but that share will decline as urbanization increases. The impact of aging on housing markets is complex, leading to both a rise in the demand for specialized housing for the elderly, and a likely decrease in household size as the surviving elderly add to the number of single person households.

These challenges and others are explored in this volume, which contains essays by scholars who specialize in China's housing market. Many of the chapters are empirical, drawing on household surveys and public data related to housing. The volume makes clear that the dynamism of the housing sector in China will continue in coming decades, while posing many policy challenges to public authorities at all levels of government.

GREGORY K. INGRAM
President and CEO
Lincoln Institute of Land Policy

Housing Policy Reform
in China

Housing Policy and Housing Markets: Trends, Patterns, and Affordability

JOYCE YANYUN MAN, SIQI ZHENG, AND RONGRONG REN

Since 1978, when the economic reform took place, China's housing policy has experienced dramatic changes. The privatization of public housing and reliance on the market for housing supply in the late 1990s, as opposed to the socialistic housing allocation system, have led to profound changes in housing distribution and consumption in urban China. This has greatly affected social and economic life. The housing reform in 1998 totally abandoned the old system of linking housing distribution with employment units. The housing sector has become a significant segment of economic activity and has provided a sizable tax base for the Chinese government. The housing conditions of urban residents, whose floor area per capita increased from 6.7 square meters in 1978 to 28.3 square meters in 2007, have greatly improved (Zheng, Man, and Ren 2009). Despite the success of the housing reform, the increase in prices and the consequent affordability problem in many cities have posed enormous challenges for the Chinese government, at both the central and local levels. In order to address issues related to housing markets and housing policies in China, this chapter provides an overview of the evolution of China's urban housing system and land market developments.

Evolution of the Urban Housing System

China's urban housing policies have experienced drastic changes since 1949. Prior to 1978, the Chinese government carried out a policy of nationalizing private housing and allocating public housing through work units under the central planning system. Most urban land was state owned, and governments monopolized all land transactions. Chinese government directly controlled the production, financing, allocation, operation, and pricing of urban housing through the work units of employees. Housing was allocated largely based on seniority, merits, and needs, and employees were required to pay heavily subsidized rent that was so low in most cases that it was not adequate to cover maintenance costs, let alone the construction of the housing (Wang and Murie 1996; Zhou and Logan 1996; Wu 1996). Home ownership and private property rights had virtually vanished prior to the economic reform that began in 1978. The consequences of such socialist housing policies were low investment in the housing sector, a chronic shortage of urban housing, substandard quality of housing, and poor living conditions for most urban residents.

Since 1978, when the transition from the centrally planned economy to a market-based system began, the housing reform has been at the top of the Chinese central government's agenda. Initially, the government restored private property rights by returning confiscated or nationalized private housing to the previous owners. Then it started to encourage urban residents to share housing costs by gradually increasing the rent they paid for public housing.

Since the 1980s the housing reform has gone through three stages. Prior to 1993, the initial stage of the reform was on a trial basis, with many experiments and pilot projects in different areas and regions. In 1988, the Chinese government introduced a nationwide reform starting the commercialization and privatization of urban public housing to encourage home ownership. A large amount of public rental housing was sold to employees in work units or *danwei* at very low prices.

The second stage of housing reform between 1993 and 1997 focused on the restructuring of housing construction, and on finance, management, and distribution systems. The work unit or *danwei* was still allowed to participate in housing construction and distribution to their employees. At the same time, the Chinese government encouraged the development of housing markets for high income groups, and subsidized the supply of the commercial housing for the middle- and low-income families. The Chinese government also allowed the private sector to participate in housing construction and development. As a result, the nature of housing was transformed from public goods and services, as a part of the social welfare package enjoyed by employed urban residents, to commodities that were privately owned and largely provided by the private sector, with rights to be traded in the market.

Starting in 1998, the third stage of the housing reform terminated welfare-based housing allocation and established a market-based system of housing provision. The State Council Document No. 23, issued in 1998, finally terminated direct public housing distribution to workers, the commonly known *danwei* housing system, and introduced cash subsidies for housing to newcomers entering the urban workforce. Since then, the direct distribution of housing through the work-unit system was abandoned, and urban residents relied upon the market for housing (Wang 2000; Wang and Murie 2000). The government also provided subsidized housing or public rental housing to selected low- and middle- income families and relied on the market-oriented commercial housing to meet the needs of higher income groups with access to mortgage financing. As a result, a vigorous urban housing market developed. Employers were allowed to offer housing subsidies to their new employees but could not involve themselves directly in housing construction, distribution, or management.

Since 2005, with urban housing prices skyrocketing, housing affordability has become an issue. Chinese governments have been called upon to increase the provision of affordable housing to middle- and low-income households. They have also attempted to stabilize urban housing prices, discourage speculative behavior of home buyers, and reduce the excessive and bad lending practices of state-owned banks and the possible financial risks associated with the housing sectors.

Housing Market Development Trends

The development of China's housing markets was accompanied by rapid economic growth during the period between 1999 and 2010, when both the gross domestic product (GDP) and urban household disposable income experienced an annual growth rate of about 10 percent on average. The rapid urbanization, from about 20 percent of the total population living in urban areas in the early 1980s to nearly 45 percent in 2007, was also a driving force behind the fast growth of housing markets in urban areas. In this section, the trends of housing market development with respect to housing supply, housing transactions, and housing prices are discussed; due to data limitations, the discussion focuses on new residential housing markets instead of housing stock.

Land Markets and Land Supply

Development of the housing market in China in the past decade has been fueled by the drastic increase in land supply by central and subnational governments. The central government is determined to stimulate economic growth by developing the real estate market and construction sectors. More land has been provided for the construction of residential and commercial property; home ownership is encouraged as a national strategy for economic growth; and the Chinese government has begun to welcome and facilitate the development of a middle class under Deng Xiao Ping's slogan "Getting rich is glorious."

In addition, the big fiscal gap between the expenditure assignment and revenue assignment of most local governments after the 1994 tax reform has forced local governments to seek other revenue sources. In the late 1990s local governments started to collect fees from land leasing, commonly known as land transfer fees, to finance public goods and services, as mandated by the central government.

In anticipation of great profits in the housing sector, a growing number of companies, both state and privately owned, have been entering the real estate market. The reorientation of China's land policy and subsequently booming land markets have contributed to the breathtaking growth of the real estate market. According to the *China Land and Resources Almanac* (2008), the quantity of land transferred for urban use increased at an average annual rate of 22.8 percent during the period from 1999 to 2007. Not surprisingly, the fees collected from land leasing by local governments also grew, at an annual rate of 31.29 percent on average during this period (Man 2010). Investment in land development experienced double-digit growth every year except 2004 between 2000 and 2007. The increased supply of land led to the rapid growth of the housing supply.

Housing Supply

During the period from 1999 to 2007, investment in real estate development increased by 21.5 percent annually, on average, while investment in residential housing development increased by 22.9 percent annually. The floor area of new construction has also increased significantly. For example, in 1999, there was only 188 million square meters of newly built floor area. Since then the number has increased every year, amounting to 788 million square meters in 2007, an increase of 320 percent (*China Statistical Yearbook 2008*).

Housing Sales and Prices

The boom in land supply and real estate investment and the consequent increase in the floor area of new construction demonstrate supply-side forces and policies. But the demand for housing is reflected in the housing transactions and the quantity of housing consumption. The total square meters of sold housing space increased from 130 million in 1999 to 701 million in 2007, an increase of 439 percent, indicating a strong demand for housing and the rapid development of a real estate market.

Although the total value of housing transactions increased significantly during the period between 1999 and 2007, the housing price per square meter did not experience a similar increase between 1999 and 2004. Starting in 2004, however, it enjoyed a double-digit increase, with a growth rate of 18.7 percent.

Patterns of Urban Housing Consumption

The National Bureau of Statistics of China (NBS) conducted the Large-Sample Urban Household Surveys in 2007 and 2010, each of which covered more than 600 cities. The data set from the survey is unique because it reveals the condition of all housing stocks in China instead of only new construction. For 2010, we studied 265 prefecture-level cities, and analyzed various housing consumption characteristics, including dwelling size, property type and tenure structure, owner-occupancy rate, and housing value. However, the survey covered only formal housing in urban areas; informal housing, such as temporary dwellings, villages in cities, and construction site shelters that are often occupied by migrant workers and low-income people, were not included. Interpretation of the findings based on the survey needs to be put within this context.

Home Ownership Rate

Home ownership rate is an important measure of the condition of the housing market. We follow the international standard by defining the home ownership rate as the ratio of owner-occupied housing units to total housing units. Based on the Large-Sample Urban Household Survey data, we found that the owner-occupied home ownership rate reached 82.3 percent in 2007 and rose to 84.3 percent in 2010. As table 1.1 shows, this figure varied widely across cities. Among the 265 prefecture-level cities in our sample, the owner-occupied home ownership rates ranged from 34.8 percent to 97.8 percent. But a majority of the sample cities (about 69.1 percent) had an owner-occupied home ownership rate exceeding the national level of 84.3 percent.

Table 1.1 reveals that the average rate of owner-occupied housing for the four largest municipalities in China was 77.1 percent, lower than the provincial capital cities (79.9 percent) and the prefecture-level cities (86.4 percent). The rate of

TABLE 1.1

Owner-Occupied Home Ownership Rate by City Type and Region, 2010

Regions	Owner-Occupied Rate (%)	Region	Owner-Occupied Rate (%)
Municipalities	77.1	East	81.6
Capital cities	79.9	West	80.5
Prefecture-level cities	86.4	Central	85.0
		Northeast	85.7
National average	84.3		

SOURCE: Calculated by authors based upon National Bureau of Statistics of China, Large-Sample Urban Household Survey, 2010.

TABLE 1.2

Owner-Occupied Home Ownership Rate by Income Group in 2007 and 2010

Income Group	Owner-Occupied Home Ownership Rate (%)		Average Floor Area (square meters)
	2007	2010	2007
Lowest 10%	72.9	79.3	67.8
2nd 10%	77.6	80.3	72.2
3rd 20%	80.5	81.2	77.5
4th 20%	83.5	83.7	83.6
5th 20%	86.0	83.6	89.6
6th 10%	86.2	85.5	96.3
Highest 10%	87.4	88.5	107.3
National average	82.3	84.3	84.5

SOURCE: Calculated by authors based upon National Bureau of Statistics of China, Large-Sample Urban Household Survey, 2007 and 2010.

owner-occupied home ownership was lower in the east and northeast regions than in the west and central regions. It may be that housing costs in the big cities and along the east coast affect the owner-occupied ownership rate in the respective areas.

It is not surprising that, as in many other countries, owner-occupied home ownership in China is highly correlated with household income. Table 1.2 reveals that among the seven income groups defined by China's National Bureau of Statistics, the rate of owner-occupied home ownership for the lowest-income group was 79.3 percent, while the highest-income group had an 88.5 percent rate, about 9.2 percentage points higher. The middle-income group had an 84.5 percent rate, about 0.2 percentage points higher than the national average. (By comparison, the American home ownership rate, according to the U.S. Census Bureau in 2000, was 66.2 percent.) This suggests that the Chinese housing reform that started in 1980 has resulted in a higher owner-occupied home ownership rate.

Quantity of Housing Consumption

In addition to the home ownership rate, the quality and quantity of housing consumption can reflect the condition of the housing market. According to the 2007 and the 2010 surveys, the average floor area of a dwelling is 84.5 square meters per household in 2007 and 91.9 square meters per household in 2010, equivalent to 63.4 and 68.9 square meters of usable living floor area per household respectively. Based on an average family size of 2.98 people per household in 2007, it can be calculated that the average floor area and the usable floor area per capita is 28.3 square meters and 21.3 square meters, respectively. This is consistent with the report of the *China Statistical Yearbook* that the per capita residential floor area was 26.1 and 27.1 square meters in 2005 and 2006, respectively. But by 2010, the per capita average floor area of a dwelling had reached 31.7 square meters, up by 3.4 square meters within three years, suggesting a rapid increase in housing consumption by city dwellers in China.

Table 1.2 shows that in 2007 the lowest-income group occupied 67.8 square meters of floor area per household unit, on average, but the highest-income group of households consumed about 107.3 square meters per unit, on average, indicating a strong correlation between household income and the quantity of housing consumption.

The housing consumption of the lowest-income group, which had 67.8 square meters of floor area, or 50.9 square meters of usable living floor area, exceeds the consumption of the low- and middle-income groups in some countries such as Singapore. This indicates that the housing reform of the past 30 years has successfully eased the chronic problem of overcrowding in the formal housing market in Chinese urban areas. It demonstrates the effectiveness of the market-based approach, as compared with the central planning system, in increasing housing production and housing services to urban residents in China. But due to the data limitations, it does not reflect housing consumption and conditions in the informal markets for migrant workers and the mobile low-income population.

Housing Tenure Structure

Table 1.3 reports the property type and tenure structure of the housing stock, according to the 2010 Large-Sample Urban Household Survey. Market-oriented commercially provided commodity houses and rental houses account for 38.1 percent of total housing stock. Privatized state-owned houses account for about 28.8 percent of the total housing stock. Affordable housing subsidized by the government and state-owned public rental housing account for 3.4 percent and 5.8 percent, respectively, indicating inadequate government support for low-income households in the area of housing consumption.

Housing Market Value

The 2007 and the 2010 household surveys report the self-estimated housing value of each household. Based on those data, we calculated the estimated mean market value of all types of residential housing to be 445,000 yuan (US$65,000; see table 1.4). Calculated by mean floor area, the estimated value is 4,844 yuan per square meter. The housing market value varies by region and jurisdiction. Not surprisingly, the

TABLE 1.3

Property Type and Tenure Structure in 2010

Marketization	Market-Oriented Housing		Subsidized Housing				
Tenure Structure	Own	Rent	Own			Rent	
Property Type	Commercial House	Rental of Private House	Original Private House	Private House Obtained from Housing Reform	Economical and Comfortable Housing	Rental of Publicly Funded House	Other
Share of total housing stock (%)	31.7	6.5	20.5	28.8	3.4	5.8	3.4
Total (%)	38.1		58.4				3.4

SOURCE: Calculated by authors based upon National Bureau of Statistics of China, Large-Sample Urban Household Survey, 2010.

TABLE 1.4

Housing Value by City Type and Region in 2010

Regions	Housing Value (10,000 yuan)	Region	Housing Value (10,000 yuan)
Municipalities	85.90	East	69.20
Capital cities	43.70	West	25.50
Prefecture-level cities	28.00	Central	26.70
		Northeast	21.80
National average	44.5		

SOURCE: Calculated by authors based upon National Bureau of Statistics of China, Large-Sample Urban Household Survey, 2010.

four largest municipalities have an average of 859,000 yuan (US$126,324) estimated market value, followed by capital cities of 437,000 yuan (US$64,265) and prefecture-level cities of 280,000 yuan (US$41,176). But the estimated housing market value for the east region is more than twice that for the western, central and northeast regions, posing political challenges for assisting the poor in the big urban areas and east regions with their basic housing consumption.

In addition to the regional disparities in housing value, there also exist large variations in the market values of residential housing among different income groups. Table 1.5 reveals that the higher-income group, the higher estimated housing value, demonstrating a strong positive correlation between income and housing consumption in urban China. The highest 10 percent income group has a market value of 644,000 yuan (US$95,000) on average, about 130 percent higher than the national average of

TABLE 1.5

Housing Value by Income Group in 2007

Income Group	Market Value of Residential Housing (10,000 yuan)
Lowest 10%	13.0
2nd 10%	15.0
3rd 20%	18.6
4th 20%	22.7
5th 20%	32.1
6th 10%	41.4
Highest 10%	64.4
National average	28.1

SOURCE: Calculated by authors based upon National Bureau of Statistics of China, Large-Sample Urban Household Survey, 2007.

FIGURE 1.1

Housing Values by Housing Type

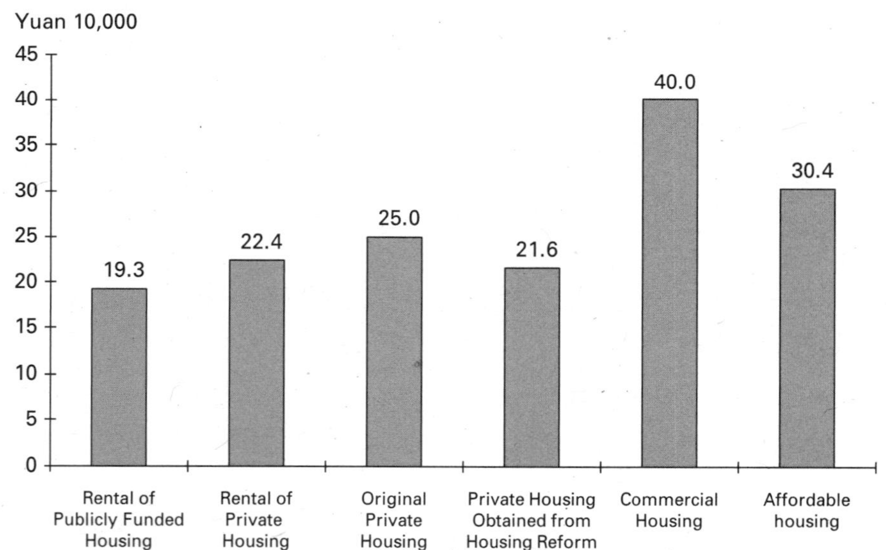

SOURCE: National Bureau of Statistics of China, Large-Sample Urban Household Survey, 2007 and 2010.

281,000 yuan (US$41,000). There is about a 400 percent difference in the market value of the housing of the richest and poorest 10 percent of urban households. This finding suggests that the wealth disparity among Chinese urban residents is alarmingly noticeable and problematic, and it may well be a side effect of the otherwise successful urban housing reform and the consequent rapid increase in housing prices in the past 10 years.

Housing value also varies by property type and housing tenure. The most expensive housing is commercial housing, which has an average price of 584,000 yuan (US$85,882), followed by affordable housing (466,000 yuan or US$68,529) and publicly funded rental housing (396,000 yuan or US$58,236).The price differences may well reflect the variations in housing characteristics such as building age, floor size, quality, and other attributes, as well as neighborhood characteristics (e.g., whether a community is gated and what services are available) and market demand (see figure 1.1).

Housing Affordability Among Chinese Cities

In the past few years, most Chinese cities have experienced a rise of housing prices to various degrees, which raises the problem of housing affordability as a major policy concern. Based on the Large-Sample Urban Household Survey in 2010, we employed the indicators of the housing price-to-income ratio (PIR) and the Housing Affordability Index (HAI) to evaluate housing affordability in 265 prefecture-level cities.

Housing Price-to-Income Ratio

The housing price-to-income ratio is the basic affordability measure for housing in a given area. It is generally the ratio of the median house price to the median family income. In the Global Urban Observatory Databases of UN-HABITAT (Flood 2001), PIR is one of the urban indicators. UN-HABITAT regards ratios of 3 to 5 as normal or satisfactory.

Demographia (2009) conducts an annual housing affordability survey that covers more than 200 markets in Australia, Canada, Ireland, New Zealand, the United Kingdom, and the United States. PIR is an important indicator that is commonly used to evaluate housing affordability across cities or countries. Housing affordability is rated in four categories based on the value of PIR: If PIR is equal to or greater than 5.1, the rating is "Severely Unaffordable"; if PIR ranges from 4.1 to 5.0, the rating is "Seriously Unaffordable"; if PIR ranges from 3.1 to 4.0, the rating is "Moderately Unaffordable"; and if PIR is equal to or below 3.0, the rating is "Affordable."

Table 1.6 shows Demographia's survey results for the third quarter of 2008. Among 265 cities surveyed, the highest value of PIR is 9.6, while the lowest is 1.8. Housing was rated as Severely Unaffordable in 64 cities. The PIR for the United States, from a sample of 175 cites surveyed, is 3.2, falling in the category of Affordable; only 22 percent of the surveyed cities are rated Seriously Unaffordable or Severely Unaffordable.

Based on the 2010 Large-Sample Urban Household Survey, we calculated PIR for China as a whole and for each of 265 prefecture-level cities in China. The results indicate that the median price-to-income ratio (PIR) nationwide in 2010 was 7.07, and the mean PIR for all the cities in China was 8.79. Both figures go beyond the normal or satisfactory level defined by UN-HABITAT. They fall in the category of Severely Unaffordable.

By studying the price-to-income ratio for 265 prefecture cities, we find that in 2007 the median PIR is 5.21, and the average PIR for the sample cities is 5.54. Among 265 prefecture-level cities, only 10 percent are affordable, with PIR below 3.0. Nearly 52 percent of all the prefecture-level cities in China are suffering from a Severely Unaffordable problem, and about 21 percent are Seriously Unaffordable. As table 1.6 shows, the situation in 2010 worsened. The number of cities that have

TABLE 1.6

Price-to-Income Ratio for Selected Countries and China

Nation	Affordable (<3.0)	Moderately Unaffordable (3.1–4.0)	Seriously Unaffordable (4.1–5.0)	Severely Unaffordable (>5.1)	Total Cities	Median PIR
Australia	0	0	3	24	27	6.0
Canada	10	15	5	4	34	3.5
Ireland	0	0	2	3	5	5.4
New Zealand	0	0	1	7	8	5.7
United Kingdom	0	0	6	10	16	5.2
United States	77	59	23	16	175	3.2
China	3	31	47	184	265	6.25
(2010)	(1.1%)	(11.7%)	(17.7%)	(69.4%)	(100%)	

SOURCES: Demographia, 2009, for all countries except China; the data for China were calculated by the author based on National Bureau of Statistics of China data sets.

the Severely Unaffordable problem increased to 184, 69.4 percent among all the 265 prefecture-level cities. In comparison, according to Demographia (2009), only 9 percent of 175 American cities had the rating of Severely Unaffordable; 13 percent of surveyed cities were Seriously Unaffordable, and about 44 percent were Affordable.

Housing Affordability Index

The Housing Affordability Index (HAI) has been published monthly by the National Association of Realtors of America (NAR) since 1981. The HAI assumes that borrowers make a 20 percent down payment and that the maximum mortgage payment is 25 percent of gross monthly income for the household. The HAI has a value of 100 when the median-income family has sufficient income to purchase a median-priced existing home. A higher index number indicates that more households can afford to purchase a home.

Based on the 2010 Large-Sample Urban Household Survey, we calculated HAI in 265 prefecture-level cities in China. The parameters used in the formula of HAI are as follows: The down payment is 30 percent, the maximum mortgage payment is 25 percent of gross monthly income for the household, the lending rate is 6.84 percent, and the length of maturity is 30 years. The HAI for 265 prefecture-level cities in 2010 was 70.7, much lower than 100, indicating severe unaffordability for the households living in those cities on average. From HAI calculation based on the 2007 Large-Sample Urban Household Survey, we found only 94 cities of the 256 had HAI values of more than 100. About 63.3 percent of the cities had a HAI below 100, indicating that the households in those cities with median income did not have sufficient income to purchase a median-price house in the city of their residence.

Major Findings

Prior to 1978, China nationalized the housing sector and eliminated property rights and housing markets in urban areas. Urban residents mostly rented housing from their work units as part of their benefits; housing shortages, poor quality, overcrowding, and underinvestment in the housing sector were among the main characteristics of the socialist urban housing system. After the economic reform started in 1978, China's urban housing policy shifted toward a market-oriented system, promoting property rights, home ownership, privatization of work-unit housing, and private investment in housing production and distribution. Since 1998, when the socialist housing distribution system was terminated, the housing market in China has grown rapidly, and housing-related sectors, including construction and steel industries, have become major contributors to the economic growth in China.

Analyses of the trends and patterns of housing markets during the period from 1999 to 2010 reveals that the housing boom in China was fueled by the significant increase in land supply and the growing land markets in China. The quantity of land transferred for urban uses experienced more than a 20 percent annual growth rate on average during this period, as did investment in land development in urban areas. The increased supply of land and rapid expansion of urban areas led to an increase in investment in residential housing development, at an annual growth rate of 20 percent on average. All of this led to a boom in housing construction, housing supply, and housing consumption.

Due to the urbanization and the rapid increase in disposable income, the floor area of new constructions grew by over 300 percent during the period from 1999 to 2010. But housing prices also increased considerably, especially after 2004. The price of housing per square meter nearly doubled between 1999 and 2010, which demonstrates a steady and strong demand for housing and the rapid development of a real estate market in China.

Based on the 2007 and the 2010 Large-Sample Household Surveys' data, we found that the home ownership rate in China, on average, increased from 82.3 percent in 2007 to 84.3 percent in 2010, exceeding the rate in many developed and developing countries in the world. Despite considerable variation in the home ownership rate across the 256 prefecture-level cities in our sample, a majority of the sample cities (about 69.1 percent) had an owner-occupied home ownership rate exceeding the national level. Almost all income groups have benefited from the privatization of housing sectors in China, albeit to different extents. Even the lowest 10th percentile of income groups enjoys nearly an 80 percent home ownership rate in 2010, suggesting the effectiveness and success of government policy in encouraging home ownership in urban China. The housing reform has also increased the floor area of housing construction and eased the chronic problem of overcrowding and poor living conditions of many urban residents.

The rapid development of China's housing market and drastically increased housing supply have not kept up with the housing demands, real or speculative, in urban areas, particularly in big cities and east coast regions. The housing price grew faster than the urban residents' disposable income in the past ten years. The median price-to-income ratio for China as a nation has put urban China in a category of "Severely Unaffordable" according to international standard. In only three out of 265 cities in this study is housing affordable to local residents. Nearly 70 percent of all the prefecture-level cities examined in our sample are "Severely Unaffordable." This finding is also supported by our calculation of the Housing Affordability

Index, indicating that urban households in many cities with median income do not have sufficient income to purchase a median-price existing house in the city of their residence. These results demonstrate that housing affordability has become a big problem for many Chinese homebuyers in urban areas, even though it is calculated using the housing stock data. If the newly constructed housing data is used, the housing affordability problem is more severe.

In conclusion, by analyzing quantitative data, this study produced a number of results and findings with respect to the current state of housing markets and affordability issues in the urban areas of China. It demonstrates that China's housing reform has resulted in a large increase in land supply, housing supply and consumption, home ownership rate, and the rapid development of housing markets. The successes of the housing reform have been accompanied, however, by the problems of inequality among income groups and regions in housing consumption, wealth, and affordability. Housing has become severely unaffordable in China, posing risks and challenges that may threaten the sustainability of economic growth and the stability of the society. This situation is contrary to China's goal of becoming a harmonious society and will be a focus of the Chinese government in its search for a sound housing policy.

This Volume

In 2007, a joint initiative created The Peking University–Lincoln Institute Center for Urban Development and Land Policy to give Lincoln Institute of Land Policy's China program a presence in China's political capital. This volume collects the proceedings and papers from the 2009 conference entitled "Housing Policy and Housing Markets in China" as well as some scholarly research funded by the joint center.

The thirteen chapters in this volume address four dimensions of housing policy and housing markets in urban China. Part 1 focuses on China's housing policy reform and outcomes in the past 30 years. Two chapters in this part review the transition of housing provision from a socialist welfare distribution system to a market-based system. The current state of housing markets and housing affordability is discussed in detail. The research shows that housing reform in China has had a positive impact in many respects but has resulted in some social and economic problems, as well. The interactions of land use, fiscal policy, and housing markets are discussed in part 2. The five empirical chapters link the housing market in China with the country's land use practices and its fiscal policy. The authors explore the effect of factors such as income, local taxes and expenditure, and employment and social security on the prices of and demand for housing, as well as the determinants of second home ownership in Chinese cities. Part 3 focuses exclusively on China's low-income housing policy, which is designed to provide assistance and support to middle- and low-income groups after housing prices experienced a rapid increase following the housing reform started in 1980. The outcomes of reform and the current challenges facing middle- and low-income groups and Chinese governments are evaluated in three chapters written from different perspectives. Each of the three chapters in part 4 takes a comparative approach to housing policy in China. The practice of low-income housing provision has precedents in many other countries, including developed countries like Britain and the United States, and developing countries. The authors draw implications from international experiences to determine what China can learn from the successes and mistakes of other countries, and what principles are appropriate to guide future housing reform and policy making in China.

This chapter provides a brief overview of the evolution of the housing reform in urban China and an analysis of the trends and patterns of China's land and housing markets during the housing reform. Affordability and equity issues are evaluated. This study finds that there have been significant increases in land supply, investment in real estate development, housing provision and consumption, and a high home ownership rate, indicating positive outcomes of the housing reform. The housing market in China has witnessed an increase in total square meters sold and a skyrocketing of housing prices, reflecting strong demand for housing. However, affordability has become an economic and social issue. Of the total housing stock, affordable housing only accounts for a very small portion, implying inadequate government support for low-income households. Further, based upon the calculation of Housing Affordability Index and the median price-to-income ratio, this suggests that China's housing falls into the category of being "severely or seriously unaffordable." China's housing reform has resulted in many positive changes, but it has also caused inequality among income groups and across regions. Government policy should correct the distortion of the original reform purposes.

In chapter 2, Ya Ping Wang looks at the distribution of benefits and losses, as well as the spatial stratification, as a result of the reform. He observes that the housing reform in China has resulted in a differentiation of residency based on socioeconomic status, with the poorer people concentrating in peripheral areas and government employees and economically advantaged people in the more expensive neighborhoods. This spatial pattern is a result of the privatization of previously government-provided housing. Professionals, managers, and civil servants have benefited the most from the housing reform, which is critical to maintaining the stability of the communist rule. Housing for the urban poor and low-income people in general has been neglected, and only recently has become a top priority on the policy agenda.

In chapter 3, Chow and Niu apply the standard theory of consumption to analyze the demand for and supply of China's urban housing. They find that the income elasticity of demand for urban housing in China is about 1.0, the price elasticity of demand 0.5–0.6, and the price elasticity of supply about 0.74. According to this calculation, the increases in housing prices are the result not of speculation, but rather of increased income based on the annual data from 1987 to 2006. The authors conclude that there was no housing bubble in the country during their sample period up to 2006.

Chapter 4, by Fu and Zheng, looks at the demand side of the housing market in China. They used data from a national large-scale urban household survey to estimate the income elasticity of housing demand for different population groups. The authors find that when housing prices increase with quality of life in a neighborhood, the income elasticity of spending on housing also increases. The study indicates that the low level of education and lack of social security of most migrants diminishes their demand for quality of life in the host cities. The authors recommend that in order to enhance the willingness of migrant workers to pay for urban housing and contribute more to domestic demand, policies are needed to improve employment and social security.

Logan, Fang, and Zhang investigate the distributive consequences of China's housing reform in chapter 5. They compare the dual tracks of the privatization of public housing and the development of the private housing sector. Rents and prices of public housing in China are of considerable variability and have been well below market prices. Using 2000 census data, their study estimates the housing subsidy received by renters and purchasers of public housing. It shows that the biggest winners in the housing reform are those who were favored in the previous system; based on such factors as residence status, education, and occupation, they are paying less for better housing by virtue of state subsidies.

Chapter 6, contributed by Huang and Yi, studies the patterns of second home ownership in Chinese cities. The authors argue that second home ownership in Chinese cities both shares similarities with and bears major differences from the experience in the West, due to the coexistence of increasingly mature housing markets and unique institutions from the socialist legacy. Using China's 2005 General Social Survey, the authors reveal that, as in the West, large and higher income households are more likely to own a second home. The *hukou* system is proved again to be important to second home ownership. Political status and work units are also important, as people with a high job rank and party membership are more likely to own a second home. Residents in municipalities and provincial capitals are less likely to own second homes, probably due to higher housing prices in large cities. The authors' findings provide important policy implications for future government decision making and housing reform in promoting efficiency and equality of resource allocation and housing provision.

In chapter 7, Man and Zheng analyze the effect of local taxes and public expenditure on residential property values, using data from over 200 Chinese cities. This study tests the Tiebout model in a country where local tax and expenditure structures are quite different from those in the United States. Their findings are nevertheless consistent with the prediction of the model: Local public services and tax liability affect the choice of residence by households in China. Controlling for other conditions, the value of residential properties has a significant positive relationship with local public expenditure and a negative correlation with taxes on land, property, and personal income in Chinese cities.

Chapter 8, by Deng and Fei, analyzes the development and performance of the nascent housing finance system in China. They point out that there is a dual-channel housing finance system in China: a policy-driven mechanism of the Housing Provident Fund, as well as commercial mortgage lending. All mortgage loans issued in China are adjustable rate mortgages without a cap. The number of default cases in China is quite small, and mortgage foreclosure is difficult to enforce. The authors conclude that stock market fluctuations and Chinese borrowers being "uncertainty averse," as well as the swift changes in related housing and finance policies and regulations all have an impact on mortgage borrowers' prepayment and default decisions.

Chapter 9 explores the intricate interactions between urban expansion, land conversion, and delivery of affordable housing in Chinese cities. Angel, Valdivia, and Lutzy selected Zhengzhou, a middle-sized city, as a case study. They found that although housing is adequate and different types of housing satisfy basic needs, housing built on land transacted at current market prices is not affordable for the majority of urban households in Zhengzhou. While urban villages provide a pragmatic solution to affordable housing for poor families, the current land conversion policy destroys this option. They present a radical recommendation that the conversion of cultivated land to urban land should not be restricted and villagers should be able to sell land directly to developers.

In chapter 10 Song asks how the presence of urban villages affects the local housing market. Using the city of Shenzhen as a case, this empirical study shows that most urbanizing villages are seen as disamenities by home owners nearby, but perceived positively by renters as a special type of affordable housing. Some urban villages have a higher level of establishment and are marketed toward "white-collar" workers. Such villages are more assimilated with the urban environment. The author believes that in the short run, the urban villages are an effective solution in providing affordable housing to rural migrants. In the long run, however, concentration of rural migrants, particularly those with lower income, in these villages may be the prelude to a new form of residential segregation in urban China. The author recommends a comprehensive approach that incorporates community development and economic development strategies.

Reingold and Xu review the policy and management of low-income housing in China in chapter 11. The authors compare it with similar programs in the United States along three dimensions: intergovernmental relations, rural-urban migration, and ethnic-regional conflict. The two countries have distinct political frameworks and social structures, and the housing programs work through different mechanisms. Nevertheless, drawing from the U.S. experience, the authors conclude that in order to minimize social disruption in low-income housing programs in China, a professional nonprofit sector is needed to represent the interests of the poor.

Chapter 12, by Jing, begins with the assumption that social policies and practices have been converging in the age of globalization. Therefore, analyzing the similarities and differences between the long-developed British social housing programs and China's recent social housing provision could shed light on the prospects for China's program. The author first reviews the history of the programs in Britain and China, then moves on to compare the physical features of social housing and the social profiles of tenants in both countries. She points out that some mistakes, such as placing priority on quantity rather than quality in low-income housing provision, seen before in Britain, are being repeated in China. Learning from the British experience, she cautions China against developing extremely large-scale peripheral social housing projects. Jing argues that voluntary groups, local communities, and private developers should be involved in such initiatives, rather than the government alone.

In chapter 13, Renaud examines the largest constraints and policy risks that can negatively affect the long-term development of China's housing and urban system. Dr. Renaud evaluates seven core areas of the development of Chinese housing markets: property rights and tenure, housing financing, taxation and subsidies, the supply of serviced urban land and infrastructure, land use, the organization of real estate, and the performance of central and local government. He cites experiences from other transitional economies, Latin American countries, and the United States to caution China against a myopic housing policy. He recommends that short-term actions to stimulate the economy should not distract from the long-term housing policy, and that an integrated safety net, including support in the areas of employment, education, health, and old-age security, is much more important than housing provision alone for low-income groups.

This book is a collection of studies done by international scholars and domestic researchers who specialize in the areas of urban and housing economics and policy, with interests in promoting the understanding of China's housing policy and markets. The information in this book is of interest to government officials and practitioners, academic researchers, students, and members of the general public who are concerned with government housing policy, market conditions related to the housing sector, and the strategic directions for building a harmonious and sustainable society beneficial to all residents in China. University instructors will find this book useful as a supplemental textbook for urban and real estate economics, policy analysis, and economic development courses.

REFERENCES

Demographia. 2009. The 5th Annual Demographia International Housing Affordability Survey. http://www.demographia.com/dhi.pdf.

Flood, Joe. 2001. Analysis of urban indicators. Global Urban Observatory Databases. UN-HABITAT. http://ww2.unhabitat.org/programmes/guo/guo_analysis.asp.

Man, Joyce Y. 2010. China's land public finance: Overview. PLC Research Brief. Beijing: Peking University–Lincoln Institute Center for Urban Development and Land Policy.

Ministry of Land and Resources. 2009. *China Land and Resources Almanac*. Beijing.

National Association of Realtors. Affordable Housing Real Estate Resource: Housing Affordability Index. http://www.realtor.org/wps/wcm/connect/725764004d02a073a8a7ee8d0a12d865/REL08Q4G.pdf?MOD=AJPERES&CACHEID=725764004d02a073a8a7ee8d0a12d865.

National Bureau of Statistics of China. 2008. *China statistical yearbook*. Beijing: China Statistics Press.

Wang, Ya Ping. 2000. The process of commercialization of urban housing in China. *Urban Studies* 33(6):971–990.

Wang, Ya Ping, and Alan Murie. 1996. The process of commercialisation of urban housing in China. *Urban Studies* 33(6):971–989.

——— 1999. Commercial housing development in urban China. *Urban Studies* 36(9):1475–1494.

———. 2000. Housing reform and its impacts on the urban poor in China. *Housing Studies* 15(6):845–864.

Wu, F. 1996. Changes in the structure of public housing provision in urban China. *Urban Studies* 33(9):1601–1627.

Zheng, Siqi, Joyce Man, and Rongrong Ren. 2009. The state of housing markets and affordability in urban China. PLC Working Paper. Beijing: Peking University–Lincoln Institute Center for Urban Development and Land Policy.

Zhou, M., and J. R. Logan. 1996. Market transition and the commodification of housing in urban China. *International Journal of Urban and Regional Research* 20(3):400–422.

Recent Housing Reform Practice in Chinese Cities: Social and Spatial Implications

2

YA PING WANG

The housing provision system has experienced many changes in Chinese cities over the past 60 years. Between 1949 and 1978, the pre-communist system based on private home ownership and rentals was gradually changed into a socialist welfare housing provision system. By the end of the 1970s, about 80 percent of urban residents lived in public-owned houses. Although this system followed basic socialist principles, it had many problems, including severe housing shortages, lack of investment, unequal and corrupted distribution, and inefficient management and maintenance (Wang and Murie 1996). To solve these problems, the government began to put forward reform policies to change the urban housing provision system beginning in the early 1980s. After 30 years of continuous reform, an urban housing market was established in all cities. The majority of urban residents now rely for housing on the market rather than the government or their employers. Most public housing units built under the old system have been sold to sitting tenants. The processes of housing development, allocation, distribution, exchange, and maintenance have been commercialized. A new housing investment and finance system has also been established. In the past, housing development was a major burden for the government and a drain on the public finance system. Now housing and related real estate development have become an important part of the property-led urbanization and one of the main pillars of the national and local economies.

Urban housing reform, however, does not solve all housing problems in cities. The market approach, on one hand, has brought significant improvement of the general living conditions in cities, especially among the rich and the emerging middle class; on the other hand, the inflated housing prices in cities have created an enormous affordability problem, particularly among the low-income people and the poor. It has become clear that housing reform policies from 1998 to 2006 have given too much emphasis to the market. The style and level of housing consumption were not very compatible with the development stage of the country and the income level of the majority of the urban population. Excessive waste (e.g., luxury cottages for the rich and second homes that were left empty most of the time) has created huge burdens on the environment. At the end of the 1970s, the housing shortage and inequality of access to housing in cities were important factors that threatened the legitimacy of the communist government. Currently, housing price inflation, affordability, and inequality are again causing instability in cities. Over the past several years, important policy adjustments have been made to correct the imbalance in the urban housing system. Greater attention has been paid and resources made available to develop social housing for low-income groups.

There is a rich literature on the early stage of housing reform in Chinese cities (Chen 1996; Chiu 1996; Huang 2004a; 2004b; Leaf 1997; Lee 2000; Li 2000a; 2000b; Logan, Bian, and Bian 1998; Wang 1992; 1995; 2000; 2001; 2003; 2004; 2007; Wang and Murie 1996; 1999b; 2000; Wu 1996; Zhang 1997; Zhou and Logan 1996), but there has been no systematic review of recent housing reform policies or evaluation of their social and spatial impacts. This chapter updates our understanding of the urban housing reform in Chinese cities and focuses on the impact of recent policies. It identifies the winners and losers of these policies and assesses their contributions to the spatial stratification of the fast-expanding urban areas. Discussion and analysis are based on recent fieldwork in several cities. Data sources include central and local government housing documents, official housing statistics, research reports, and other secondary materials published in Chinese.

Development of Housing Reform Policies

China has followed a pragmatic approach to housing reform. Throughout the 1980s, a series of reform programs were implemented and tested at various locations. These included experiments with the sale of new housing to urban residents at construction cost (1979–1981); experiments with the subsidized sale of new housing (1982–1985); and experiments with comprehensive housing reform (1986–1988). The publication, by the central government, of the document *Implementation Plan for a Gradual Housing System Reform in Cities and Towns* (State Council 1988; World Bank 1992) marked the turning point of housing reform from pilot tests and experiments in selected cities to overall implementation in urban areas. The plan aims to realize housing commercialization according to the principles of a socialist planned market economy. The plan was interrupted in 1989 by economic and political problems (Wang and Murie 1996).

The beginning of the 1990s was marked by further policy moves toward a market economy. In 1991, a major national housing reform conference was held in Beijing and issued the resolution *On Comprehensive Reform of the Urban Housing System,* compiled by the State Council's Housing Reform Steering Group (General Office of the State Council 1991). This document reinforced the 1988 implementation plan, and required all urban authorities to carry out housing reform. This resolution (and a 1993 policy document) led to the large-scale sale of existing public housing at very low prices. In late 1993, concern about the low prices of public housing led the government to suspend the housing reform program. Another important and comprehensive policy document on housing reform, *The Decision on Deepening the Urban Housing Reform,* was published in 1994 (Housing Reform Steering Group of the State Council 1994). Specific policies included changing the housing investment, management, and distribution systems and establishing

- a dual housing provision system;
  (a government-subsidized social housing supply providing economic and comfortable housing to middle- and low-income households, and a market housing supply for high-income families)
- a public and private housing savings system;
- housing insurance, finance, and loan systems that would enable both policy-oriented and commercial developments; and
- a healthy standardized and regulated market system of property exchange, repair, and management. (Wang and Murie 2000)

These policies were gradually implemented in all urban areas, formalizing several special arrangements to help urban households participate in the new housing market. The first important arrangement involved the establishment of a Housing Provident Fund system based on the Singapore model, through which the employer and employee each make a contribution to the employee's housing savings fund. The savings could be used only to purchase housing or for housing repairs until the employee retired. Other important changes included the introduction of subsidized commercial housing for low- and middle-income families. Central government loans and free land allocations were used as the main mechanisms for the development of affordable housing (the *anju,* or peaceful living, project, later renamed *jingji shiyong fang*—economic and comfortable housing).

Taken together, these policies resulted in important changes in housing construction, distribution, and management and significantly improved housing conditions in cities. These reforms, however, did not manage to separate housing from employment. House sales, rent increases, and setting up various housing funds were all done through the work unit that employed the person concerned. On one hand, work units sold their existing housing stock to employees at a heavily subsidized price; on the other hand, they continued their house-building program or purchased new housing from commercial developers at full market prices, then distributed them to employees for renting and privatization. Most commercially built housing during the early 1990s actually ended up in the old welfare system (Wang 2000).

The most important set of housing reform policies was introduced by the central government in July 1998 (State Council, 1998). These policies included three main objectives:

- To end direct housing distribution by employers and introduce housing cash subsidies to new and essential employees.
- To create a diversified housing supply system with state-supported affordable (low-cost) housing as the main form.
- To set up a new housing finance system to help developers and individuals with loans and mortgages.

The policies prescribed a model of an urban housing system based on home ownership. The housing requirements of public-sector employees in work units would be met directly through the housing market. To reduce commercial housing prices and support public-sector employees, affordable housing was to be built with government support. The government planned to make this type of housing accessible to most urban residents (around 70 percent). The higher-income households in urban areas (about 15 percent) would be encouraged to obtain high-standard commercial housing (*shangpin fang*) through the market; and poor urban families would be given subsidized social rental housing (*lianzu fang*) by their employers or the municipal government (State Council 1998). Social rental housing targets families that have a monthly per capita income below the municipal poverty line and floor space per person of less than the minimum standard set by municipal governments (e.g., 7 square meters in Beijing).

Considering China's development stage and the income level of the majority living in cities, the 1998 policies were appropriate. They aimed for a more equal and moderate level of housing consumption, and the government promised to maintain an important and active role in urban housing provision. Developments in the following years quickly led to a change in policy direction, however. First, there were dramatic increases in the urban population. In 1997, the urban population was at 394.5 million (31.9 percent of the total population). By the end of 2002, the urban population had reached 502.1 million (39.1 percent) (National Bureau of Statistics of China 2007). Although this population increase was mainly a result of rural to urban migration, and most newcomers often stayed in poor-quality private rental housing, the increase of over 100 million people in urban areas did have an important impact on the housing system. It put great pressure on the social housing and affordable housing supply. Second, there were large increases in salaries for mainstream urban residents. The average annual salary in urban areas in 1997 was 6,440 yuan. By 2002, that had nearly doubled, to 12,373 yuan. Salaries in the state sector and privately owned large companies grew particularly fast. This increased the division between the rich and the poor. Fast income growth among the rich made commercial housing accessible to a large group. Wealthier residents began to invest in larger houses or buy second homes.

The scale of personal income growth and the great demand for the more expensive commercial housing exceeded the expectations of the 1998 policy makers. The purchasing powers of some residents increased the demand for commercial housing and began to push up housing prices in large cities. In September 2003, a national conference on housing and the real estate industry was held in Beijing. A document issued by the State Council after the conference in effect changed the housing reform direction set in 1998 (State Council 2003). It made ordinary commercial housing the main urban housing provision system. There is, however, no clear definition for *ordinary commercial housing* at the national level. It was left to local housing authorities to make their own definition and decide on their support policies. This 2003 policy adjusted the seemingly unrealistic expectations for affordable housing and tried to slow the expansion of large and luxury houses. For various reasons, many local governments did not make a difference between ordinary commercial housing from other market housing; some of the special policies for "ordinary housing" were applied to other commercial housing. Some developers and investors artificially pushed up housing prices to make money. Ordinary residents, particularly middle- to low-income people, found it more and more difficult to get into the housing market. At the same time, the prospect of an urban property bubble began to threaten the general performance of the national economy. Table 2.1 lists the main housing policies in China.

Problems of Implementation

The 1998 housing reform policies, on one hand, reflected the experiences gained from early housing reform experiments, and on the other hand, were responses to the special global and national economic conditions at that time. Beginning in 1997, East Asian countries were in a severe financial crisis, which had serious impacts on China's economy. Export and international demands (the main engine of development in the 1990s) slowed dramatically, and GDP growth showed signs of decline for the first time since the early 1990s. China's central government tried to find ways to reduce the negative effects of this international crisis by increasing domestic and internal demands and consumption. Budgetary and monetary policies were put forward to create and foster new growth poles, or sectors. Housing and property development was identified as one such new economic sector, which policy makers believed could bring about demands in many other economic sectors, including construction materials, metals, chemicals, and manufacturing. Housing development was expected to create employment opportunities, increase investment, and accelerate consumption. It could create a large internal market with a fast input-output circle and make a major contribution to general economic growth.

The urban housing system at the time was, however, still modeled on the socialist welfare system, with public-sector employers playing a major role. Housing investment came mainly from public sources. Many urban residents were reluctant to spend their money on housing. This seriously prohibited housing development and consumption in cities. The 1998 policies made a big breakthrough and abolished the public provision system once and for all. This major step toward housing commercialization saw some immediate effects. In Beijing, for example, more than three-quarters of commercial houses were sold to employers and work units before 1998. Sales to individual families increased very quickly after 1998. By 2000, about 90 percent of new commercial houses were sold to individuals (Cheng 2006). Despite this positive effect, the overemphasis on urban housing development and reform sowed the seeds for many of the subsequent housing problems.

Housing Subsidies

Most purpose-built public houses were privatized during the 1990s, and no new work-unit housing was allowed. Housing subsidies became the most important direct contribution employers could give to their employees. The implementation of this policy was very slow. In many cities, detailed implementation plans were made only for the civil servants and public institutions financed directly by the government. Private and enterprise sectors, including state-owned enterprises (SOEs), were

Urban Housing System Changes and Reform Policies

Years	Main Policy Document	Policies and Orientations
Socialist Welfare Housing Provision: 1949–1977		
1949–1957	Various	Regulation of the private rental market, rent control, and confiscation of properties owned by warlords.
1958–1977	Various	Nationalization of properties owned by large landlords; development and distribution of public housing by the government through work units as a welfare service.
Reform Experiments with Commercialization: 1978–1993		
1978–1987	Various	Major period of expansion of public housing, particularly work-unit housing. Pilot urban housing experiments in selected cities, aimed to diversify the welfare housing provision by restoring private property rights and encouraging individuals to share housing costs.
1988	State Council 1988, Document No. 11	Turning point of housing reform from pilot experiments to comprehensive implementation in all urban areas, aimed to realize housing commercialization according to the principles of a socialist planned market economy. Reform policies included rent increases in the public sector coupled with housing subsidies and the sale of public housing.
1991	General Office of the State Council 1991, Document No. 73	Aimed at increasing the housing investment from different sources, focusing on rent reform in the public sector, encouraging sales of public housing, increasing housing construction.
1993	State Council 1993	Modified the 1991 strategy, giving priority to sales of public housing over rent reform. This led to the large-scale sale of existing public housing at very low prices.
Move from Welfare Provision to Housing Market: 1994–1998		
1994	State Council 1994, Document No. 43	For the first time, policy aimed to establish an urban housing market: to change the housing investment, management, and distribution systems and to establish a two-track housing provision system, with social housing for middle- and low-income households and commercial housing for high-income families.
1998	State Council 1998, Document No. 23	Ended direct housing distribution by employers and introduced housing cash subsidies to new and essential employees; created a diversified housing supply system with state-supported affordable (low-cost) housing as the main form.
Housing Market Formation: 1999–2006		
2003	State Council 2003, Document No. 18	Adjusted the affordable housing approach and promoted an extreme market system based on so-called ordinary commercial housing, in which the majority of the urban population would rely on the market.

(continued)

TABLE 2.1 *(continued)*

Years	Main Policy Document	Policies and Orientations
2005–2006	Various	Housing affordability problem emerged, particularly among low-income groups; housing problems began to cause social and economic instability in cities; policies focused mainly on stabilizing urban housing prices through taxation and land and planning policies.

Multiple Housing Provision Systems: Since 2007

Years	Main Policy Document	Policies and Orientations
2007	State Council 2007, Document No. 24	Adjusted to the extreme market approach and reemphasized the requirement of social housing provision.

encouraged to adopt policies designed for the administrative sector. In practice, not all private firms and SOEs attempted to apply this policy. The few that did were mainly in the more profitable sectors such as oil, finance, and insurance.

Housing subsidies offered by employers are an important cause of housing inequality in cities. Wealthy and powerful organizations and businesses could afford to issue sizable cash subsidies to their employees, while poor organizations and enterprises could give little housing support to their employees. Within the same organization, housing subsidies may have been offered to senior and essential staff, while junior and temporary staff were excluded (Wang 2000; Wang, Wang, and Bramley 2005). Housing subsidies were aimed at those who either had not benefited at all or had not benefited enough from public housing. In the past, because of housing shortages, some employees lived in work-unit housing, while others waited in the queue. Theoretically speaking, subsidies avoided this inequality. However, the level of subsidy was based mainly on office status, a key housing distribution factor in the prereform system. In practice, housing subsidies became an extra source of income to well-positioned managers and professionals. Though they enhanced the original inequality in housing consumption, subsidies did play an important role in the development of the urban housing market by earmarking a significant proportion of employment income for housing. They improved the purchasing power of many professional families.

Social Rental Housing

The progress of social rental housing has been very slow because there has been no clear source of funds to implement this policy. The central government sees the social housing provision as an important part of the social protection system, while many local authorities see subsidized rental housing as a temporary measure to solve a short-term problem and an unprofitable, resource-draining activity. For several years, local housing officials were engaged in discussion about the nature of social rental housing and local standards to separate those who were entitled to it from those who were not.

Beijing City had an early start on this. Policies were produced swiftly following the 1998 reform. Demonstration social rental houses were provided to some of the very poor families living in the city. In 2001, the housing authority carried out a survey among the 32,097 registered low-income and poor households in the city and identified a total of 21,876 families that required government support to improve their living conditions. Between 2001 and 2005, 4,391 families applied to the government for housing support; of those, 3,032 families received rent support, and 319 families moved into government-provided social housing (Beijing Municipal Construction Commission 2006). In 2005 the government carried out another survey, which identified 38,300 households living in overcrowded conditions (less than 7.5 square meters of floor space per person). By October 2007, only 5,831 families had applied for housing support (Beijing Municipal Construction Commission 2007). This was only 15 percent of the poor families identified through the survey. Obviously, this was far below the original target of 10–15 percent of the total population—well over 10 million. Many other cities had not taken any action on this for several years after the central policy was issued. Not many housing officials expect that the policy will cover 10–15 percent of the urban population. In most cities that have implemented this policy, fewer than 2 percent of households have actually received some kind of help. The nature of the help also shifted away from the direct public housing provision with a low rent; most municipal housing authorities preferred to provide cash subsidies to low-income households and allow them to find their own rental accommodations in the market.

Affordable Housing

The 1998 regulations stipulated that affordable housing should be the main type of housing in cities. As such it was to be made available to most public-sector employees, especially teachers, doctors, nurses, policemen, and low-level civil servants. However, this policy was found to be too ambitious and unrealistic. First, it was difficult to define "middle- to low-income" households. In some cities, as long as the purchasers were not obviously rich, they would be qualified to buy. In other cities, there were strong official objections to the affordable housing idea, because it reduces municipal income from land and other sources. Very few affordable housing developments were built (figure 2.1). Shanghai City, for example, started an affordable housing program only recently. Guangdong Province, where the urban housing market was well established and very dynamic, built few affordable houses (0.5 percent of 2006 completions). Western and inland provinces and regions built a higher proportion of affordable housing. In the Tibet Autonomous Region, for example, 84 percent of new housing was affordable; in Xingjiang, it was 36 percent.

Some cities divided the residents originally targeted for affordable housing into two groups: a low-income group (around 30 percent of the urban population above the urban poor), which would qualify for affordable housing; and a middle-income group, which would not qualify for affordable housing but would be given access to a new category of housing—*ordinary commercial housing*. While affordable housing development will receive the same level of government support as before (e.g., free land allocation, controlled development profits, and reduced government charges), ordinary commercial housing can benefit from reduced land use fees and

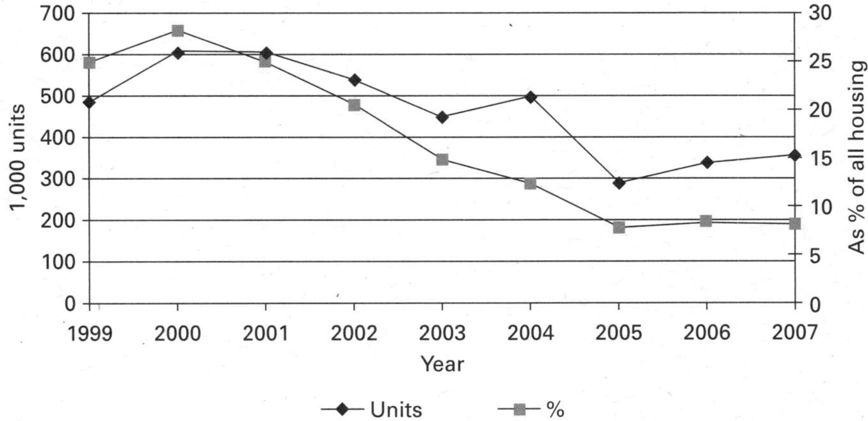

SOURCE: National Bureau of Statistics of China, 2007, 2008.

government charges and favorable land allocation. In Beijing another category of restricted commercial housing was promoted—*liangxian fang*. This type of housing, whose size and selling price are restricted by the government by giving developers some favorable conditions (including land price), aims to fill the gap between affordable housing and ordinary commercial housing.

Housing Provident Fund

The Housing Provident Fund is an important part of the urban housing reform package. Employers and work units play a very important role in managing individual Housing Provident Funds. Housing Provident Funds were used initially as short-term loans to work units, housing cooperatives, and developers for the development of affordable housing. Subsequently, they were used more in line with their original purpose—to help individuals buying, renting, or building houses (e.g. through a mortgage) (Wang 2005). By the end of 2007, the total accumulated Housing Provident Fund had reached 1,623 billion yuan. About 72 million urban employees across the country were contributing to the fund. About 40 percent of the money was withdrawn by contributors for housing purposes, 53 percent was used for mortgage loans for 8.3 million individuals; the rest was invested in either government bonds or development companies. Mortgage lending had a slow start but increased rapidly (Ministry of Housing and Urban-Rural Development 2008).

Although the Housing Provident Fund was aimed at all urban employees, those who benefited most tended to be public-sector employees, especially government officials, civil servants, academics, and professionals. Public-sector employers were funded by the government, and it was not difficult for them to budget the required contribution to the housing fund. There were also steady increases in salaries in those sectors. The monthly contributions have become a sizable amount of money for employees. In contrast, private and other employers found it difficult to set up this fund for their employees. In the private sector, most employees, especially the manual and unskilled workers (including most rural migrants) stayed out of the system.

Mortgages and Home Loans

The sale of public housing during the 1980s and 1990s involved substantial discounts. Most public-sector employees were able to pay the asking price from family savings. After the middle 1990s, house prices, particularly commercial house prices, increased quickly. This made any outright purchase of a properly built house beyond the reach of most ordinary urban residents. The mortgage emerged as an important kind of financial arrangement in the urban housing market. Three different types of mortgages were promoted by the government:

- Housing Provident Fund mortgage.
- Commercial bank mortgage.
- A combination of the two.

Provident fund mortgages were related to the amount of funds accumulated and had a relatively lower interest rate. In 1997, China's central bank, the People's Bank, issued a policy document, *Provisional Management Methods of Mortgages*, which allowed all commercial banks to do mortgage business. To encourage borrowing, the People's Bank reduced the basic interest rate seven times between 1996 and 1999. It also introduced a 20 percent income tax on bank interest earned from savings in 1999. The mortgage interest rate was reduced six times, from 10.53 percent in 1997 to 5.76 percent in 2002 (Cheng 2006). State banks also adjusted terms and conditions on mortgage borrowing and extended the normal period of a loan from 20 to 30 years in November 1999.

As in every other country, mortgage lending can help only the people who have a steady income and employment. The emerging middle class in Chinese cities, including civil servants and all sorts of professionals employed by public-owned institutions and large private firms, is the main group to benefit. For most low-income people, including rural migrants, borrowing from a bank to purchase housing is not an option. More important, most of the people who could borrow from a bank are those who are entitled to receive a housing cash subsidy from their employers and who also have accumulated a sizable amount of savings in the Housing Provident Fund.

Price Inflation and Affordability

Most housing reform policies encouraged urban households to increase their housing consumption and improve their living conditions. As a result, money from every direction has poured into the urban housing system. These policies, coupled with major increases in individual earnings in cities (particularly in the mainstream public sectors), led to a continuous and steady increase in the provision of urban housing. The average housing floor space per person in cities increased from 17.8 square meters in 1997 to 22.8 in 2002. Between 2000 and 2002, over 2 million new homes were built in Chinese cities each year. Urban housing development has also helped China to successfully handle the Asian financial crisis. Indeed, the real estate industry has become one of the key national economic sectors; in some cities, it was responsible for more than half of the total local GDP.

Housing price inflation, however, became a problem in most cities in 2004. Faced with the danger of the collapse of the overheated housing and property market and complaints from middle- and low-income urban residents, the government intensified its macroeconomic adjustment program beginning in 2005. The first initiative came in March 2005 with the publication of the General Office of the State Council's *Circulation on Stabilising Housing Price* (2005a). A month later, a detailed policy document prepared by the Ministry of Construction and a few other ministries was issued by the same office, the so-called *guo ba tiao*, or State Council's eight points (General Office of the State Council 2005b). Adjustment policies included giving priority to the development of affordable housing; introducing financial and taxation measures to discourage speculative investment in the housing market; tightening housing development loans for developers and mortgage lending to individuals; and encouraging the development of higher-density, smaller, and low-priced ordinary housing through favorable planning, land, finance and taxation policies.

Though the policies were comprehensive, their effect on stabilizing housing prices was limited. Housing prices in most cities continued climbing in late 2005 and early 2006 (figure 2.2). At the same time, several other issues caused the government concern. The proportion of commercial houses, particularly the expensive ones, was still too high, while affordable housing for the middle- to low-income groups

FIGURE 2.2

Average Salaries and Housing Prices in Urban Areas, 1997–2006

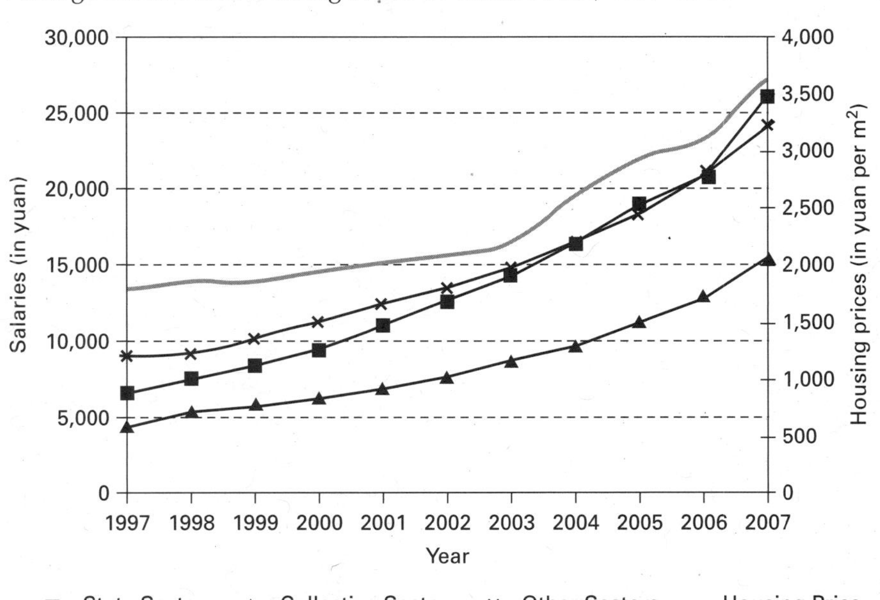

SOURCE: National Bureau of Statistics of China, 2007, 2008.

was far from enough. Urban low-income families found it very difficult to get involved in the housing market. Some families, especially families with an income just above the poverty line, were excluded from all forms of official housing provision. They were not qualified for social rental housing but could not afford to buy or rent a decent house.

In May 2006, another policy document was issued. Apart from reiterating some of the policies in the 2005 document, the six-point regulations significantly tightened the rules on mortgage down payments and housing transactions. As of June 2006, the minimum down payment for a new apartment larger than 90 square meters was raised from 20 percent to 30 percent; the period for charging a transaction tax on sales was extended from two years to five years; all new commercial housing projects were required to be at least 70 percent housing units smaller than 90 square meters; banks were instructed to provide loans only to housing developers that have more than 35 percent of the funds for the proposed project; developers that have a large unsold stock were not to be given additional loans for housing construction; and local governments were required to ensure a sufficient land supply for middle-size to small and mid- to low-priced ordinary commercial housing, affordable housing, and low-rent social housing projects. The annual land supply for these types of housing should be over 70 percent of the total housing land supply; for affordable housing projects, developers should tender not only for the land price, but also for the final house price; and penalties on land waste and holdings should be increased. Construction should start within one year of approval; a vacant land fee should be charged from one to two years; after two years, land should be withdrawn without compensation; all cities should be required to make a plan for the construction of low-rent social housing. A proportion of the income from land development must be used as the funding source.

Despite these efforts, house prices rose continuously in late 2006 and 2007. Housing prices in the coastal region were much higher than those in the inland regions. Average house prices in Beijing and Shanghai were the highest, at 7,375 and 7,039 yuan per square meter, respectively, in 2006, more than double the national average (3,119). During the first four months of 2007, housing prices climbed even faster. The average housing price in October was 10.6 percent higher than that of a year before. Prices in some large cities increased much faster than in others; for example, Shenzhen prices increased at 19.5 percent, Beijing at 15.1 percent, and Chongqing at 10.2 percent.

The huge housing price inflations were welcomed by some property owners, property developers, and local governments, as they brought substantial benefits. However, they brought great pressure on the people who had not stepped onto the housing ladder. As the urban housing market had a relatively short history, not many urban households had bought a commercial housing unit. Although the proportion of home ownership has increased substantially, most of these home owners actually live in the so-called *fanggai fang*, or privatized public housing. As the old public (work-unit) housing units were small and poorly designed, there are great demands among this group to improve their living conditions. The income of these people is affected by their age and their particular social economic profile. High housing prices made homes unaffordable to most of them. New and young employees in the public sector and professional services are another group of people who have a strong interest in buying new commercial housing. Despite their higher than average income and housing subsidies, the inflated prices made it very difficult to buy, even with parental support.

Social and Spatial Implications

The Winners and Losers

In 2000, we determined that

- housing reform in China has had a very limited impact on rural society;
- housing reform is also almost irrelevant to the large numbers of rural migrants in the cities;
- housing reform has had a limited direct impact on people who are traditional home owners and are not employed by the state sector; and
- the people most affected by housing reform have been employers and employees in the public sector.

Although the objective of early housing reform was to improve housing conditions in general, the heart of the reform policy is a more fundamental adjustment of social and economic distribution within the public sector. The policy was to share housing provision costs within the current public sector between the state, work units, and individuals with a progressive increase in the costs borne by individuals. However, the specific impact of housing reform depends upon the individual's current situation. Under the old system people employed by the public sector waited in the housing queue and improved their housing conditions step by step. With privatization, what housing people were in at the time of the reform was crucial. People in good-quality apartments would gradually secure their position in those apartments. They would obtain the property rights through a subsidized purchase and become home owners. People who were seeking to enter the housing system for the first time would increasingly have to obtain housing through the market with or without a subsidy. People who worked in work units that had not been performing well and had not invested substantially in housing were more likely to live in poorer-quality housing. People who had suffered under the old system would not find their circumstances changed under the new one. To this extent the early housing reform policies reinforced existing inequalities within China (Wang and Murie 2000).

In a follow-up study on housing reform in state-owned enterprises in 2004, we confirmed the above findings. Well-performing enterprises implemented more elements of the housing reform policies and provided their employees with many different housing benefits, while poorly performing enterprises had little to contribute to housing reform (table 2.2).

While the above assessments still stand, there have been important changes in the social and economic organization of Chinese urban societies (table 2.3). The

TABLE 2.2

Housing Reform in State-Owned Enterprises

Housing Reform Policy	State-Owned Enterprises			
	Nearly Bankrupt SOE	Poorly Performing SOE	Reasonably Well-Performing SOE	Well-Performing and Profitable SOE
Sale of existing public housing	Poor housing stock and delayed sale program	Better housing conditions and early/cheaper sale of housing to occupiers		
Establishing and contributing to Housing Provident Fund (HPF)	Very low and irregular level of HPF contribution	HPF contribution at standard rate set by municipal governments		Generous HPF contribution, well above the local recommended level
Building new housing for sale		Building new housing with workers bearing the full costs	Building for sale with some contribution from employees	Buying high-standard commercial houses for key and senior staff, then "privatizing" them cheaply
Setting up housing cooperative			Setting up housing cooperatives to build housing for their employees	
Issuing housing cash subsidy				Issuing housing subsidies to employees following similar rules applied to civil servants

SOURCE: Based on Wang, Wang, and Bramley, 2005.

private sector has become a much more important sector and employs a larger proportion of the urban labor force. Many private employers were privatized state companies or organizations. Owners and senior managers of these private firms have joined government officials and professionals in the urban elite group. Marginalization of the traditional working class employed by state-owned enterprises and institutions has increased. Housing policies (including major housing reform policies) are still relevant to the mainstream employees in traditional state sectors and to owners and managers in the new private sector. These people (the emerging middle class in Chinese cities) tend to have steady jobs and above-average incomes.

Housing reform policies placed a lot emphasis on the provision of social rental housing and affordable housing. If properly implemented, they could have a major impact on the living conditions of semiskilled and unskilled industrial workers (the new working class). Unfortunately, post-1998 practices have moved away from the reform policies and allowed the market to play a dominant role in housing supply.

TABLE 2.3

Changing Social and Economic Groups and Class Division in Cities

Prereform Major Urban Social Groups and Ranking	Postreform and Emerging Social Groups and Ranking	Social Classes
Leading government and party officials	Owners of large private companies and leading government and party officials	Emerging middle class
Directors and managers of SOEs and organizations	Managers of joint ventures and private companies, and major SOEs	
Middle- and low-rank officials, professionals, and academics employed by SOEs	Middle- and low-rank government leaders and civil servants, academics, and professionals in both public and private sectors	
Managers of collective enterprises	Small and family business owners	New working class
Workers of SOEs	Workers and general staff employed by SOEs and private companies	
Workers of collective enterprises	Employees of small private businesses	
Other general or unemployed urban residents	Low-paid rural migrants, unemployed and laid-off workers	Urban poor

For most traditional working-class families, without enough money to buy a new house, living conditions remain poor and assets remain small. Price inflations further increased the gap between the working class and the middle class. Working-class families are the losers of the recent housing development and reform. As China is a largely industrial society, the working class is large. If housing reform policies miss this group, their effect will be limited.

Another group that received limited benefits from the marketized housing provision is the traditional and emerging urban poor. Despite the central government's policies on social rental housing for the urban poor, implementation was very slow, as indicated in the previous section. Only a very small proportion of the poor received housing support from some cities. Many others were left in the market to find their own housing solutions. The urban poor includes unemployed and laid-off workers of the collective and state-owned enterprises and most rural-to-urban migrants. The traditional urban poor did not have good access to public housing under the old system; this led to a poor deal for them due to housing privatization and very limited assets. Most rural migrants did not receive any housing support from the government. They live in poor-quality rental housing, concentrated in the so-called urban villages.

Spatial Impacts

Research on the emerging spatial patterns of Chinese cities in the 1990s identified three different zones (Wang and Murie 1999a; 2000):

1. Traditional central areas built during the precommunist period, which hosted relatively poor residents in private houses and underwent quick redevelopment and upgrading.
2. Intermediate zones of socialist work units, which shared some common features during the prereform period and were substantially differentiated by the sectors in which they were engaged during the reform period.
3. Suburban commercial housing estate zones built during the economic reform period and "urban villages" transformed by the urbanization process.

This division still provides a useful framework for analyzing the spatial patterns of Chinese cities. However, important changes that have taken place in recent years require a more detailed analytical framework. Increased economic and social divisions have resulted in more obvious contrasts between different areas in cities. The homogeneous and concentric zone system has been broken into many different neighborhoods and areas. First, in all cities, we can identify two types of land uses: the finely designed areas of the modern city; and the simultaneously developed urban villages, which represent an informal development. Within the officially planned areas, several changes have happened in the last few years. In the central areas, most old neighborhoods have been redeveloped, and poor residents have been dispersed and relocated to peripheral areas. The socialist work-unit zone has been diversified, with most large publicly owned institutions consolidating their positions through their own internal redevelopment programs and traditional industrial factories relocating. Urban sprawl has resulted in more rural land being turned into various development and high-tech zones, shopping centers, science parks, university towns, and—more important—commercial housing developments for various social and economic groups. Of all the communities created, there are the barbed-wire fenced and gated communities of the rich; semigated communities of the ordinary commercial housing developments; modified old work-unit housing areas; and remaining old traditional neighborhoods in various corners.

The following list shows the main residential areas in cities:

- Modern gated communities.
    - Luxury cottage housing estates.
    - Cottage housing estates.
    - Luxury apartment housing estates.
- Modern semigated communities.
    - Ordinary commercial housing estates.
    - Economic and comfortable housing estates (affordable housing).
    - Urban-renewal relocation housing estates.
- Modified work-unit housing estates.
    - Housing cooperatives and work unit built housing estates.

Privatized old work-unit housing areas.
Professional and administrative sectors.
State enterprise sectors.
- Remaining old inner-city neighborhoods.
- Urban villages.
Original villagers' living quarters (gated settlements for landlords).
Modernized private rental housing quarters.
Traditional rural housing quarters.

The impacts of housing reform policies on each of these communities are summarized in table 2.4. It is clear that most reform policies (particularly the supporting policies) are only highly relevant to the areas occupied by the mainstream employees of the public sector. Policies that support the housing market are more relevant to areas of government officials, professionals, and managers employed in both the public and private sectors. Social housing is more relevant to the work-unit housing areas and the remaining old neighborhoods. Urban villages occupied by farmers and migrants have no relation with housing reform at all.

Readjustment of the Reform Direction

Post-1998 housing reform policies and practices started with an emphasis on the government's role of providing social rental and affordable housing. Influenced by the economic conditions at the time, however, housing policies and practices gradually moved away from this public-led approach to a market-led approach focused on the development of commercial housing. At the policy level, several types of housing have been defined that in theory would cover the whole spectrum of the urban population, from the very poor to the very rich. In practice, the number of people who benefited from each of the policy elements is very small, particularly at the initial stage of policy implementation. As a result, not all populations are covered by these policies; various gaps emerged between different provision systems. Because of the lack of funding, social rental provision, for example, focused on the very poor. Affordable housing, rather than targeting 70–80 percent of the population, was made available only to the people who had a steady income but not enough to purchase a full-priced commercial house (table 2.5).

This policy shift resulted in a huge housing price inflation and affordability problems among the majority of urban residents and led to hot debate. The emerging property bubble between 2005 and 2007 eventually led to the publication of another important State Council document—*Suggestions on Solving Urban Low- and Middle-Income Families' Housing Difficulties* (2007). The document, while recognizing the achievement in urban housing development and the improvement of living conditions in cities, pointed out several major problems of the urban housing system:

- Slow progress in social rental housing provision.
- Imperfect affordable housing system.
- Some urban low-income families still living in poor conditions.

Social and Spatial Impacts of Housing Reform Policies

				Relevance of Main Housing Reform Policies							
Category of Community	Type of Housing	Location	Type of Residents	Social Rental Support and Subsidies	Affordable Housing	Cash Subsidy for Housing	Housing Provident Fund	Mortgage Support	Policy to Reduce Housing Prices	Policy to Encourage Smaller Units	Transitional Housing for New Staff
Modern gated communities	Luxury cottage	Suburban	Super rich	O	O	O	L	L	L	O	O
	Other cottage	Suburban	The rich; second homes of professionals	O	O	L	L	H	L	O	O
	Luxury apartment housing	Inner city/ central	Emerging middle class; second homes	O	O	L	H	H	H	L	O
Modern semigated communities	Ordinary commercial housing	Peripheral	Middle to high income	O	L	H	H	H	H	H	O
	Affordable housing	Peripheral	Public-sector employee	O	H	H	H	H	H	H	L
	Urban-renewal relocation housing	Peripheral	Traditional private home owners	H	H	H	H	H	H	H	L

Modified work-unit residences	Housing cooperatives and work units built with individual contribution new housing	Inner city	Public-sector workers, civil servants, professionals	H	H	H	H	H	H	H	H
	Privatized old work-unit housing areas	Inner city	Cadres and workers, including retired ones	H	H	H	H	H	H	H	H
Remaining old inner-city neighborhoods		Central	Traditional home owners, collective sector workers	H	H	O	L	L	L	H	O
Urban villages	Original villagers' quarters (gated)	Peripheral/ suburban	Land owners, original village residents and their families	O	O	O	O	L	O	O	O
	Rebuilt rental housing quarters	Peripheral/ suburban	Migrants with stable jobs	L	L	L	L	O	O	L	L
	Traditional poor-quality housing quarters	Peripheral/ suburban	Poor rural migrants	O	O	O	O	O	O	O	O

NOTE: O=policy is not very relevant to the areas/estates (communities) and has no impact on most of the residents living there; L=policy has some relevance to the areas/estates (communities) and has minor impacts on the main residents living there; H=policy is highly relevant to the areas/estates (communities) and has important impacts on the main residents living there.

TABLE 2.5

Urban Housing Provision System: 1998 Model and Current Practice

Percentage of Urban Households According to Income (from low to high)

5	10	15	20	25	30	35	40	45	50	55	60	65	70	75	80	85	90	95	100

1998 Policy

Social housing or rent subsidy	Affordable housing	Commercial housing

2003 Adjustment

Social housing	Affordable housing	Ordinary commercial housing	Luxury commercial housing

Gaps of Coverage in Practice and 2007 Adjustment

Social housing provision	Rent subsidy	Affordable housing	Controlled commercial housing	Ordinary and small commercial housing	Moderate housing Consumption encouraged	Luxury commercial housing

SOURCE: Modified from Wang, 2007.

The new policies adjusted the 2003 market-oriented approach and gave the government more responsibilities and resources in housing provision. They provided many specific instructions to local authorities in dealing with low-income families. The first priority of the new policies was to establish and enhance the social housing provision system: By the end of 2007, all cities should provide rental housing or a cash subsidy to all qualified poor families. All county towns should achieve this target by the end of 2008. Richer cities should extend the coverage to include low-income families. The funding sources of social housing were clarified for the first time:

- Local government budget allocation.
- Net earnings from local Housing Provident Fund savings (after various charges).
- No less than 10 percent of net income from all land leases.
- Rent income from social rental housing.
- Central government social housing fund allocation (to poor inland provinces).

These policies had some immediate effects. According to statistics produced by the Ministry of Construction, the total investment for social rental housing in the country in 2007 reached 7.7 billion yuan, more than the total investment in the previous eight years. It has helped 681,000 low-income households (China Real Estate News 2008). The second main area of the 2007 policies focused on the affordable housing system. It clarified many areas that were not defined in earlier documents:

- The target of affordable housing should be the low-income groups in cities; in addition, affordable housing should cover all low-income residents after the very low-income groups are included in the social rental system.

- Families that benefited from welfare housing in the past are no longer qualified for it.
- The floor space of affordable housing should be around 60 square meters per unit.
- The purchasers of affordable housing have limited property rights. Affordable housing should not be traded on the market within five years of purchase. If no longer required by the owner, it should be "sold back" to the government at a price that reflects the age of the building and local market prices. It can be sold on the open market after five years, but the owner must pay a proportion of the price difference between the affordable housing and ordinary commercial housing in the area, as a land use fee.

The 2007 documents provide regulations for housing cooperatives (including work unit organized housing building), old neighborhood redevelopment, and policies to improve the living conditions of rural-to-urban migrants. The documents also restated a 2006 policy that aimed at regulating the commercial housing market and encouraging small houses of less than 90 square meters of floor space. Local authorities are required to provide at least 70 percent of the land for small housing units, and each new housing scheme should be at least 70 percent small units. In 2008, local governments were instructed to produce housing development plans, particularly to state the proportions, and locations, of low-rent and affordable housing, price-controlled commercial housing, and low-priced and smaller commercial housing (China Real Estate News 2008).

To implement these new policies, both national and local housing authorities were reorganized. The Ministry of Construction was changed to the Ministry of Housing and Urban-Rural Development (MHURD). Housing has been promoted to a ministerial status. In Beijing City, a Municipal Social Housing Provision and Regulation Office was established. It has 19 district- and county-level offices, and 311 township- and street-committee-level offices. The new arrangement marked a change of government emphasis, from promotion of housing development and construction management to safeguarding the housing requirements of low-income groups and the management of social housing.

By late 2008, it became clear that the global financial crisis had begun to affect China. While exports slowed down fast, the government had to stimulate internal consumption again to maintain economic growth. Again, housing was seen as the biggest source of internal consumption and real estate development as a key economic sector that could provide some stability for the urban economy. In December 2008, another major housing policy document was published by the General Office of the State Council (2008). The new policies aim to do the following:

- To implement the national strategy of increasing internal demand and ensuring steady economic growth.
- To increase social housing development and improve the living conditions.
- To promote the healthy development of the real estate industry.

The main policies in this document focused on the development and provision of government-supported social and affordable housing. As part of a large-scale increase of capital investment to maintain economic growth for the next three years, housing investment was increased substantially. The central government increased its contributions to social housing and slum area redevelopment, especially for the central and the western regions. Local governments were required to follow the central government's advice and increase the social housing supply in their areas and to ensure land supply for social housing projects. Commercial banks were encouraged to increase their lending to social housing development projects. To support the housing market, the policy lowered the level of deposit for home buyers and gave a preferred mortgage interest rate for people in overcrowded housing to buy a second home to improve their living conditions. The policy also reduced the housing transaction tax for a year in 2009, reversing the increases made in 2006 to the 2005 level (e.g., the transaction tax liability period was reduced from five years to two years). These policies reversed the trend of housing price decline. By early 2009, housing prices began to increase in some large cities again.

Conclusions

The minister for Housing and Urban-Rural Development, Jiang Weixin, gave a speech, "On Establishing and Improving the Chinese Urban Housing Policy System," at the China Development Forum 2008 in March of that year (Jiang 2008). He summarized the main achievements of housing reform since 1998:

- It abolished housing as a material distribution to public-sector employees.
- It commercialized the urban housing provision system.
- More recently, it introduced a new social housing support system to ensure housing provision to low-income and poor populations.

He also outlined some outstanding problems:

- Social rental and government-supported affordable housing development lagged behind.
- The structural adjustment of the housing market progressed slowly, with the middle-size and small houses still a small proportion.
- The affordability problem of middle- to low-income families was very serious.
- The urban housing market was still immature; commercial housing prices had increased too fast, and there was a serious imbalance in the housing supply.
- The use of advanced technology in house building was very low; housing development and consumption exceeded the environmental and resource capacity.

Overall, the minister felt that after many years of experiment and reform, China had found a suitable urban housing policy framework, in which both the government and the market could play an active role. The discussions and analysis in this chapter support this view. Housing development, distribution, and consumption in Chinese cities now is very different from that at the end of the 1990s. Since 1998, 2–4 million new housing units have been constructed each year in cities and towns. Most of them have been built by commercial developers and sold directly to people through the market. These new houses and their associated infrastructures have helped to modernize the urban landscape and improve the living conditions of many millions of families.

In early studies, the programmatic nature of the Chinese housing reform and the dynamics between continuation and change in policy development and practice were emphasized:

> Economic and housing reform resulted in a social and spatial reorganization of cities and the widening of the gap between the poor and the rich. . . . Although housing reform has brought significant changes to the housing provision system and improved many urban residents' living, it has . . . yet to break through the old institutional framework and to fully develop a commercial housing market independent of work units. Reform has to a large extent been carried out within work units. Nevertheless, housing reform has very different impacts on different social and economic groups with the leaders, managers and professionals in the public sector benefiting most and industrial workers gaining less. In this sense, housing reform in China has sustained current patterns of benefit. (Wang and Murie 2000, 414)

Some of these early findings still stand. The gap between the rich and the poor has increased dramatically during the past 10 years. There are important changes in the institutional framework and the development of the urban housing market. The work units (particularly the public-sector work units) still play important roles in housing provision, not through direct distribution, but through cash subsidies to their senior staff and managers, through self-organized house building with qualified individual employees' contributions, and through their influence over the distribution of social and affordable housing. The job-related housing entitlement is still very much alive. The representation of this entitlement is not a house anymore, however, but several housing benefits such as cash subsidies, Housing Provident Funds, and access to affordable housing. The main beneficial groups of the reform policies are still the mainstream urban population, including government officials, civil servants, and professionals employed by various public institutions. There is an increase of private- and other nonstate-sector employees among the beneficial group. Their benefits come more from policies to support the urban housing market than from housing reform policies.

Housing reform and market expansion are beginning to break the links between employment and residence and have led to the differentiation of neighborhoods according to the social and economic status of residents. Poor, low-income, and less powerful people began to concentrate in the less desirable peripheral areas of cities, such as urban villages, old dilapidated inner-city neighborhoods, and the poorly maintained and privatized former public and work-unit housing estates, where low-profit housing is cheaper. Government workers and core groups in the economy began to group in more expensive and higher-status neighborhoods.

The continuous support of the mainstream urban population through housing policies and reforms helped to maintain the delicate relationship between the people and the government and between the people and the Communist Party. Theoretically speaking, abolishing socialist welfare housing and replacing it with high-priced commercial housing are in contradiction to communist principles, and the change of mainstream urban residents from proletarians and socialist workers into petty bourgeois and property owners may weaken the base of the communist administrative socialist system. The housing supports and benefits offered to professionals, managers, and civil servants have helped to preserve the communist administrative system under a free-market economic system.

The insufficient support to the traditional socialist industrial workers and their families has not caused a big problem in the past because that group has been declining and becoming marginalized. Its contribution to the urban economy has been replaced by that of the rural migrants. After about 10 years' support of the market approach and the neglect of housing provision for the low-income and the poor, the living conditions of the working class and migrants became intolerable, not only to the residents themselves, but also to many party and government leaders. As a major step toward a harmonious society, housing for the urban poor and low-income people has become a top policy agenda over the last two years.

Housing, as an important social policy, has a very strong relationship with China's economic development policies. A well-selected housing reform direction could easily be sidetracked to suit the demands of the national and local economies. The post-1998 practice was a good example. When housing had been identified as a major economic sector to offset the negative effects of the Asian financial crisis, the less profitable social housing had to give way to commercial housing; when the low-income and the poor found it difficult to purchase the government-supported affordable housing, relatively well-off people were allowed to buy. There was a commonly accepted official view at the time that if the poor and low-income populations have no power to pull the urban economy forward, let the rich people do it. China is now in the middle of another international financial crisis. Urban housing again has been identified as a key economic sector to increase internal demand to compensate for the loss of exports. Public spending has been seen as an effective way out of this crisis. Luckily, China has accumulated a huge savings and foreign reserves. This enables the government to promote its harmonious society idea and make very large-scale investments in social and affordable housing this time. This new initiative will pay back some of the policy debts and help the low-income population gain some ground in improving their living conditions.

REFERENCES

Beijing Municipal Construction Commission. 2006. Report of survey on housing conditions among the lowest-income households in Beijing. Unpublished policy document in *Macroadjustment and social housing development document collection*. Beijing.

———. 2007. Working plan for achieving the target of full provision of social housing to qualified families by end of 2007. Unpublished policy document in *National and Beijing municipal policy collections on solving the housing problems of low-income households, market regulations and implementation of the macro-adjustment policies*. Beijing.

Chen, Aimin 1996. China's urban housing reform: Price-rent ratio and market equilibrium. *Urban Studies* 33(7):1077–1092.

Cheng, Jianhua. 2006. Analysis of the progress and problems of social housing provision in Beijing City. Speech at a local policy conference (November 9).Unpublished policy document in *Macro-adjustment and social housing development document collection*. Beijing: Beijing Municipal Construction Commission.

China Real Estate News. 2008. The low profile launch of the Department for Social Housing by the Ministry of Housing and Urban-Rural Development. http://www.ydfcj.gov.cn/Article/ShowArticle.asp?ArticleID=320 [in Chinese].

Chiu, Rebecca. 1996. Housing affordability in Shenzhen special economic zone: A forerunner of China's housing reform. *Housing Studies* 11(4):561–580.

General Office of the State Council. 1991. *On comprehensive reform of the urban housing system.* Document No. 73. Beijing.

———. 2005a. *Circulation on stabilising housing price.* Document No. 8. Beijing.

———. 2005b. *Suggestions on works of stabilising housing price.* Document No. 26. Beijing.

———. 2008. *Some suggestions on promotion of the healthy development of housing and property market.* Document No. 131. Beijing.

Housing Reform Steering Group of the State Council. 1994. The decision on deepening urban housing reform. In *Urban Housing System Reform,* ed. Housing Reform Steering Group of the State Council. Beijing: Reform Press.

Huang, Youqin. 2004a. Housing markets, government behaviors and housing choice: A case study of three cities in China. *Environment and Planning A* 36(1):45–68.

———. 2004b. The road to homeownership: A longitudinal analysis of tenure transition in urban China (1949–1994). *International Journal of Urban and Regional Research* 28(4):774–795.

Jiang, Weixing. 2008. On establishing and improving the Chinese urban housing policy system. Speech at the China Development Forum 2008. http://www.cin.gov.cn/ldjh/jsbfld/200803/t20080324_165587.htm [in Chinese].

Leaf, Michael. 1997. Urban social impacts of China's economic reforms. *Cities* 14(2):v–vii.

Lee, James. 2000. From welfare housing to home ownership: The dilemma of China's housing reform. *Housing Studies* 15(1):61–67.

Li, Simin. 2000a. Housing consumption in urban China: A comparative study of Beijing and Guangzhou. *Environment and Planning A* 32:1115–1134.

———. 2000b. The housing market and tenure decisions in Chinese cities: A multivariate analysis of the case of Guangzhou. *Housing Studies* 15(2):213–236.

Logan, John, Fuqin Bian, and Yianjie Bian. 1998. Tradition and change in urban Chinese families: The case of living arrangements. *Social Forces* 76(3): 851–882.

MHURD 2008. Review of Housing Provident Fund saving and use in 2007. http://www.cin.gov.cn/hydt/200803/t20080313_164189.htm.

National Bureau of Statistics of China. 2007. *China statistical yearbook 2007.* http://www.stats.gov.cn/tjsj/ndsj.

National Bureau of Statistics of China. 2008. *China statistical yearbook 2008.* http://www.stats.gov.cn/tjsj/ndsj [in Chinese].

State Council. 1988. *Implementation plan for a gradual housing system reform in cities and towns.* Document No. 11. Beijing.

———. 1998. *The notice on further reform of the urban housing system and speeding up housing development.* Document No. 23, July 3. Beijing.

———. 2003. *On further promotion of the sustainable and healthy development of the housing and property market.* Document No. 18. Beijing.

———. 2007. *Suggestions on solving urban low- and middle-income families' housing difficulties.* Document No. 24, August. Beijing.

Wang, Ya Ping. 1992. Private sector housing in urban China since 1949: The case of Xian. *Housing Studies* 7(2):119–137.

———. 1995. Public sector housing in urban China 1949–1988: The case of Xian. *Housing Studies* 10(1):57–82.

———. 2000. Housing reform and its impacts on the urban poor in China. *Housing Studies* 15(6):845–864.

———. 2001. Urban housing reform and finance in China: A case study of Beijing. *Urban Affairs Review* 36(5):620–645.

———. 2003. Progress and problems of urban housing reform. In *Social policy reform in China: Views from home and abroad,* ed. C. J. Finer, 176–190. Aldershot, U.K.: Ashgate.

———. 2004. *Urban poverty, housing and social change in China.* Oxon, U.K.: Routledge.

———. 2005. Low-income communities and urban poverty in China. *Urban Geography* 26(3): 222–242.

———. 2007. From socialist welfare to support of home ownership: The experience of China. In *Housing and the new welfare state,* eds. Richard Groves, Alan Murie, and Christopher Watson. Aldershot, U.K.: Ashgate.

Wang, Ya Ping, and Alan Murie. 1996. The process of commercialisation of urban housing in China. *Urban Studies* 33(6):971–989.

———. 1999a. Commercial housing development in urban China. *Urban Studies* 36(9):1475–1494.

———. 1999b. *Housing policy and practice in China.* Basingstoke, U.K.: MacMillan.

———. 2000. Social and spatial implications of housing reform in China. *International Journal of Urban and Regional Research* 24(2):397–417.

Wang, Ya Ping, Yanglin Wang, and Glen Bramley. 2005. Chinese housing reform in state owned enterprises and its impacts on different social groups. *Urban Studies* 42(10):1859–1878.

World Bank. 1992. *China implementation options for urban housing reform.* Washington, DC.

Wu, Fulong. 1996. Changes in the structure of public housing provision in urban China. *Urban Studies* 33(9):1601–1627.

Zhang, Xingquan. 1997. Chinese housing policy 1949–1978: The development of a welfare system. *Planning Perspectives* 12(4):433–455.

Zhou, Min, and John Logan. 1996. Market transition and the commodification of housing in urban China. *International Journal of Urban and Regional Research* 20(3):400–421.

Land Use, Fiscal Policy, and Housing Markets

Residential Housing in Urban China: Demand and Supply

GREGORY C. CHOW AND LINLIN NIU

Ever since residential housing in urban China became commercialized in the late 1980s, the price of houses has increased rapidly, from 408.18 yuan per square meter in 1987 to 3,119.25 in 2006, an annual growth rate of 11.3 percent. (See table 3.1.) Such a price increase has been a great concern to the Chinese government and the Chinese people. At times the government has attempted to regulate the housing market because it believed that the rise in prices was due to speculation. For example, purchasers of new houses were not allowed to resell them within two years without paying a penalty of 5 percent in the form of a business tax on the total transaction price; also, a 40 percent down payment is required for second mortgages. A main purpose of this chapter is to show that the price of urban housing in China is determined mainly by the basic economic forces of demand and supply. If the price increase is partly due to the upward shift in demand resulting from the rapid increase in disposable income, and partly due to the upward shift in the supply curve resulting from the rapid increase in construction cost, any government interference with the market price will lead to an inefficient allocation of resources in the housing market. (Although construction cost, as measured by the building materials industry price index, did not increase after 1992, the average land purchase price as a major component of construction cost increased at an annual rate of 11.8 percent from 1997 to 2007.) Furthermore, government regulation is unlikely to be effective in controlling the price of housing because the basic forces of demand and supply—namely, changes in disposable income and construction prices—are more powerful than government action.

The standard theory of demand for and supply of consumer durable goods is applicable to urban housing in China after the late 1980s, when the market for housing was established. Although previous studies (e.g., Hu et al. 2006; Zhang, Weng, and Zhou 2007) have examined the determination of housing prices in China, none has estimated the demand and supply equations for urban housing in

"

TABLE 3.1

Residential Housing Time Series Data, 1987–2006

Time (year)	Urban Residential Floor Space per Capita (m²)	Commercial Residential Housing Sales Price (yuan per square meter)	CPI Urban (1978=1)	Urban per Capita Disposable Income (yuan)	Building Materials Industry Price Index (1986=1)
1987	12.7	408.18	1.562	1,002.1	1.056
1988	13.0	502.90	1.885	1,180.2	1.198
1989	13.5	573.50	2.192	1,373.9	1.480
1990	13.7	702.85	2.220	1,510.2	1.474
1991	14.2	756.23	2.333	1,700.6	1.564
1992	14.8	996.40	2.534	2,026.6	1.738
1993	15.2	1,208.23	2.942	2,577.4	2.481
1994	15.7	1,194.05	3.678	3,496.2	2.670
1995	16.3	1,508.86	4.296	4,283.0	2.841
1996	17.0	1,604.56	4.674	4,838.9	2.963
1997	17.8	1,789.80	4.819	5,160.3	2.951
1998	18.7	1,853.56	4.790	5,425.1	2.851
1999	19.4	1,857.02	4.728	5,854.0	2.785
2000	20.3	1,948.43	4.766	6,280.0	2.774
2001	20.8	2,016.75	4.799	6,859.6	2.746
2002	22.8	2,091.72	4.751	7,702.8	2.685
2003	23.7	2,359.50	4.794	8,472.2	2.674
2004	25.0	2,197.35	4.952	9,421.6	2.768
2005	26.1	2,548.61	5.031	10,493.0	2.786
2006	27.1	3,119.25	5.106	11,759.5	2.838

NOTE: CPI=consumer price index.

a simultaneous equations framework and provided estimates of price and income elasticities of demand and price elasticity of supply.

Beginning with the study of Chow (1957; 1960), economists have accepted the proposition that the demand for total stock of a consumer durable good such as automobiles and housing can be treated in the same way as the demand for nondurables and services. To explain the change in the stock of a durable good, Chow (1957; 1960) introduced and found evidence to support the partial adjustment hypothesis—namely, that the actual change in the stock in one year is a fraction b of the difference between the "desired stock" and the stock of the preceding period, where the "desired stock" is determined by a demand equation for the services generated from the stock, with income and price as the most important explanatory variables.

Theoretical Framework

The major variables determining the demand for the total stock of housing, as measured by housing space, are real income and relative price (price of housing divided by a general price index). The income effect is positive, and the price effect is negative. The same income and price variables are assumed to affect the demand for residential housing by government units and the subsidized housing provided by commercial enterprises to their employees. The quantity of housing is measured in per capita terms to avoid the scale effect of an increase of population. Without any theory to explain the demand for housing, one would expect that doubling the size of the population would double the quantity of housing demanded. Demand theory applies to the behavior of a representative consumer. It explains mean demand of consumers by mean income and relative price.

The supply equation explains the same quantity variable by the same price variable and cost of construction. The price effect is positive, and the effect of construction cost is negative. Although in China land is collectively owned and the use of land for construction is controlled by local government officials, we assume that the same factors that affect the supply of housing in a market economy apply to China; resources required in the construction of housing are acquired in the same way as in a market economy. Since the quantity variable includes both new construction and the amount of existing housing made available for sale, the price elasticity of supply under our theoretical framework is smaller than the elasticity of supply of new housing alone.

Both demand and supply equations will be approximated by linear functions or equations linear in the logarithms of the variables.

If the standard theory of consumer demand is applied to explain the consumption of a durable good as measured by the quantity of service it generates, and if the latter is assumed to be proportional to the stock of the durable good in existence, strictly speaking we have to consider two components of the stock—the stock owned by the consumer and the stock rented by the consumer. In the latter case, the price of housing should be measured by the rent per unit of housing stock. Without introducing rent as a separate variable, our study assumes that rent is approximately proportional to the price index we use. Also, concerning the appropriate price variable affecting demand, if many consumers purchase their housing units by a mortgage loan, the rate of interest will affect the price of consumption of housing service; we have not introduced the interest rate as a component of the price variable. This assumption is justified if historical changes in the interest rate are small and less frequent as compared with the changes in the price index for housing that we use. As we have pointed out, the price of urban housing increased at an average annual rate of 11.3 percent from 1987 to 2006. The annual change in the mortgage rate was much smaller. According to the *China Statistical Yearbook 2007,* table 20-9, interest rate of loans five years and longer varied between 5.76 percent per year and 8.01 percent per year in the period from 1 July 1998 to 19 August 2006. According to *China Statistical Abstract 2002–2008,* between June 1999 and 2006, there were three changes in the commercial bank mortgage rates, with the rate for five years and above varying between 5.04 percent and 6.12 percent. To the extent that the above two simplifying assumptions concerning the price of consuming services of housing are invalid, errors would be introduced in the measurement of our price variable, and a downward bias would result in our estimation of price elasticity.

The demand and supply equations can be written as

$$\text{Demand:} \quad q_t = b_0 + b_1\, y_t + b_2\, p_t + u_{1t} \tag{1}$$

$$\text{Supply:} \quad q_t = c_0 + c_1\, p_t + c_2\, c_t + u_{2t} \tag{2}$$

where q_t denotes housing space per capita, y_t denotes real disposable income per capita, p_t denotes relative price of housing, and c_t denotes real construction cost. These are two structural equations.

The reduced form equations are derived by solving the structural equations for the endogenous variables q_t and p_t. They can be expressed algebraically as

$$p_t = d_0 + d_1\, y_t + d_2\, c_t + v_{1t} \tag{3}$$

$$q_t = r_0 + r_1\, y_t + r_2\, c_t + v_{2t} \tag{4}$$

The first reduced form equation (3) will be used to explain the rapid rise in the price of urban housing in China by the forces of demand and supply. The predicted value of p_t by equation (3), denoted by p_t^*, will also be used to estimate the demand equation (1) for q_t by the method of two-stage least squares. Because p_t and q_t are determined by the reduced form equations with v_{1t} and v_{2t} as residuals, and because the residuals u_{1t} and u_{2t} of the structural equations are algebraically related to v_{1t} and v_{2t}, p_t in the demand equation (1) for housing stock is correlated with its residual u_{1t}. Hence we cannot obtain consistent estimates of the coefficient b_2. On the other hand, p_t^* is a function of the exogenous variables y_t and c_t, which are assumed to be uncorrelated with the residuals of both the structural and reduced form equations. We apply the method of two-stage least squares to estimate the demand equation (1) by first estimating p_t^* from (3) as stated above and then, in the second stage, estimating the demand equation (1) by least squares after substituting p_t^* for p_t.

The above theory of demand and supply and of housing price determination assumes that the market for housing is in equilibrium all the time. If we allow for a partial adjustment process by which the actual price p_t adjusts toward its equilibrium level p_t^* as determined by equation (3) by only a fraction d of the difference $p_t^* - p_{t-1}$ we obtain the following equation to explain the change in p_t:

$$p_t - p_{t-1} = d(p_t^* - p_{t-1}) = d(d_0 + d_1\, y_t + d_2\, c_t) - d p_{t-1} \tag{5}$$

Similarly we can assume a partial adjustment process for the actual stock of housing q_t to adjust within a year by only a fraction b to its equilibrium level q_t^* as determined by its demand equation (1), namely

$$q_t - q_{t-1} = b(q_t^* - q_{t-1}) = b(b_0 + b_1 y_t + b_2 p_t) - b q_{t-1} \tag{6}$$

We can obtain estimates of the coefficients of equations (3) and (1), respectively, by estimating equations (5) and (6), as discussed in the section on statistical results.

In this study, the Chinese urban housing market is treated as one market, although prices in different cities vary substantially. For example, as reported in table 6-38 of the *China Statistical Abstract 2007*, in 2006 average prices of commercialized residential housing sold in different provinces and municipalities ranged from 1,584 to 7,375 yuan per square meter. The average price in China stood at 3,119 yuan per square meter. Beijing topped the country with 7,375 yuan per square meter, while southwest China's Guizhou Province had the cheapest housing, with an average cost of 1,584 yuan per square meter. When we use a time series of housing price to estimate the demand and supply of housing, our series is an average across different cities. This treatment of housing price and the corresponding treatment of the quantity of housing as floor space per capita are valid, as we are estimating a demand equation for an average Chinese urban consumer across different cities.

The Data

The time series analysis is based on annual data from 1987 to 2006. Before 1987 housing for urban residents was provided to a large extent by their employing units at rents well below the market price. The market forces of demand for and supply of housing began to operate after 1987.

Data on housing space per capita for urban residents are found in table 10-35 of the *China Statistical Yearbook 2007* and its earlier editions and reported in the second column of table 3.1 in this chapter. (In the *China Statistical Yearbook 2008*, released recently, per capita housing space for urban residents in 2007 is missing. Hence we are constrained to rely on the *China Statistical Yearbook 2007* and earlier editions for data up to 2006.) Urban residents in the definition of housing space per capita do not include migrant workers, nor are they included in the definition of disposable income per capita mentioned below.

Data on the sales price of commercialized residential housing are calculated by dividing the total sales revenue of commercialized residential housing by the total floor space sold. Both series are found in table 6–36 of the *China Statistical Yearbook 2007* for the period from 1991 to 2006. For the period from 1987 to 1990, no data on commercialized residential housing are available and we use data for the total commercialized buildings sold in table 5–35 of the *China Statistical Yearbook 1996* as an approximation. This is valid, as total commercialized buildings sold contain commercialized residential housing sold as the major component; the two price series are very close for the period from 1991 to 1993, with a difference of up to merely 1 percent (table 6–36 of the *China Statistical Yearbook 2007*). Therefore, we assume that the two price series are also almost identical from 1987 to 1990 and use the commercialized buildings price as the commercialized residential housing price for those years. The sales price of commercialized residential housing so obtained is reported in column 3 of table 3.1. The price variable p is the ratio of the above price series divided by the urban consumer price index (CPI; 1978 = 1) presented in column 4 of table 3.1 and found in table 9–2 of the *China Statistical Yearbook 2007* and its earlier editions.

The income data are the per capita disposable income of urban residents, found in the online database of the National Bureau of Statistics of China and given in column 5 of table 3.1. The income variable y_t is the ratio of the above income series divided by the same urban CPI.

For construction cost, we use the building materials industry price index found in table 9–12 of the *China Statistical Yearbook 2007* and its previous editions. Since this price index takes the previous year as the base year, we calculate a price index accordingly, taking its value in 1986 as 1. The series is shown in the last column of table 3.1. The cost variable c_t is the ratio of this price index divided by the same urban CPI. It should be pointed out that some other important components of construction cost are omitted due to data availability. These include labor cost, operational cost, land purchasing price, and related expenditures. Land cost in particular accounts for a sizable proportion of the total cost in major cities, but annual data on average land purchasing cost can be obtained only after 1997 from the *China Statistical Yearbook*. The omission of land cost does not significantly affect our estimates of elasticities of housing demand with respect to income and price, as will be shown in the section on statistical results.

For the estimation of income elasticity by cross-section data, we use table 10–7 of the *China Statistical Yearbook 2007*, which provides for each of the seven income groups the mean total consumption expenditures per capita and the mean expenditure for housing per capita for the year 2006, as reported in table 3.2.

Statistical Results

Using annual data from 1987 to 2006, as presented in the previous section on data, the linear reduced form equation (3) is estimated to explain the price of housing space by the predetermined variables to yield

$$p_t = -86.065 \ (91.562) + 0.215 \ (0.017) \ y_t + 352.842 \ (120.185) \ c_t$$
$$R^2/\text{s.e} = 0.930/26.992 \tag{7}$$

TABLE 3.2

Cross-Section Data: Per Capita Annual Expenditure of Urban Households, 2006

Income Group	Housing Expenditure (yuan)	Total Consumption Expenditures (yuan)
1	427.16	3,422.98
2	530.06	4,765.55
3	655.61	6,108.33
4	799.32	7,905.41
5	1,009.55	10,218.25
6	1,341.89	13,169.82
7	2,196.59	21,061.68

The numbers in parentheses are standard errors of the corresponding coefficients. (The Newey-West standard errors of the two coefficients of explanatory variables that allow for second-order autocorrelation in the regression residuals are respectively 0.012 and 70.989, smaller than the OLS standard errors reported above. OLS standard errors will continue to be reported in the remaining equations.) This equation shows that the price of urban residential houses can be well explained by the forces of demand (per capita real income y_t) and supply (real cost of construction c_t). The coefficients of these variables have the correct sign and are statistically significant.

Although some important components of cost, such as land cost, are missing due to availability, our chosen explanatory variables already account for 93 percent of the total variance of price. According to table 6-30 of the *China Statistical Yearbook 2007*, we can divide the total value of land purchased by the land space developed by real estate enterprises to obtain the average land purchasing cost from 1997 to 2006, which is highly correlated with the per capita disposable income of urban residents during the same period. Omitting this variable will lead to an upward bias for the coefficient of income in equation (7); however, it has little effect for predicting price p_t^* and for using p_t^* in the second stage to estimate the demand equation.

Figure 3.1 compares the actual price with the price p_t^* predicted by the demand equation. The residuals are plotted at the bottom of the graph.

FIGURE 3.1

Relative Housing Prices, Fitted Values, and Residuals

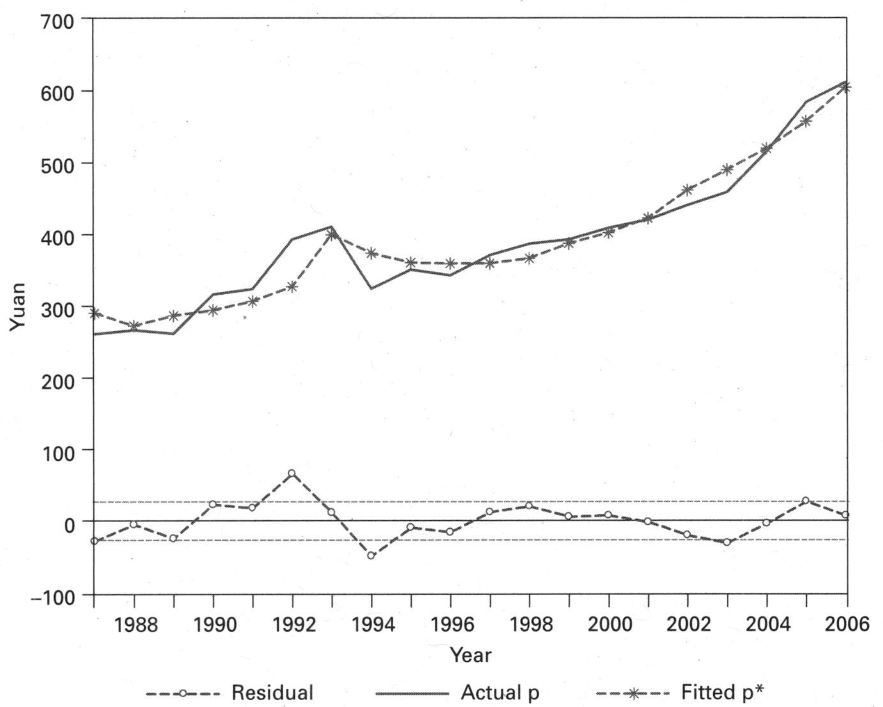

To allow for the partial adjustment of price we have estimated equation (5) to explain the annual change of housing price:

$$p_t - p_{t-1} = -79.254 \,(104.440) + 0.216 \,(0.069)\, y_t$$
$$+ 359.182 \,(191.015)\, c_t - 1.030(0.338)\, p_{t-1} \tag{8}$$
$$R^2/\text{s.e} = 0.450/27.623$$

The reported R-square 0.450 shows that 45 percent of the variance of $p_t - p_{t-1}$ is explained by demand and supply. The fact that the coefficient of p_{t-1} is close to 1 implies that adding lagged price to equation (7) will give a coefficient of p_{t-1} close to zero and has no added value besides y_t and c_t in predicting p_t. Hence we retain the specification of equation (7) for the explanation of housing price. Figure 3.2 shows the observed values of $p_t - p_{t-1}$ and the predicted values. We observe from the value of the R-square and figure 3.2 that even the annual change in housing price is fairly well explained by the forces of demand and supply.

We proceed to estimate the demand equation (1) for housing using the method of two-stage least squares by regressing q_t on y_t and p_t^* as estimated by equation (7). The result is

$$q_t = 10.343 \,(1.126) + 0.01153 \,(0.00111)\, y_t - 0.01450 \,(0.00610)\, p_t^* \tag{9}$$
$$R^2/\text{s.e} = 0.990/0.483$$

An estimate of income elasticity at the mean is the coefficient 0.01153 of y_t multiplied by the mean 1,191.539 of y_t and divided by the mean 18.39 of the dependent

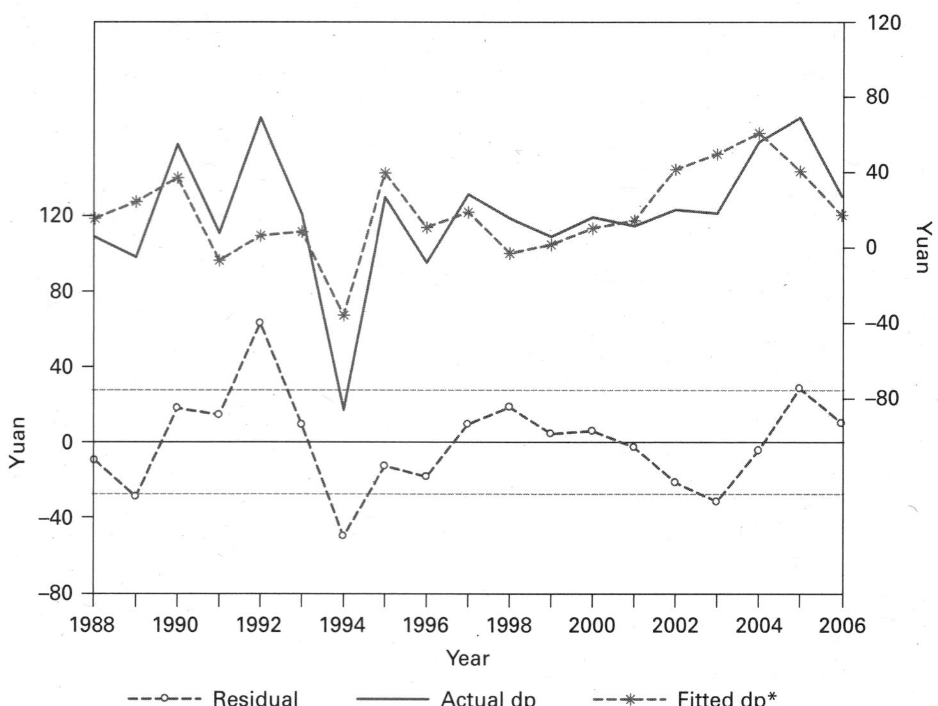

FIGURE 3.2

Price Changes, Fitted Price Changes, and Residuals

variable q_t, yielding 0.747. Similarly, an estimate of price elasticity at the mean is the coefficient -0.01450 times the mean 392.085 of p_t and divided by 18.39, yielding -0.309.

By adding q_{t-1} to both sides of equation (6) we obtain an equation to explain q_t after allowing for partial adjustment in the change in q_t:

$$q_t = 2.299 \ (2.076) + 0.00286 \ (0.00215) \ y_t - 0.00536 \ (0.00425) \ p_t^*$$
$$+ 0.838 \ (0.196) \ q_{t-1} \tag{10}$$
$$R^2/\text{s.e} = 0.996/0.310$$

Comparing with equation (6), which is just a transform of equation (10), we can derive from equation (10) the partial adjustment coefficient $b = (1 - 0.838) = 0.162$. Dividing the coefficients of income and price in equation (10) by b, we obtain estimates of the coefficients of the demand equation (1) for the stock of housing—that is, 0.01765 and -0.03309. These coefficients are converted to elasticities at the means, as in the last paragraph. The results are 1.144 and -0.705 for income and price elasticities, respectively. The magnitudes of these elasticities are larger than the estimates from equation (9) because they allow for the effects of income and price to work out through time; they measure long-run elasticities, whereas 0.747 and -0.309 are short-run elasticities. The same phenomenon occurs for the demand equation linear in the logarithms of the variables as will be reported below.

To find out how sensitive the statistical results are to the functional form chosen, we have also approximated the demand and supply equations by functions linear in the logs of the variables. The equation explaining $\log p_t$ is

$$\log p_t = 1.629 \ (0.379) + 0.657 \ (0.065) \log y_t + 0.602 \ (0.472) \log c_t$$
$$R^2/\text{s.e} = 0.903/0.079 \tag{11}$$

To compare how well this equation explains the price of housing as compared with equation (7) in linear form, we observe that the standard error of equation (11) is 7.9 percent for the explanation of price, whereas the standard error of equation (7) is 26.992. If we convert the latter to percentage terms by dividing it by the mean value of the price series 392.085, we obtain 6.9 percent. As in the linear case, adding $\log p_{t-1}$ to the right-hand side of (11) yields a coefficient that is not significantly different from zero.

Denoting the estimated $\log p_t$ resulting from the above equation by $(\log p_t)^*$, we estimate the demand equation for housing stock by two-stage least squares as given below:

$$\log q_t = -0.489 \ (0.224) + 0.764 \ (0.053) \log y_t - 0.333 \ (0.097) \ (\log p_t)^*$$
$$R^2/\text{s.e} = 0.995/0.019 \tag{12}$$

The income elasticity is estimated to be 0.764 with a standard error of 0.053. The price elasticity is estimated to be -0.333 with a standard error of 0.097. These estimates are close in magnitude to the estimates 0.747 and -0.309 obtained by using a linear demand equation (9) without allowing for partial adjustment.

To compare the goodness of fit of the equations in linear form and in log form, the standard error of regression (12) gives 1.9 percent as the standard deviation of the errors in estimating q_t. Equation (9) in linear form has a standard error of 0.483. Converted to percentage terms by dividing by the mean floor space q_t, it becomes $0.483/18.39 = 0.026$, or 2.6 percent. These results show that both the linear demand equation and the log-linear demand equation explain the demand for urban housing well.

If we assume a partial adjustment process for the change in $log\, q_t$ as a fraction of the difference between the desired $log\, q_t$ as determined by demand theory and $log\, q_{t-1}$, we obtain a partial adjustment model as follows:

$$log\, q_t = -0.147\,(0.176) + 0.333\,(0.133)\, log\, y_t - 0.170\,(0.087)\,(log\, p_t)^*$$
$$+\,0.600(0.176)\, log q_{t-1} \tag{13}$$
$$R^2/\text{s.e} = 0.997\,/\,0.013$$

Given an estimate of the adjustment coefficient b to be $1 - 0.600 = 0.400$, we estimate the income and price elasticities of demand for housing stock by dividing the coefficients of the income and price variables in the above equation by 0.400, yielding 0.833 and -0.425, respectively. As in the case of linear equations, these estimates are larger in magnitudes than 0.764 and -0.333, obtained by estimating the demand equation directly, but only slightly larger. In conclusion, using the model of partial stock adjustment, we have estimated the income elasticity of demand for urban residential housing to be approximately 1 (1.144 in the linear equation and 0.833 in the log-linear equation) and the price elasticity to be about -0.57 (-0.705 in the linear equation and 0.425 in the log-linear equation), allowing for estimation errors.

To provide further evidence on income elasticity, we have examined cross-section data. In table 10-7 of the *China Statistics Yearbook 2007*, data for 2006 are provided on expenditure on housing per capita ($p_t\, q_t$) and total expenditure per capita (y_t) for families of seven income groups, as given in table 3.2. Taking logarithms of these variables, we find the seven points in the scatter diagram to fall very close to a straight line. The estimated regression is

$$log(p_t\, q_t) = -1.382\,(0.345) + 0.904\,(0.038)\, log\, y_t$$
$$R^2/\text{s.e} = 0.991/0.058 \tag{14}$$

The coefficient 0.904 can be interpreted as total expenditure elasticity, which is close to income elasticity. Strictly speaking, to obtain this total expenditure elasticity we should regress $log\, q_t$ on $log\, y_t$ and $log\, p_t$ or equivalently regress $log(p_t\, q_t) = log\, p_t + log\, q_t$ on $log\, y_t$ and $log\, p_t$. The latter regression will yield the same coefficient of $log\, y_t$ as equation (14) if $log\, p_t$ is uncorrelated with $log\, y_t$ as we assume. This assumption is justified if consumers in different income groups pay the same price for housing of a given quality.

It is interesting to observe that our estimates of income elasticity of demand for housing are similar to the estimates of 0.940 (0.032) for Peking (in 1927) and 0.714 (0.046) for Shanghai (from 1929 to 1930) given in Houthakker (1957, table 3). In concluding his paper to compare income elasticities of demand for four major categories of consumption goods—namely, food, clothes, housing, and fuel—and all other items in 35 countries and cities, Houthakker (1957, 551) wrote, "If no data on the expenditure patterns of a country are available at all we would not be very far astray by putting the partial elasticity with respect to total expenditure at .6 for food, 1.2 for clothing, .8 for housing and 1.6 for all other items combined." Hence, our estimates of 0.747, 0.764 from the time series without partial adjustment effect, and 0.904 from the cross-section are reasonable. We summarize our estimates of income and price elasticities of housing demand from various specifications in table 3.3.

To complete our study of demand and supply we have estimated a supply equation of housing in log-linear form as follows:

$$log\ q_t = -2.385\ (0.128) - 0.700\ (0.049)\ log\ c_t + 0.831\ (0.024)\ (log\ p_t)^* \tag{15}$$
$$R^2/s.e = 0.995/0.019$$

Both coefficients are of the correct signs and highly significant. The price elasticity of supply is estimated to be 0.831. As pointed out in the section on theoretical framework, since the quantity variable includes both new construction and the amount of existing housing made available for sale, the price elasticity of supply under our theoretical framework is smaller than the elasticity of supply of new housing alone.

Before closing this section we note that our estimates of price elasticity may be biased downward. As pointed out, housing consists of two components: (1) owner-occupied housing; and (2) rental housing. For (1), the appropriate price variable is a function of our price of housing variable p_t and of the rate of interest for those requiring a mortgage to purchase the house. For (2), the price of consuming housing service is rent. In our statistical analysis, we use only the price of housing p_t as the price variable. Our price variable p_t is a good approximation of the true price if the rate of interest changes much more slowly than p_t (for which we provided supporting evidence) and if rent is approximately proportional to p_t. To the extent that these two assumptions are invalid, our price variable p_t equals the true price variable plus a measurement error. Estimating a regression equation with measurement errors in an independent variable yields a downward bias for its coefficient. Thus our estimates of price elasticity are likely to be biased downward unless the above two assumptions concerning the price variable are valid.

TABLE 3.3

Estimation of Income and Price Elasticities of Housing Demand

Equation\Elasticity	Income Elasticity	Price Elasticity
Linear	0.747	−0.309
Linear partial adjustment	1.144	−0.705
Log	0.764	−0.333
Log partial adjustment	0.833	−0.425
Cross-section	0.904	

Conclusions

We have applied the standard theory of consumer demand supplemented by a partial adjustment mechanism to explain the demand for and supply of urban residential housing in China. The demand for housing is explained by real income and relative price. The supply of housing is explained by relative price and the cost of construction. The interaction of demand and supply can explain the annual price of urban housing at the aggregate level in China very well. This result helps dispel the notion that urban housing prices in China are mainly the result of speculation. We have found the (long-run) income elasticity of demand for urban housing to be about 1, and the price elasticity of demand to be between −0.5 and −0.6. The price elasticity of supply of the total stock of housing is about 0.83.

In applying the standard theory of consumer demand to the demand for durable goods, we have adopted two simplifying assumptions. First, the rent of housing is approximately proportional to the price variable for housing that we use. Second, the movement of the rate of interest that affects monthly mortgage payment is small and infrequent relative to the movement of prices. While these two assumptions may introduce errors in the price variable in our model, the fact that the simple model of demand and supply employed in this chapter has succeeded in providing elasticity estimates of correct signs and reasonable orders of magnitude is reassuring. Our estimates of income elasticity are similar to those found in other countries and in China in the early 1930s. This study is an example of the applicability of standard economic analysis to the Chinese economy. Numerous other examples can be found in Chow (2007).

If the past increase in the price of urban housing in China was the result mainly of increase in income and not of speculation, we can conclude that a housing bubble did not occur during our sample period up to 2006. There would be no evidence of a bubble in housing price after 2006 unless the rate of increase in housing price after 2006 is outside the range predicted by equations (7) and (8). This remark applies to urban China as a whole and does not rule out a housing bubble in particular cities.

ACKNOWLEDGMENTS

We would like to express our thanks to Professor Vernon Henderson of Brown University for helpful comments; Ms. Lai Chu Lau of the City University of Hong Kong for providing expert help in data collection; and Wei Yang, a student at the Wang Yanan Institute for Studies in Economics, Xiamen University, for his excellent research assistance. Acknowledgment with thanks also go to the research support from the Gregory C. Chow Econometric Research Program of Princeton University.

REFERENCES

Chow, Gregory C. 1957. *Demand for automobiles in the United States: A study in consumer durables.* Amsterdam: North-Holland.

———. 1960. Statistical demand functions for automobiles and their use for forecasting. In *Demand for durable goods*, ed. Arnold C. Harberger, 149–178. Chicago: University of Chicago Press.

———. 2007. *China's economic transformation*, 2d ed. New York: Wiley.

Harberger, Arnold C., ed. 1960. *Demand for durable goods*. Chicago: University of Chicago Press.

Houthakker, H. S. 1957. An international comparison of household expenditure patterns, commemorating the centenary of Engel's Law. *Econometrica* 25:532–551.

Hu, Jianying, Liangjun Su, Sainan Jin, and Wanjun Jiang. 2006. The rise in house prices in China: Bubbles or fundamentals? *Economics Bulletin* 3(7):1–8.

Muth, Richard. 1960. The demand for non-farm housing. In *Demand for durable goods*, ed. Arnold C. Harberger, 29–96. Chicago: University of Chicago Press.

National Bureau of Statistics of China. *China statistical yearbook 2007*. Beijing: China Statistics Press.

———. *China statistical abstract from 2002 to 2008*. Beijing: China Statistics Press.

Zhang, Hong, Shaoqun Weng, and Xuan Zhou. 2007. Housing price fluctuations across China: An equilibrium mechanism perspective. *Tsinghua Science and Technology* 12(3):302–308.

4

Housing Demand of Migrants in Chinese Cities

YUMING FU, SIQI ZHENG, AND RONGRONG REN

Since the liberalization of Chinese urban housing and labor markets two decades ago, in the wake of the urban economic reform and growth led by manufacturing and export, over 100 million rural migrants in China have found their way to urban employment. But few of those migrant workers expect to make the city their home.[1] The *hukou* system, put in place in the 1950s to register people by their hometown origin and by urban versus rural status for the purpose of regulating migration, remains a barrier for rural migrants to become urban citizens (see, for example, Wang and Zuo 1999). Many local public services, such as public education and health care, and social security benefits, such as unemployment insurance, public pensions, and Housing Provident Fund schemes, which are provided and administered by local governments, are rationed by *hukou* and are not portable. Migrants without urban *hukou* thus can be denied local public services and social security benefits in a city. What are the implications of *hukou* for housing demand in Chinese cities?

Economic theory tells us that the demand for housing is derived from the more fundamental demand for shelter and for access to employment, public services, and amenities (e.g., Rosen 2002). Migrants move to cities for better access. The benefits of cities other than their capacity to provide productive employment opportunities are increasingly recognized. Lucas (2004) and Glaeser and Mare (2001), for example, highlight the benefits of human capital spillovers that reduce the cost of learning in cities. Glaeser, Kolko, and Saiz (2001), Costa and Kahn (2003), and Rappaport (2009) show the increasing importance of urban amenities for residential location choices in developed economies as rising income increases the demand for

---

[1] A recent survey by Renmin University in Beijing found that about a third of migrants in their 20s aspired to build a house in their home village rather than buy one in a city. Only 7 percent identified themselves as city people (see Migration in China: Invisible and heavy shackles. *The Economist*, May 6, 2010).

quality of living. In the context of developing economies, Zheng, Fu, and Liu (2009) find an increasing demand for quality of living in China, as revealed by individuals' differential willingness to pay for housing in different cities. Rappaport (2008) shows that living in larger cities means consumption of more amenities; for example, the difference in amenity consumption between the second most dense and the least dense U.S. metropolitan areas is about 30 percent of average consumer expenditure.

The importance of access to human capital spillovers and to quality of living with respect to the benefits of living in cities suggest a model of housing demand that involves both consumption and investment motives. The dichotomy of those motives has been emphasized in the housing literature (e.g., Henderson and Ioannides 1983), but the traditional dichotomy makes no distinction between the consumption of shelter services (structural attributes) and location qualities or between financial and nonfinancial returns on the housing investment. Such distinctions help us to understand the role of *hukou* with respect to housing demand in Chinese cities. Locations accessible to good public services would have little value to migrants who would be denied these services for want of urban *hukou*. Furthermore, deprivation of local public services and social security benefits deters migrants from long-term stays in cities, diminishing their incentives to invest in human capital that would produce returns in the long run. Accordingly, the value of locations that offer good access to social interactions and human capital spillovers, which reduce the cost of learning, is diminished to migrants without urban *hukou* in the city.

The objective of this chapter is to investigate the extent to which individuals' *hukou* status in Chinese cities affects their housing demand. In particular, we decompose housing consumption into two components—(1) expenditure on shelter services, as determined by the structural attributes of a home; and (2) expenditure on quality of housing location—so that the importance of *hukou* status for accessing local public services and as an incentive to invest in human capital can be assessed in terms of the effect of *hukou* on housing demand.

Many studies have examined labor migration incentives in the context of China's recent economic development (e.g., Liang and White 1997; Wu and Yao 2003; Poncet 2006). Fu and Gabriel (2010), in particular, find low-skill migrants, with little chance of obtaining urban *hukou* in destination cities, to attach considerably less importance to potential human capital spillover benefits in migration destination choices than high-skill migrants. Our study shows that residents without urban *hukou* have a significantly lower demand for the location quality of housing, providing further evidence on the adverse effect of the *hukou* system on human capital investment incentives of migrants. Given the importance of migration for raising labor productivity in China's economic development and structural change, such an adverse effect of the *hukou* system could be costly for China's long-term economic growth.

Empirical Analysis

Our empirical analysis employs household survey data and consists of four steps. Step 1 involves a hedonic regression to decompose home value into two components: the value of shelter services and the value of location quality (access to employment, public services, and amenities). Similar decomposition is used in Rapaport (1997) and Zabel (2004). In this setup, the location premium of housing prices would increase the cost of shelter services. Step 2 applies Mincerian wage regression to decompose household employment income into a permanent income component, predictable by demographic and human capital attributes of the household, and a transitory shock component. Step 3 estimates a probit model of housing tenure choice. And step 4 estimates the household demand for housing shelter services (the value of building in structural attributes) and for housing location quality, taking into consideration household permanent income and tenure choice.

The empirical analysis is applied to a sample of Beijing households derived from the 2007 Urban Household Survey (UHS). UHS is conducted by the National Bureau of Statistics of China (NBSC) in cities across the country. The UHS samples 30–40 households in randomly selected neighborhoods (called *ju wei hui*, or JWH) in each of the 152 precincts (*jie dao*, or JD) in Beijing. Among the 2,459 households in our sample, 91.5 percent have Beijing urban *hukou*, 5.8 percent have urban *hukou* from other cities, and 2.7 percent have agricultural *hukou* from other places. Beijing is regarded as one of the most restrictive cities in China in terms of offering urban *hukou* to migrants from rural areas and from other cities.

Decomposition of Home Value

The home value of a household in the UHS, H_VALUE, is assessed according to the market value of similar homes recently sold in adjacent locations. It averages about 600,000 yuan in our Beijing sample, about 20 times the average household total annual income (see table 4.1). The home size, H_SIZE, ranges from 6 square meters to 240 square meters and averages 75 square meters. To decompose the home value into the components corresponding to housing services produced by structural attributes and by location quality, respectively, we regress $\ln(H\_VALUE)$ on $\ln(H\_SIZE)$, building type H_TYPE, cooking fuel type H_FUEL, property right type H_TITLE, and jie dao fixed effects JD_FE. We allow the marginal value of $\ln(H\_SIZE)$ to vary by location price premium (JD_FE). The Ordinary Least Squares (OLS) hedonic estimates are reported in table 4.2.[2] The price per square meter declines with the size of total living area and the marginal contribution of H_SIZE to the home value is proportionally smaller in more expensive locations, where the fixed portion of home value is higher.

We define the (relative) value of housing services produced by location quality to be JD_FE and that produced by the structural attributes (size of living area, building type, fuel type, and unobserved attributes), H_SV, to be $\ln(H\_VALUE)$ minus JD_FE and H_TITLE effects. The sample statistics of JD_FE and H_SV are reported in table 4.1.

---

[2] We first estimate the equation without the interaction between JD_FE and $\ln(H\_SIZE)$ to obtain an initial estimate of JD_FE equal to jie dao fixed effects. The hedonic equation is reestimated to include the interactive term $JD\_FE^*\ln(H\_SIZE)$, and the value of JD_FE is updated. The process is repeated until JD_FE values converge.

Variable Description and Sample Statistics

Variables	Description	Mean	Median	Max.	Min.	SD
H_VALUE	Estimated market value of the home (10,000 yuan)	60.8	52.0	500.0	1.0	41.3
H_SIZE	Living area of the home (m^2)	75.3	70.0	240.0	6.0	32.1
HHLINC	Household annual employment income (yuan)	26,034	21,000	267,200	0	23,315
HHLINCF	Household permanent income (yuan), predicted by Mincerian regression	20,434	18,055	62,346	4,770	8,277
HHTINC	Household total income (yuan)	32,047	26,220	267,200	0	24,792
HHSIZE	Number of people in the household	2.8	3.0	8.0	1.0	0.8
H_TYPE	Home building type: 1=single-family, 2=high-rise condo, 3=old-style building with shared kitchen and bathroom, 4=old-style single-story building					
H_TITLE	Type of housing property rights: 1=leased private housing, 2=leased public housing, 3=old private, 4=converted public to private, 5=new private (commodity housing), 6=new low-income housing, 7=other					
H_FUEL	Type of cooking fuel: 1=electricity, 2=town gas, 3=natural gas, 4=liquefied petrol gas, 5=coal, 6=other					
AGE	Age of household head	45.2	46.0	64.0	20.0	10.2
GENDER	Gender of household head: 1=male, 2=female	1.4	1.0	2.0	1.0	0.5
EDU	Years of schooling of household head	12.9	12.0	19.0	6.0	3.0
HUKOU	*Hukou* status of household head: 1=local urban *Hukou*, 2=local agricultural *Hukou*, 3=nonlocal urban *Hukou*, 4=nonlocal agricultural *Hukou*					
RENT	Binary housing tenure indicator: 1=rent, 0=own	0.2	0.0	1.0	0.0	0.4
CBD_EMP	Binary indicator of household head employment industry: 1=industry centrally located in the city (including finance, insurance, real estate, telecom, IT), 0=otherwise	0.1	0.0	1.0	0.0	0.3
JD_FE	Jie dao fixed effects from hedonic regression, measuring housing location quality	−0.883	−0.764	0.602	−5.130	0.782
H_SV	Housing shelter service value=ln(*H_VALUE*) − *JD_FE* − *H_TITLE* effects	4.842	4.870	6.604	0.390	0.699
IM_R	Inverse Mills ratio with respect to renting: normal density over probability of renting predicted by the probit regression of tenure choice	0.341	0.306	1.336	0.099	0.150
IM_O	Inverse Mills ratio with respect to owning: normal density over probability of owning predicted by the probit regression of tenure choice	1.450	1.486	2.109	0.385	0.230

NOTES: The sample statistics are calculated using 2,459 observations taken from the Beijing sample of the 2007 UHS. SD=standard deviation.

TABLE 4.2

OLS Estimation of Hedonic Equation

Dependent Variable	ln(*H_VALUE*)	Sample Mean
Constant	0.929 (3.6)***	
ln(*H_SIZE*)	0.960 (44.1)***	
*JD_FE**ln(*H_SIZE*)	−0.081 (3.9)***	
H_TYPE: high-rise condo	−0.534 (2.2)**	87.3%
H_TYPE: old-style, shared kitchen and bath	−0.523 (2.2)**	2.7%
H_TYPE: old-style, single story	−0.567 (2.4)**	9.8%
H_FUEL: town gas	0.007 (0.1)	0.8%
H_FUEL: natural gas	0.009 (0.2)	68.8%
H_FUEL: liquefied petrol gas	−0.038 (1.0)	27.9%
H_FUEL: coal	−0.260 (2.4)**	1.3%
H_FUEL: other	−0.100 (1.8)*	0.04%
H_TITLE: leased public	0.040 (1.8)*	4.6%
H_TITLE: old private	0.142 (3.5)***	3.8%
H_TITLE: converted public	0.033 (2.1)**	33.7%
H_TITLE: new private	0.095 (4.5)***	33.8%
H_TITLE: new low-income	0.040 (1.7)*	7.6%
H_TITLE: other	−0.062 (0.9)	1.7%
Jie Dao fixed effects	151 fixed effects	
R-square	0.932	

NOTES: t-statistics based on White Heteroskedasticity-Consistent Standard Errors & Covariance are in parentheses. ***=1% statistical significance; **=5% statistical significance; *=10% statistical significance. Number of observations is 2,459. The regression is iterated for *JD_FE* to converge.

Household Permanent Income

Since housing is a durable consumer good, the demand for housing services depends not only on a household's current income but also on its expected long-term income, called permanent income. According to a standard Mincerian wage model, household employment income *HHLINC* is regressed on household demographic attributes and human capital for the purpose of predicting the household permanent income; the OLS estimates are reported in table 4.3.

Other things being equal, households headed by a female make about 7.5 percent more from employment than those headed by a male. Moreover, each year of schooling by the household head increases household employment income by about 12.5 percent; the incremental effect of schooling is somewhat smaller for older household heads. In addition, we find migration (*hukou*) status to have little effect on household employment earning or return to schooling, suggesting no labor market discrimination with respect to *hukou* status. The estimates in table 4.3 are used to compute the permanent income measure *HHLINCF* (the age effect, which is small, is excluded so that the predicted employment income is invariant with respect to the age of household head). *HHLINCF* varies between 4,770 yuan and 62,346 yuan in the sample (see table 4.1).

TABLE 4.3

OLS Estimation of Permanent Income Equation

Dependent Variable	ln($HHLINC$)
Constant	7.684 (54.0)***
Female household head	0.075 (2.6)***
AGE	0.003 (1.4)
ln($HHSIZE$)	0.567 (13.0)***
EDU	0.125 (21.0)***
Nonlocal *hukou*	0.286 (1.4)
EDU*(AGE>35)	−0.007 (2.0)**
EDU*(nonlocal *hukou*)	0.002 (0.2)
R-square	0.257

NOTES: t-statistics are in parentheses. ***=1% statistical significance; **=5% statistical significance. Number of observations is 2,459.

Housing Tenure Choice

The housing literature predicts that the likelihood of home ownership increases with a household's income and decreases with its mobility (e.g., Henderson and Ioannides 1983; Fu 1991). We estimate a probit model of housing tenure choice, taking into account household income, household demographic attributes, and migration status. The estimates reported in table 4.4 show that the probability of owning increases with permanent income *HHLINCF* and, to a lesser extent, with transitory income (computed as the log difference between household total annual income *HHTINC* and the predicted household permanent income *HHLINCF*). Households headed by a female are more likely to rent. *Hukou* status has a significant impact on housing tenure choice; households with nonlocal *hukou* are significantly more likely to rent, but, among nonlocal households, those with urban *hukou* are more likely to buy than those with agricultural *hukou*. The results suggest that households without local urban *hukou* anticipate greater residential mobility.

The predicted latent index of propensity to rent from the probit regression is used to compute inverse Mills ratios to account for potential selection bias in housing demand: *IM_R* equals the normal probability density over the probability of renting, and *IM_O* equals the normal density over the probability of owning. A high *IM_R* value indicates an unlikely renter, whereas a high *IM_O* value indicates an unlikely owner.

Housing Demand: Shelter Services Versus Location Quality

To evaluate the importance of *hukou* status on housing demand, we estimate two demand equations, one for shelter services *H_SV* and the other for location quality *JD_FE*, taking into account household income, demographic attributes, and housing tenure choice, as well as *hukou* status. The estimates are reported in table 4.5.

TABLE 4.4

Probit Estimates of Housing Tenure Choice

Binary Dependent Variable	Rent
Constant	2.581 (3.0)***
ln($HHLINCF$)	−0.355 (3.9)***
ln(($HHTINC$+1)/$HHLINCF$)	−0.131 (3.2)***
35<AGE<=50	0.109 (1.2)
AGE>50	−0.008 (0.1)
$HHSIZE$	−0.045 (1.1)
Nonlocal *hukou*	1.136 (6.9)***
Nonlocal urban *hukou*	−0.501 (2.5)**
Female household head	0.171 (2.8)***
LR statistic (8 df)	127.3

NOTES: z-statistics are in parentheses. ***=1% statistical significance; **=5% statistical significance. Number of observations is 2,459.

In the demand equation for H_SV, the location price premium JD_FE is also included to control for price differences for shelter services. We find a highly significant negative price elasticity of demand for shelter services, as expected; a 10 percent increase in the location price premium reduces the demand for shelter services by about 5 percent. The permanent income elasticity is positive and significant, as is the transitory income elasticity, though much smaller in magnitude. Renters have a significantly smaller demand for housing shelter services, but household size, household life cycle (according to the age of the household head), and, notably, *hukou* status have little effect on the demand for shelter services. In addition, the H_SV demand does not appear to be affected by tenure choice selection bias.

The demand for housing location quality (JD_FE) behaves quite differently from that for shelter services in many respects. First, the elasticity estimates with respect to both permanent income and transitory income are much larger in magnitude and in statistical significance. The demand rises over the household life cycle but declines with household size. Renters, especially those with local *hukou*, have a greater demand for location quality. Those working in finance and IT-related industries pay a higher location premium for homes nearer to central business districts to save commuting cost. *Hukou* status is important for the demand for housing location quality, as suggested by the potential effect of *hukou* status on human capital accumulation incentives; households without local urban *hukou*, especially those with agricultural *hukou* from outside of Beijing, have a significantly weaker demand for housing location quality. Finally, the selection bias with respect to housing tenure choice also appears important: Unlikely renters tend to sacrifice housing location quality, whereas unlikely owners tend to buy in high-quality locations. The finding suggests that home ownership, which would indicate an expectation for long-term stays in the city, elevates incentives to invest in human capital accumulation.

TABLE 4.5

OLS Estimates of Demand for Housing Shelter Services and Location Quality

Dependent Variable	H_SV	JD_FE
Constant	1.715 (2.6)***	−10.118 (13)***
JD_FE	−0.506 (32.0)***	
ln(HHLINCF)	0.289 (5.1)***	0.842 (13.0)***
ln((HHTINC+1)/HHLINCF)	0.089 (3.4)***	0.375 (10.0)***
35<AGE<=50	0.015 (0.5)	0.154 (3.3)***
AGE>50	0.005 (0.2)	0.404 (8.3)***
HHSIZE	−0.003 (0.2)	−0.051 (2.4)**
Nonlocal hukou	0.027 (0.2)	−1.089 (4.8)***
Nonlocal urban hukou	0.170 (1.3)	0.435 (3.0)***
RENT	−1.108 (2.7)***	3.757 (7.3)***
RENT*(nonlocal hukou)	0.064 (0.5)	−0.495 (2.7)***
CBD_EMP		0.172 (3.5)***
IM_R *RENT	0.271 (1.2)	−1.704 (5.7)***
IM_O *(1-RENT)	−0.250 (0.7)	2.171 (5.5)***
R-square	0.494	0.175

NOTES: *t*-statistics based on White Heteroskedasticity-Consistent Standard Errors & Covariance are in parentheses. ***=1% statistical significance; **=5% statistical significance. Number of observations is 2,459.

Conclusions

Analysis shows important differences between determinants of the demand for housing shelter services and those of the demand for housing location quality. The latter is found to be more sensitive to household income and *hukou* status, reflecting the importance of both the consumption (of public services and urban amenities) and investment (with respect to human capital) motives of housing location choice. The findings indicate not only consumers' strong willingness to pay for local public services and amenities as their income rises, but also the welfare cost of the *hukou* system in China, which discourages migrants in Chinese cities from investing in human capital.

ACKNOWLEDGMENTS

Earlier versions of this chapter were presented at the the Lincoln Institute of Land Policy conference "Housing Policy and Housing Markets in China," May 2009, and at the Asia Pacific Real Estate Research Symposium at USC Lusk Center, July 2009. We thank Vernon Henderson, John Quigley, and the conference participants for valuable comments and suggestions.

REFERENCES

Costa, Dora L., and Matthew E. Kahn. 2003. The rising price of nonmarket goods. *American Economic Review* 93:227–232.

Fu, Yuming. 1991. A model of housing tenure choice: Comment. *American Economic Review* 81(1):381–383.

Fu, Yuming, and Stuart A. Gabriel. 2010. Migration and economic growth in China: The role of knowledge and human capital spillovers. Working Paper. Los Angeles: UCLA Anderson School of Management.

Glaeser, Edward L., Jed Kolko, and Albert Saiz. 2001. Consumer city. *Journal of Economic Geography* 1:27–50.

Glaeser, Edward L., and David C. Mare. 2001. Cities and skills. *Journal of Labor Economics* 19:316–342.

Henderson, J. Vernon, and Yannis M. Ioannides. 1983. A model of housing tenure choice. *American Economic Review* 73:98–113.

Liang, Zai, and Michael J. White. 1997. Market transition, government policies, and interprovincial migration in China: 1983–1988. *Economic Development and Cultural Change* 45:321–339.

Lucas, Jr., Robert E. 2004. Life earnings and rural-urban migration. *Journal of Political Economy* 112:S29–S59.

Poncet, Sandra. 2006. Provincial migration dynamics in China: Borders, costs and economic motivations. *Regional Science and Urban Economics* 36(3):385–398.

Rapaport, Carol. 1997. Housing demand and community choices. *Journal of Urban Economics* 42(2):243–260.

Rappaport, Jordan. 2008. Consumption amenities and city population density. *Regional Science and Urban Economics* 38:533–552.

———. 2009. The increasing importance of quality of life. *Journal of Economic Geography* 9:779–804.

Rosen, Sherwin 2002. Markets and diversity. *American Economic Review* 92:1–15.

Wang, Feng, and Xuejin Zuo. 1999. Inside China's cities: Institutional barriers and opportunities for urban migrants. *American Economic Review* 89(2):276–280.

Wu, Zhongmin, and Shujie Yao. 2003. Intermigration and intramigration in China: A theoretical and empirical analysis. *China Economic Review* 14:371–385.

Zabel, Jeffrey E. 2004. The demand for housing services. *Journal of Housing Economics* 13:16–35.

Zheng, Siqi, Yuming Fu, and Hongyu Liu. 2009. Demand for urban quality of living in China: Evolution in compensating land-rent and wage-rate differentials. *Journal of Real Estate Finance and Economics* 38(3):194–213.

The Winners in China's Urban Housing Reform

5

JOHN R. LOGAN, YIPING FANG, AND ZHANXIN ZHANG

In the early 1980s the Chinese government announced that the national policy of economic reform would be extended to the housing sector, first by raising public housing rents to market prices and then by privatizing housing production and consumption. These reforms would radically change a system in which most urban residents relied on their work units or on municipal housing authorities to provide shelter at highly subsidized rents (Logan, Bian, and Bian 1999). An apartment allocated by a person's employer was almost free, but it was also likely to be small, poorly equippéd, and hard to obtain. Reform could require people to pay more for housing (compensated only partly by rising wage levels), but it could also spur investment in a housing stock that had fallen far behind people's needs (World Bank 1992; Kosareva and Struyk 1993). It also had the potential to weaken workers' lifelong dependency on their employers.

More than two decades later, it is possible to evaluate the privatization process and, in particular, to investigate its distributive consequences. Not surprisingly, the transition to a market system has been only partial. There is an emerging private rental housing market due to increasing labor mobility and rapid economic development. The growth of a new affluent class of entrepreneurs and professionals has also supported an expansion of housing construction for sale at market prices. Yet a considerable (if declining) share of public housing continues to be occupied by renters, and purchasers of public housing have been highly subsidized. This means that there are effectively at least two kinds of systems operating today in China. Sato (2006) describes these as an "internal" market that has developed from within the welfare system and an "open" market that is still being created. It is unclear how long the system will continue in this transitional phase, or at what point people will be making housing choices largely in terms of the standard market criteria of price, quality, and location.

This chapter appeared in *Housing Studies* 25, 1 (2010):101–118.

In the meantime the kind of housing that people live in depends not only on their market resources but also—and in fact mostly—on their position in the pre-reform system. Similar to the experience in several other countries, privatization of public housing took the form of transferring ownership to tenants. In the Chinese case this had to be accomplished in an economy where most people had little access to capital, with only the beginning of a system of home mortgages and no recent history of market pricing. Privatization had to be subsidized, while public rental housing continued to be priced below market levels.

Who were the winners in this particular phase of China's "marketization" policy? This question can be pursued through analysis of census data for the year 2000 from eight major cities that include information on types of housing tenure, various measures of quality, and cost. The question is: Who is paying less for better housing by virtue of state subsidy?

Similar questions have been raised in other countries where public housing underwent privatization. It has been widely reported that the privatization of public housing in Eastern Europe and the Russian Federation after 1990 represented substantial transfers of wealth, in the form of giveaways and discounted sales of public housing apartments, to sitting tenants. Discounted sales and the free transfer of public housing to sitting tenants are rationalized as enabling strategies that restore housing market demand and increase mobility and housing choice (Angel 2000). It is also said that the policy is a form of payback for a process of many years when households "financed capital subsidies for past investment with forced savings through the wage repression mechanism" (Buckley 1996, 40). However, since not all citizens benefit from the privatization policy, it is essential to evaluate more carefully the distributional impacts.

Kosareva and Struyk (1993, 95) note that evidently "housing privatization potentially involves an enormous transfer of wealth to individual households." In major Russian cities in 1992, for example, they estimated the market value of an average public housing unit at more than six times the average annual family income. To achieve rapid privatization the prices were highly subsidized. For example, in Hungary about 35 percent of the public housing stock existing in 1990 had been privatized by 1993 at prices between 15 percent and 40 percent of market value (Hegedüs and Tosics 1993). Pickvance (1994, 435–436) points out that in Hungary even before privatization of public housing people with higher occupational status benefited from both the original socialist system and the expansion of the private housing stock: first by being allocated the most attractive state housing, then by cashing in on the value of these apartments by selling occupancy rights to new tenants, and finally by purchasing on favorable terms in the private sector. Kosareva and Struyk (1993) make a similar evaluation for Russia, that higher-income households occupied the more valuable public housing and (since prices were only modestly adjusted for quality and in any case were much lower than market valuation) therefore received larger transfers of wealth through privatization. Other research suggests that the impacts varied by country. Yemtsov (2007), for example, finds that privatization strongly increased wealth inequality in Russia and Serbia but resulted in less wealth inequality in Poland.

Low prices do not necessarily make a good investment. The actual value of public housing depends in large part on the quality of initial construction and need for repair. In Britain, for example, sometimes the better units were sold and the low-quality units had no takers. In other cases low-income families, lured by the prospect of home ownership, took on loan burdens that they could not sustain, or were unable to keep their homes in good repair (Karn and Wolman 1992). The other side of this issue is that many people remain in public rental housing, and it is necessary to consider the quality and rental rates for that housing. Again in the British case, it has been argued that housing provided by local public authorities was "worth" considerably more than the remaining tenants were paying in rent (Willis and Nicholson 1991), so those who continued to rent in this sector certainly did better than those who rented in the private sector.

Hence, to evaluate who came out ahead in housing privatization in China, it is necessary to determine what is being paid and what comparable units would cost in the private sector. For those who purchase public housing, this is the difference between their purchase prices and the prices paid by those who buy private-market housing. For those who continue to rent in the public sector, it is the difference between their rents (adjusted for quality) and the rents paid by people in the private market.

The Chinese Case

In comparison to Eastern Europe, where the overall share of state-owned housing at the end of the socialist period was only 28 percent (Hegedüs and Tosics 1996), public housing in China was absolutely dominant in urban areas before the reform. Huang (2004) reports that 75 percent of households were in the public housing sector through the socialist period, and the share might be even bigger in large cities (Logan, Bian, and Bian 1999). Because rents were set at extremely low levels (less than 1 percent of household income, according to Wang and Murie [1999]), public housing was heavily subsidized, and one motivation for housing reform was to reduce the burden on municipal and work-unit budgets (Yang and Wang 1995). Housing reform began with a policy of significant rent increases, followed by a plan to shift public housing to private ownership and promote development of market housing.

A key question for China's policy makers was how to price the sale of public housing. Their approach was to set a standard price of construction in each city, based on floor space, and to adjust it according to characteristics of the location, the building, and the housing unit itself. The discount rate was also adjusted according to characteristics of the purchaser. According to some official documents (State Council 2004), the most significant locational factor in that scheme was an assessment of land values in the neighborhood, which could vary the price by as much as 30 percent. Access to shopping and availability of public transportation and other public infrastructure were also taken into account. A building factor adjustment considered such features as the age of the structure (buildings more than 30 years old, for example, were discounted by 30 percent), building materials, elevators, and height. Unit characteristics included which floor the apartment was on (favoring the highest floors in buildings with elevators and floors 3–4 in buildings without elevators) and the direction faced by bedroom windows (with a 3 percent discount for west-facing bedrooms).

The amount of subsidy provided under the Beijing government housing regulations also depended on the employee's job rank. For the lowest-level administrative position (*Ke* and below), for example, employees were considered qualified for an apartment of 60 square meters. This meant that the tenant would receive a subsidized price on the first 60 square meters and would pay the standard price for additional space. A *Ju*-level official, in contrast, qualified for a subsidy on up to 120 square meters.

There is considerable variation in how different work units applied rules such as these. The "standard price" (not a market price) often depended on seniority. Beginning in the 1990s the state introduced a mandatory Housing Provident Fund, to which employees were required to contribute a fraction (around 5 percent) of their salary, matched by the employer, for the purpose of financing a housing purchase (Yeung and Howes 2006). An additional subsidy provided by many work units is based on the number of years that the person was working prior to establishment of the Housing Provident Fund (if the spouse was in the same work unit, those years would also be counted). In addition, work units that owned or controlled housing were free to offer different prices for different tenants. But for those who did not work for a government agency and whose work unit controlled no housing, as well as those who could not qualify for any subsidy (i.e., persons who were not employed or did not have a local urban registration), privatization offered no benefits.

As a starting point, we hypothesize that if there is a benefit to public housing purchase or remaining a public-housing renter (compared to purchasing or renting in the private market), the benefit will most likely be distributed in a way that mirrors past practices. Thus, it is important to document which workers were favored in housing allocation in the past. Formally, housing was a welfare benefit to be distributed based on merit and need. Yet there is considerable evidence that in China, as in other socialist countries (Szelenyi 1983), individuals of higher socioeconomic and political status have had privileged access to housing of good quality at a low cost. Logan, Bian, and Bian (1999) showed that housing was allocated partly on the basis of seniority through a continuous process over time of negotiating for larger or better equipped housing. Income, education, and Communist Party membership had positive effects on the size and quality of housing, as did employment in a larger and administratively more powerful work unit. Pan (2004) found that Communist Party membership was associated with larger housing size and higher housing quality in both 1988 and 1995. Davis (2003) showed that workers with more seniority in higher-ranked work units were more likely to receive better housing.

There is little research on access to housing in the post-1990 period, when the marketization policy was greatly expanded. One exception is Sato's (2006) study of prices for housing purchased from 1996 to 1999. Sato reported that seniority, education, work-unit administrative rank, and party membership resulted in reduced prices for housing purchased in the public sector. Sato also documented the disadvantages of migrants in the emerging housing market (on this point see also Logan, Fang, and Zhang 2009). Most migrant households have to rent or sublet housing owned by local households, often at very high prices. Rent and utilities amounted to an average of 26 percent of total household expenditure for migrants, compared to only 7 percent for locally registered urban households, largely because of migrants' exclusion from public rental housing.

Research Design

Similar disparities in the prices paid for housing are to be expected. This study uses 2000 census microdata (a public use sample of 0.1 percent) to quantify the differences in prices in the public and private sectors for both housing purchases and rentals. This source has the advantage of broad coverage of urban China. It includes residents of eight of the largest cities: Beijing, Chongqing, Guangzhou, Harbin, Nanjing, Shanghai, Tianjin, and Xi'an. There are significant regional differences. For example, Huang and Clark (2002; see also Li and Wu 2004) found in a national housing survey that nearly half of total variation in tenure choice is between cities. Such differences have been acknowledged by including city dummy variables in the multivariate models, so that all prices are in effect measured from the city average.

These data have important limitations. People in collective housing (e.g., migrants in work-unit dormitories), whose expenditures are not reported in the census, and people in self-built housing (the usual source for rural villagers), where the building cost is not comparable to other owner-occupied housing, have been excluded. The census identifies five tenure types that can be compared. In the public sector these are public purchases by sitting tenants and public rentals. Public purchase is compared to two tenure categories: market purchase (including most housing sold at market prices) and "economic purchase" (a form of private housing where builders pass on limited construction subsidies to qualifying buyers). The date of purchase is not reported, but we are able to control for whether people have lived in their current neighborhood for less or more than five years. Because all forms of purchase increased greatly during the late 1990s, we do not believe that rising purchase prices bias this comparison. Current (1999) rents for public and private rental housing are compared. In both the owner and renter sectors all prices are provided by the census in categories, which we code to the category midpoint. Values in the top category are coded to the category's minimum value.

Hedonic models (Rosen 1974; Follain and Jimenez 1985) are estimated to determine how purchase prices and rents in the private sector are related to characteristics of the housing unit. In such models it is expected that larger size, higher quality, existence of amenities, and better accessibility should all predict a higher housing price. Hedonic models have been applied in studies of the impact of urban green spaces in Guangzhou (Jim and Chen 2006) and Jinan (Kong, Yin, and Nakagoshi 2007). A precondition for successful application of hedonic pricing is the existence of a mature housing market that is achieving equilibrium. This is, of course, not the case for China, so the results reported here should be interpreted as a first approximation. Our purpose is to apply the hedonic model coefficients to housing units in the public sector, estimating what roughly comparable units would cost if they were in the private market. The difference between this estimated cost (or "market value") will then be treated as the subsidy received by public-sector purchasers or tenants.

Our models use all available housing characteristics from the census. Housing space is measured in square meters, and a second-order term is included to test for nonlinearity. Housing quality is an index ranging from 0 to 100, based on five equally weighted aspects of housing units: with or without kitchen, energy source for cooking (gas is treated as the favorable type), with or without tap water, type of bathing facilities (hot water supply as the most favorable type), and individual toilet. Number of rooms is also included. Having smaller but more rooms in a given space was an old fashioned design and is usually considered to be a negative quality. Building types are categorical variables: low-rise, high-rise, and courtyard housing. There are few cases of courtyard housing among market purchasers, so that housing type is excluded from the analysis of owner housing. Building age is the number of years since construction.

Based on these variables and hedonic models for private-market housing, the "market value" of apartments in the public sector and the subsidy received by public-sector participants are estimated. In turn, the personal characteristics associated with receiving higher or lower levels of subsidy are analyzed. These models also make use of the limited number of characteristics that are available from the census.

A key predictor is residence status, which uses three kinds of information. The first is whether the person was born in the current city of residence (to distinguish migrants from natives). The second adds an institutional status, whether the person has a rural or urban household registration (i.e., agricultural or nonagricultural eligibility). The third is related to migrants' length of residence in the city. A person who was living in the current city for five years or more is treated as an "established" resident; someone who has arrived within the last five years is "recent." Combining these three criteria leads to six categories of residence status: urban natives, rural villagers, established urban migrants, recent urban migrants, established rural migrants, and recent rural migrants. All cases of public purchase have urban and local registration, because there were too few such owners with rural or nonlocal registration to be studied.

A related variable is spouse's registration status, which is combined with marital status into a "living status" variable with three categories: living with a spouse with urban registration, living with a spouse with rural registration, and living without a spouse. Does the registration status of one spouse compensate for that of the other? In 1998 a reform of the *hukou* system made it easier for an urbanite's migrant spouse to apply for urban registration. However, the process is not easy, and there remained many households in 2000 where spouses had different types of registration.

Another variable relevant to trends in prices is recent relocation within the city (within the past five years). In this data set "moves" are recorded only if the person changes neighborhood (street district). "Recent movers" are defined as persons who moved across neighborhoods in the past five years.

The socioeconomic variables available from the census include education, spouse's education (for those living with their spouse), and occupation. Education is measured as years of schooling. Occupation is a set of dummy variables ranging from work-unit heads and professionals and technicians at the top to agricultural laborers at the bottom, with separate categories for persons who are retired or not employed. Following the precedent of studies of housing tenure in China, gender, age (treated as a possible nonlinear effect), and household size are introduced as demographic control variables.

Results

Table 5.1 provides descriptive statistics for the eight-city sample. By a large margin the majority of cases of owner-occupied housing and rental housing are public sector, with slightly more cases of public purchase than continuing public rental. In the period since 2000, not shown here, there has been a more pronounced shift toward public purchase, with some increase in market purchase and private rental. The table shows how the central variables in the analysis (space and quality) vary across tenure categories, as do average prices (purchase cost or rent per square meter). Market-purchased housing is subdivided into two categories: commodity housing (at full market prices) and economic purchases (at somewhat discounted prices through a limited government program). Commodity housing tends to be considerably larger than other owner-occupied housing but not of much higher average quality than public-purchased housing. Yet its price on average is nearly five times higher per square meter. Public rental housing on average is larger than private rental housing and is of much higher quality (though lower quality than any category of owner-occupied housing). Its price is less than one-quarter as much per square meter. These price comparisons and the advantage that public-sector housing represents to leaseholders and owners are the motivation for this study.

The next step in the analysis is to estimate hedonic models of housing expenditures among owners and renters in market housing. Results are presented in table 5.2. The dependent variable is the log of purchase price or monthly rent. For reference, the table provides the mean values of space, housing quality, number of rooms, and building age for both types of housing, as well as the mean values of the purchase price or monthly rent for each city. Market-purchased housing is larger, higher quality, and newer than market rentals. Purchase prices on average are lowest in Xi'an and Chongqing and highest in Guangzhou, Shanghai, and Beijing.

TABLE 5.1

Average Size, Quality, and Cost of Housing by Tenure for Eight-City Sample

	N	Per Capita Space (m²)	Quality Index	Cost per Square Meter
Purchase:				
Market				
Commodity	1,177	33.2	90.2	$252.66
Economic	722	24.9	85.6	$107.13
Public	4,594	23.6	89.5	$53.14
Rental:				
Market	1,061	14.2	58.0	$1.39/month
Public	4,303	17.3	72.3	$0.30/month

SOURCE: 2000 Census microdata tabulated by authors.

NOTE: Exchange rate in 1999: US$1.00 ≈ 8.28 yuan.

TABLE 5.2

Hedonic Model of Housing Expenditure Among Market Owners (Commodity and Economic Purchase) and Market Renters

	Market Owners		Market Renters	
	Mean	Coefficient	Mean	Coefficient
Constant		2.666**		5.065**
Area space (m^2)	76.13	.030**	28.58	.011**
Square of area space		−7.04E-5**		−1.63E-5
Housing quality index	90.23	.007**	58.33	.006**
Building type (reference category: apartment)				
High-rise		.215**		.377**
Courtyard		—		−.294**
Number of rooms	2.18	−.153**	1.33	−.023
Building age (years old)	6.39	−.037**	13.49	−.001
Economic purchase	$7,338	−.647**		—
City (reference category: Beijing)	$17,766		$36.8	
Chongqing	$7,391	−.871**	$23.5	−1.000**
Guangzhou	$23,853	.226**	$48.6	−.194*
Harbin	$10,833	−.289**	$24.4	−.743**
Nanjing	$14,396	−.029	$26.4	−.434**
Shanghai	$22,210	.387**	$24.1	−.445**
Tianjin	$15,495	.054	$20.8	−.564**
Xi'an	$6,727	−.487**	$19.8	−.766**
N		1,751		1,029
Degree of freedom		14		14
Adjusted R-square		.604		.338

NOTE: *=p < .05; **=p<.01. Cost for renters is cost per month; E-5 equals to 0.00001; exchange rate in 1999: US$1.00 ≈ 8.28 yuan.

Rental prices are lowest in Xi'an, Harbin, and Tianjin and higher in Guangzhou and Beijing.

The model for private-market owners provides remarkably good prediction with an adjusted explained variance of .604. Coefficients are significant and in the expected direction. Space in square meters has a strong positive effect, diminishing somewhat at high values. Housing quality is strongly related to purchase price. High-rise construction is more expensive, but older buildings command lower prices. For a given amount of floor space, apartments divided into more and smaller rooms cost less. The coefficient for "economic purchase" shows a substantial discount. Prices in Tianjin and Nanjing are not significantly different from those in Beijing. Guangzhou and Shanghai are considerably more expensive, while Chongqing, Xi'an, and Harbin have significantly lower prices.

The model for private-market renters is less robust but still explains .338 of the variance in rents. Rents increase linearly with space and quality. High-rise buildings have higher rents than low-rise apartments, while courtyard housing is less expensive. Surprisingly, building age is unrelated to rents, perhaps because building quality and construction type have been controlled. Rents in all other cities, especially Chongqing, Harbin, and Xi'an, are lower than in Beijing.

The final step in this analysis is to determine which residents in the public sector live in housing of higher estimated market value and who receives a higher level of subsidy (discount from market value in the actual purchase price or rent paid). One important missing variable in the private-sector models is location, because the census microdata offer no geographic detail within cities. When we apply the hedonic equations to estimate the market value of housing in the public sector, results would be overestimated if public purchase and public rental housing tended to be found in worse locations than corresponding private-market units. In fact, there is reason to believe that our approach leads to *underestimates* of the value of public-sector housing. Research on land and housing prices generally shows that inner-city locations are more highly valued. For example, Zheng and Kahn (2008) report that land prices and purchase prices for new condominiums in Beijing in 2004–2005 declined at a rate of about 4 percent per kilometer from the center of the city at Tiananmen Square. Figure 5.1 shows mapped aggregated census data for Beijing neighborhoods (*jie dao*) in 2000. The share of rental units that is public-sector housing is much higher in the inner districts than at the periphery of the urban area. The correlation between public rental share and distance from the center of the city (weighting neighborhood areas by the total number of rental units) is −0.48. Hence, public-sector rental housing tends to be found in higher-value locations. There is a smaller but not significant negative correlation between the share of owner housing that is public purchase (not counting self-built housing) and distance from the center (−0.16). Purchase of work-unit housing in factory locations outside the city partly offsets the concentration of public purchase in the inner districts.

Table 5.3 reports the estimated average discount rates for all of the cities. On average the discount on public purchase housing (compared to commodity purchase housing) was 38 percent. Discount rates varied across cities, highest in Beijing and Xi'an and lowest in Shanghai. The average discount rate on monthly rent was 28 percent, with a high of 37 percent in Guangzhou and a low of 21 percent in Tianjin. These levels of subsidy are in line with estimates cited above for Hungary in the 1990s. It is also possible to estimate the aggregate value of the subsidies in each city, applying the sample values to the full urban population. There is a substantial redistribution of wealth, nearly $30 billion for the public housing that had been purchased by tenants up to 2000 and more than $9 billion in Shanghai alone. The annual rent subsidy for those who continued to live in public rental housing was above $1.2 billion. Note from the analysis above that a majority of family households in these cities benefited from these subsidies. Those who are excluded entirely from this analysis are people in collective households, the predominant form of housing for rural-urban migrants; these people were only indirectly affected by this aspect of marketization.

The next question is, Which public purchasers and which public renters received the greatest benefit? The results for public-sector housing are presented in tables 5.4 and 5.5. In almost every case the purchase price or rent is lower than the estimated market value. We believe the exceptions represent situations where an apartment is in a particularly favorable location and the hedonic

Percent of Rental Housing in the Public Rental Sector in Beijing Neighborhoods

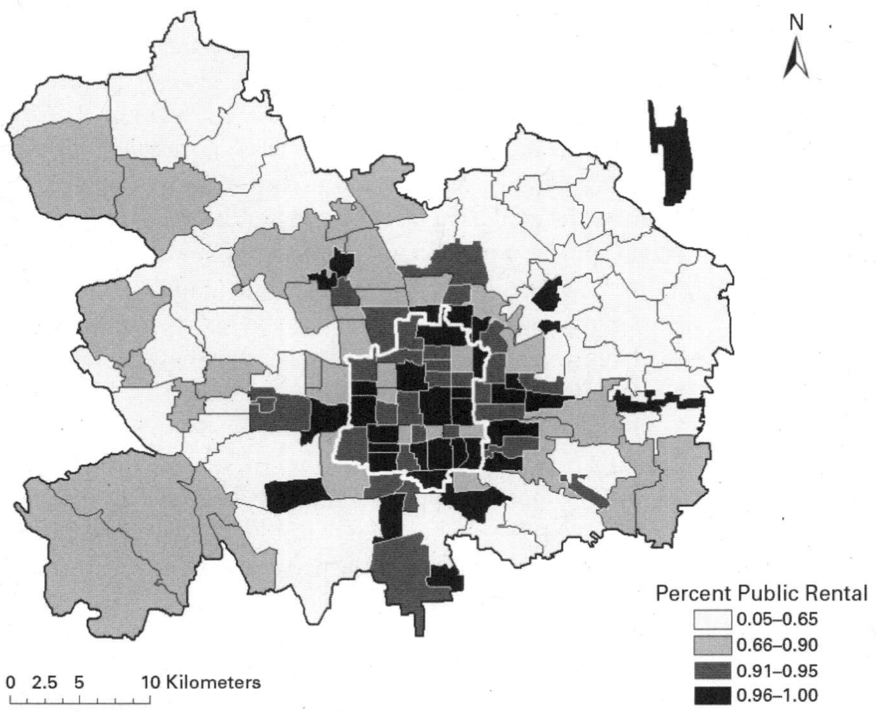

SOURCE: 2000 Population Census of China files (jie dao data), Department of Geography, Peking University, Beijing.
NOTE: The divisions represent urban neighborhood (jie dao) boundaries. The four inner-city districts are outlined in white.

Average Discounts and Estimated Total Subsidies for Public Housing

	Public Purchase Housing		Public Rental Housing	
	Mean Discount	Estimated Total Subsidy (millions)	Mean Discount	Estimated Annual Subsidy (millions)
Beijing	0.52	$5,289	0.24	$400
Chongqing	0.48	$813	0.35	$43
Guangzhou	0.35	$4,366	0.37	$79
Harbin	0.40	$1,500	0.32	$55
Nanjing	0.29	$2,303	0.23	$78
Shanghai	0.25	$9,279	0.30	$305
Tianjin	0.31	$2,030	0.21	$196
Xi'an	0.52	$849	0.31	$23
Total	0.38	$28,700	0.28	$1,247

SOURCE: 2000 Census microdata tabulated by authors.
NOTE: Exchange rate in 1999: US$1.00 ≈ 8.28 yuan.

Regression on Estimated Market Value of Public Purchase Housing and Discount Represented by Price Paid

	Housing Market Value	Discount Ratio
Constant	3.178**	.112*
City (reference: Beijing)		
Chongqing	−.831**	.037**
Guangzhou	.282**	.186**
Harbin	−.489**	.160**
Nanjing	−.083*	.234**
Shanghai	.170**	.270**
Tianjin	−.024	.220**
Xi'an	−.542**	−.003
Male or female (1 = male)	.015	.013
Household head age	.011*	.011**
Age squared	−8.02E-5	−7.98E-5**
Household size	.036**	−.002
Years of education	.022**	.003*
Spouse years of education	.013**	−.001
Occupation (reference: manual worker)		
Head of work unit	.228**	.013
Professional or technician	.068*	.011
Staff or other white collar	.180**	.007
Commercial or service	.098**	.008
Retired	−.006	.032*
Other unemployed	.019	.014
Residence status (reference: urban native)		
Established urban migrant	.047*	−.007
Recent urban migrant	.532**	−.104**
Living status (reference: living with urban registration spouse)		
Unmarried or not living with spouse	.101*	−0.031
Living with rural registration spouse	−.238**	0.013
Recent within-city move	.508**	−.048**
N	4,357	4,357
Degree of freedom	24	24
Adjusted *R*-squared	.402	.241

NOTES: *=p<.05; **=p<.01; E-5 equals to 0.00001. Dependent variable for the first model is ln(predicted market value of public purchase housing). Dependent variable for the second model is (1 − (actual cost of public purchase housing) / (predicted market value)).

model underestimates the market value. Hence, in cases with an estimated negative subsidy the discount ratio has been recoded to reflect a subsidy of at least 500 yuan for public purchase and 0.50 yuan per month for public rental. Note that in these models, all variables are characteristics of the head of household or spouse. Characteristics of the housing unit itself are summarized in the estimated market

TABLE 5.5

Regression on Estimated Market Rental Value of Public Housing and Discount Represented by Rent Paid

	Market Rental Value	Discount Ratio
Constant	5.015**	.765**
City (reference: Beijing)		
Chongqing	−.879**	−.099**
Guangzhou	−.047	−.074**
Harbin	−.422**	−.056**
Nanjing	−.236**	.030*
Shanghai	−.383**	−.044**
Tianjin	−.446**	.015
Xi'an	−.837**	−.074**
Male or female (1=male)	−.041*	−.015*
Household head age	.011**	.004**
Age squared	−8.81E-5**	−3.87E-5**
Household size	.050**	−.005
Years of education	.015**	−.001
Spouse years of education	.008**	−.002
Occupation (reference: manual worker)		
Head of work unit	.213**	−.033
Professional or technician	.086**	.018
Staff or other white collar	.070*	−.008
Commercial or service	.031	−.021*
Retired	.003	.001
Other unemployed	.025	.013
Residence status (reference: urban native)		
Rural villagers	.091	−.344**
Established urban migrants	.026	−.013
Recent urban migrants	.237**	−.183**
Established rural migrants	−.044	−.357**
Recent rural migrants	.108**	−.445**
Living status (reference: living with urban registration spouse)		
Not married or not living with spouse	.095**	−.011
Living with rural registration spouse	−.029	−.071**
Recent within-city move	.306**	−.043**
N	4,239	4,239
Degree of freedom	27	27
Adjusted R-squared	.345	.309

NOTES: *=p<.05; **=p<.01; E-5 equals to 0.00001. Dependent variable for the first model is ln(predicted market value of public rental housing). Dependent variable for the second model is (1− (actual public housing rent) / (predicted market value)).

value. The city of residence is included here, because housing policies vary across urban China and we have seen that the discount ratio also varies.

Table 5.4 provides results for people who purchased their public housing apartment. The estimated market value of such an apartment is highest in Guangzhou and

Shanghai and lowest in Chongqing, Harbin, and Xi'an. Older household heads and those with larger households live in more valuable apartments. Education of both the household head and spouse has significant positive effects. Not surprisingly, people who are the head of their work unit own the most valuable housing, followed by staff workers (cadres). Manual workers and retired and unemployed people live in the least valuable homes. Residence status has a substantial effect. Note that this analysis includes no one with rural or nonlocal registration. But compared to a native person with urban and local registration, recent migrants with similar registration purchased more valuable apartments, as did established migrants to a lesser degree. People living without a spouse own more valuable apartments than people married to a spouse with urban registration, but those whose spouse has a rural registration own significantly less valuable homes. Finally, recent movers within the city (those who changed neighborhoods in the past five years) live in substantially more valuable homes, which may partially reflect recent construction.

These results are consistent with expectations about who could afford a better apartment or had been living in a better public rental apartment and was therefore in a position to purchase it. A separate question is how large a subsidy they received when they purchased. This discount ratio is analyzed in table 5.4, showing that the discount ratio was higher in every other city than in Beijing, with the exception of Xi'an. The highest subsidies were in Shanghai, Tianjin, and Nanjing. Older people received a higher subsidy (a nonlinear effect that may be related to seniority). Few other variables are significant. There are significant positive effects of higher education and being retired (possibly associated with age and seniority). Recent migrants received a smaller subsidy, as did those who moved more recently within the city.

Patterns are somewhat different among public housing tenants (table 5.5). City effects show that tenants in Beijing occupy the most valuable housing, with the lowest values in Chongqing and Xi'an. Male heads of household rent less valuable apartments, while older people and larger households rent more valuable apartments. Education (both for head of household and spouse) and high-ranked occupation (work-unit heads, administrative staff, and professionals and technicians) are positively related to estimated rental value. In the public rental sector there are some rural villagers and migrants who have rural registration. Compared to urban natives, recent migrants with urban registration live in more valuable apartments, while the apartments of established rural migrants are less valuable. Unexpectedly, there is a positive coefficient for recent rural migrants, and having a spouse with rural registration does not affect rental value. People living without a spouse occupy more valuable rentals. Finally, recent movers within the city rent more valuable apartments.

Why do recent rural migrants live in more valuable public rental housing than do urban natives? A starting point is the observation that recent rural migrants are unlikely to have access to public rentals because under usual circumstances they do not qualify. In some cases, however, migrants are offered work-unit housing tied to their jobs. Recent migrants in public rental housing, whether with urban or rural registration, tend to live in newer units, which tend to be built to a higher standard,

Yet recent rural migrants have a disadvantage relative to urban natives in the price they pay. Residence status counts heavily in predicting the discount ratio for public rentals. Compared to urban natives, all other categories of people receive smaller rent subsidies, although the gap for established urban migrants is small. Recent rural migrants receive the lowest subsidies. People married to a spouse with rural registration also receive smaller subsidies, as do recent movers.

We also find that men receive a smaller discount from estimated market value than women, while older people receive higher discounts. Subsidy of public housing rents is highest in Nanjing and lowest in Chongqing. Although higher education and occupation are associated with living in more valuable apartments, they are not related to the level of subsidy. We suspect (though we do not have information to test this explanation) that workers with higher education and occupation levels are more likely to be employed in higher-ranked work units, which historically have been able to provide higher-quality housing for their employees. In that case, employees' access to better housing would be based not on their individual privilege but on the standing of their employer,

Conclusions

For potential beneficiaries the opportunity to take advantage of these housing deals, either to continue living in public rental housing or to purchase that apartment, is time limited. Comparing tabulations from the Population Census of China 2000 with data that have been made available from the 2005 mini census, we find that the share of rental housing that is in the public sector declined from over 70 percent to under 40 percent in just five years. By 2005 only 8 percent of urban housing units were public rentals, leaving few tenants with prospects for purchasing their unit. At the same time, the share of market housing purchased with no discount nearly doubled, and it seems clear that most newly constructed owner-occupied housing in the future will be in the private sector. Hence, in the space of about 20 years, starting slowly around 1990 and now nearly complete, China has achieved its intended restructuring of the urban housing system.

We find, consistent with most results elsewhere and the expectations of Chinese urban researchers (Chen 1996), that this policy has brought a windfall to those who could take advantage of it. We also find that those who have been able to remain in public rental housing for the time being receive better accommodation at lower rents than people who rent in the private sector. What were the distributional impacts of these benefits?

If the question were simply who could purchase public housing, the answer would be self-evident—it would be those who had been able to qualify for public rental housing (or better-quality housing) under the previous system. This is why, for example, in table 5.3 there are no cases of rural migrants. They had been largely excluded from public housing in the socialist period, and even those rural migrants who received public rental housing were not eligible to buy it. Our analysis mainly addresses a second-level question: Among those who qualified to purchase their public housing units, and among those who continued to rent public housing in 2000, who got the best housing and who received the most favorable terms?

The allocation of the best nonmarket housing in 2000 (estimated in terms of its market worth) closely matches the priorities for allocation of apartments under socialism, and here patterns are similar for public purchase and public rental. One criterion of need stands out: household size. People who were better placed in their work unit (older people with more seniority, those with higher education, work-unit leaders and administrative staff or professional and technical workers) were favored. Migrants and people with rural registration did worse, as did those whose spouse had rural registration. It may seem surprising that there is one category of migrants who fared well. These are migrants with urban registration, people some scholars have called "permanent migrants" (Wu 2002). The Chinese term is *qianyi* (permanently migrated), different from *zanzhu* (temporarily settled). People can gain entitlement to this change if they are recruited by a state-owned enterprise or by enrollment in an institution of higher education, thereby gaining full legal access to all city public resources. Urban migrants have done better in the urban housing system than natives with urban registration.

We anticipate that studies using other data sources will show that other privileged groups in the socialist housing system also have been able to obtain more valuable housing. These would be especially members of the Communist Party and employees of larger and more highly ranked work units. These hypotheses cannot be tested with census data.

Although previously favored groups obtained the best housing in the public sector, they did not necessarily get it with a higher discount from its market value. In both the public purchase and public rental models, older persons receive greater benefit. Education counts in the purchase model but not for rentals. No occupational differences are found in the rental model, and for purchase it turns out to be retired people rather than work-unit heads, staff, or professionals and technicians who got a higher subsidy. This means that in many respects the *pricing* of public-sector housing did not redistribute resources. Indeed, one could argue that, aside from the cumulative prior advantages of some groups under socialism, the privatization process was carried out in an equitable way. Possibly the application of bureaucratic criteria such as those described above for government-controlled housing in Beijing generally succeeded in translating housing characteristics into prices.

There is, nevertheless, one dimension of state policy that factors heavily into housing outcomes, and that is residence status. Among purchasers of public housing, there are no rural villagers or rural migrants. Recent urban migrants and recent movers received smaller discounts in purchasing public housing. Rural villagers, rural migrants, and persons whose spouse has rural registration are substantially disadvantaged in the pricing of public rental housing. It is not migrant status in itself that matters, since migrants with urban registration may even have some advantages. The continuing state policy to distinguish between urban and rural registration has placed citizens with the latter status at a severe disadvantage in the process of housing reform. In this respect our findings reinforce other studies that focus particularly on the rural-urban divide in Chinese social policy.

REFERENCES

Angel, Shlomo. 2000. *Housing policy matters: A global analysis.* Oxford, U.K.: Oxford University Press.

Buckley, Robert M. 1996. *Housing finance in developing countries.* New York: St. Martin's Press.

Chen, Aimin. 1996. China's urban housing reform: Price-rent ratio and market equilibrium. *Urban Studies* 33(7):1077–1092.

Davis, Deborah. 2003. From welfare benefit to capitalized asset: The re-commodification of residential space in urban China. In *Housing and social change: East-west perspectives,* eds. Ray Forrest and James Lee, 183–198. London: Routledge.

Follain, James R., and Emmanuel Jimenez. 1985. Estimating the demand for housing characteristics: A survey and critique. *Regional Science and Urban Economics* 15(1):77–107.

Hegedüs, József, and Iván Tosics. 1993. Changing public housing policy in a Central European metropolis: The case of Budapest. Paper presented at the European Network for Housing Research Conference, Budapest (September).

———. 1996. Urban Institute and Metropolitan Research Institute (Budapest, Hungary), *Transition of the housing sector in the Central-East European countries.* Washington, DC: Urban Institute.

Huang, Youqin. 2004. The road to homeownership: A longitudinal analysis of tenure transition in urban China (1949–1994). *International Journal of Urban and Regional Research* 28(4):774–795.

Huang, Youqin, and William A. V. Clark. 2002. Housing tenure choice in transitional urban China: A multilevel analysis. *Urban Studies* 39(1):7–32.

Jim, Chiyong, and Wendy Y. Chen. 2006. Impacts of urban environmental elements on residential housing prices in Guangzhou (China). *Landscape and Urban Planning* 78(4):422–434.

Karn, Valerie A., and Harold Wolman. 1992. *Comparing housing systems: Housing performance and housing policy in the United States and Britain.* Oxford, U.K.: Clarendon Press and Oxford University Press.

Kong, Fanhua, Haiwei Yin, and Nobukazu Nakagoshi. 2007. Using GIS and landscape metrics in the hedonic price modeling of the amenity value of urban green space: A case study in Jinan City, China. *Landscape and Urban Planning* 79(3–4):240–252.

Kosareva, Nadezhda, and Raymond Struyk. 1993. Housing privatization in the Russian Federation. *Housing Policy Debate* 4:81–100.

Li, Siming, and Fulong Wu. 2004. Contextualizing residential mobility and housing choice: Evidence from urban China. *Environment and Planning A* 36(1):1–6.

Logan, John R., Yanjie Bian, and Fuqin Bian. 1999. Housing inequality in urban China in the 1990s. *International Journal of Urban and Regional Research* 23(1):7–25.

Logan, John R., Yiping Fang, and Zhanxin Zhang. 2009. Access to housing in urban China. *International Journal of Urban and Regional Research.* Forthcoming.

Pan, Zhenfeng. 2004. Housing quality of Communist party members in urban China: A comparative study. *Housing Studies* 19(2):193–205.

Pickvance, Chris G. 1994. Housing privatization and housing protest in the transition from state socialism: A comparative study of Budapest and Moscow. *International Journal of Urban and Regional Research* 18:433–450.

Rosen, Sherwin. 1974. Hedonic prices and implicit markets: Product differentiation in pure competition. *The Journal of Political Economy* 82:34–55.

Sato, Hiroshi. 2006. Housing inequality and housing poverty in urban China in the late 1990s. *China Economic Review* 17(1):37–50.

State Council. 2004. Guidelines for price assessment in the sales of public housing among Beijing Central Government institutions. In *Government Offices Administration of the State Council.* http://www.ggj.gov.cn/zfggs/zfggsfggw/200510/t20051020_2042.htm.

Szelenyi, Iván. 1983. *Urban inequalities under state socialism.* New York: Oxford University Press.

Wang, Yaping, and Alan Murie. 1999. *Housing policy and practice in China.* New York: MacMillan.

Willis, Ken G., and M. Nicholson. 1991. Costs and benefits of housing subsidies to tenants from voluntary and involuntary rent control: A comparison between tenures and income groups. *Applied Economics* 23(6):1103–1115.

World Bank. 1992. *China: Implementation options for urban housing reform.* A World Bank Country Study. Washington, DC.

Wu, Weiping. 2002. Migrant housing in urban China: Choices and constraints. *Urban Affairs Review* 38(1):90–119.

Yang, Lu, and Yukun Wang. 1995. *Housing reform: Theory rethinking and reality selection.* Tianjin: Tianjin People's Press.

Yemtsov, Ruslan. 2007. Housing privatization and household wealth in transition. Research Paper No. 2007/02. United Nations University, World Institute for Development Economics Research. http://www.wider.unu.edu/publications/working-papers/research-papers/2007/en_GB/rp2007-02/.

Yeung, S. C. W. and Rodney Howes. 2006. The role of the Housing Provident Fund in financing affordable housing development in China. *Habitat International* 30(2):343–356.

Zheng, Siqi, and Matthew E. Kahn. 2008. Land and residential property markets in a booming economy: New evidence from Beijing. *Journal of Urban Economics* 63:743–757.

Patterns of Second-Home Ownership in Chinese Cities

YOUQIN HUANG AND CHENGDONG YI

Launched nationwide in 1988, the housing reform in Chinese cities has transformed the welfare-oriented housing system into a market-oriented system dominated by private home ownership. According to the 2007 Urban Household Survey, the rate of home ownership in Chinese cities had reached 82 percent, while two decades before, it was less than 20 percent (Huang 2004; Zhen 2007). China is becoming a nation of homeowners. Due to rapidly rising incomes and high returns on real estate investment during the recent housing boom, second- and multiple-home ownership is also emerging in Chinese cities, where housing shortages prevailed and public rentals dominated for decades. According to the State Statistical Bureau (SSB), about 6.6 percent of urban households owned two or more homes in 2002 (Chou 2003), and the percentage increased to 15 percent in 2007 (calculated using the 2007 Urban Household Survey data). Based on a small-scale survey in Beijing, Feng and Zhou (2004) estimated that about 24 percent of households owned second homes in 2002, and about 50 percent of households hoped to own second homes. Fueled by the provocative argument made by a well-known economist in China, Professor Yining Li, that second home ownership should be promoted to stimulate the economy, there has been a heated debate on second homes (e.g., Li 2002). Despite massive media coverage and anecdotal evidence, we know very little about second homes in Chinese cities. Yet second homes represent an important dimension of the increasingly severe housing inequality and have a significant impact on local economies (especially housing markets) and local communities; thus, they have important policy implications. It is the goal of this chapter to understand the patterns of second homes in Chinese cities.

Some of the findings in this chapter appeared in Consumption and tenure choice of multiple homes in transitional urban china. *International Journal of Housing Policy* 10, 2 (2010): 105–131.

Defining second homes can be difficult due to their transient and fluid nature. In general, a second home is a property owned or rented on a long lease as the occasional residence of a household that usually lives elsewhere; it is mainly for leisure use by household members or family and friends on a noncommercial basis (Coppock 1977). Thus, a second home is defined mainly based on its relationship to the primary home (e.g., is spatially separated from the primary home, used only occasionally), its tenure (owned or on a long lease), and how it is used (e.g., for leisure) rather than on the characteristics of the dwelling. In this chapter, a second home is defined as an owned dwelling that the owning household does not currently live in; the dwelling that the household currently lives in is called the primary home, assuming it is the household's usual residence. This definition was determined by the following question in the survey used in this chapter: "Besides this dwelling, do you own additional dwellings elsewhere with partial or full rights?"[1] Thus, we do not know the frequency of occupancy (whether it is for occasional occupancy), usage (whether it is for leisure-related self-consumption, for lease as an investment, or even unoccupied), or location (whether it is in a different city or area than the primary home). A second home could also be a third or even fourth home for some households. Owners of second homes in Chinese cities may own or rent their primary homes. This is different from the West, where owners of second homes usually own their primary homes but may rent with a long lease or own a second home. The conventional definition of second home (an additional home owned by homeowners) cannot fully describe the reality in China. Thus, the definition is expanded here to include additional homes owned by households regardless of their tenure (renting or owning) of their primary home. The concept of second home in this chapter is broader than that in the Western literature.

There are limitations with this definition of second home. For example, the current home or primary home that a household lives in at the time of the survey may turn out to be temporary or secondary. Because the frequency of occupancy or use of either current dwellings or additional homes is unknown, it is impossible to differentiate which home can be considered as a second home using the Western definition. Thus, this chapter assumes that the current dwelling a household lives in is its usual residence and primary home, and any additional dwellings it owns are second homes.

While the rich and noble in China have always owned second homes (Feng and Liu 2000), the massive second-home ownership by emerging middle-class Chinese households is a new phenomenon, mainly driven by the recent housing and economic reforms, which have led to rapidly rising incomes and changing lifestyles (higher private auto ownership, more leisure time, and a faster pace of urban life). Yet the

---

[1] Houses and apartments in China are sold with different bundles of property rights based on how households purchase their homes. If households purchase their houses from the market and pay market prices, they enjoy "full property rights," which include right of occupancy, right to extract financial benefits, right to dispose of the property through resale, and right to bequeath it to others (Davis 2003). If households purchased previously public housing or private housing at subsidized prices such as affordable housing (*jingji shiyong fang*), they have only "partial property rights," which means homeowners only have the right of occupancy and the right of use; they are not allowed to sell their homes on the market for profit within the first five years unless they pay the gap between the discounted and market prices.

practice of having a second home also emerges from the transitional housing system, in which the socialist legacy endures (Huang and Yi 2010). First, despite the official end of the provision of public housing in 1998 (State Council 1998), resourceful work units such as universities and ministries continue to provide subsidized housing (rental or owned) to their employees. Even if a household can afford or has already purchased private housing on the market, few people would say no to such subsidies in a society with extremely high housing prices and an increasing problem of affordability. It is not uncommon for people like professors and government employees to live in subsidized rental housing close to their workplace (and other services such as schools) for convenience and purchase another home in the same city for occasional use or investment. In addition, subsidized housing in the owning sector often offers partial property rights which makes it difficult for households to sell, and thus encourages second home ownership.

Second, the household registration (*hukou*) system, one of the most important institutions that defines a person's socioeconomic status and access to welfare benefits (Cheng and Selden 1996), continues to favor urban residents with nonagricultural *hukou* registered locally, while migrants with *hukou* (agricultural or nonagricultural) registered elsewhere are severely constrained in accessing subsidized housing, education, and medical services. When some cities allowed migrants to purchase houses and obtain a *hukou* status similar to that of local urban residents, such as the "blue stamp" *hukou,* many households rushed to capture the opportunity. At the same time, they continued to have access to collectively owned land in their home villages for housing construction; migrants often build or own houses back home for eventual return even though they now live and work in cities. Furthermore, good infrastructure and services are not distributed evenly across neighborhoods within the city. It is increasingly common for households to buy or rent another dwelling as a primary home, so that their children can attend a superior school nearby. All these factors have encouraged the rapid growth of second homes in Chinese cities. Yet we know virtually nothing about second homes in China. The existing literature on second homes has focused on the West and on leisure and recreation as the main driving force for second homes.

Literature Review

Since Coppock's pioneering work in 1977, there has been a large body of literature on second home ownership, mostly derived from leisure and tourism studies, rural studies, planning studies, and cultural studies. First, second homes as leisure consumption stand out in the literature. People purchase second homes to facilitate their leisure and recreational activities. While there is tremendous regional variation, most second homes are located in tourism or resort communities, scenic or rural areas; and in many regions, second homes have played an important role in the growth of the tourism industry (Davies and O'Farrell 1981; Tress 2002). Rising disposable income, widespread car ownership, changing lifestyles, retirement migration, counter-urbanization, and growing dissatisfaction with the "urban" environment are considered reasons for the growth of second-home ownership (Coppock 1977; Robinson 1990; Butler 1998; Paris 2006). There are signs of growth in second-home ownership for leisure in London, Barcelona, and coastal cities (Paris 2006). Affordability, accessibility, and economic growth, as well as the beauty of a city's hinterlands and its proximity to a major city are identified as the key factors (Direct Line 2005).

A related factor is the opportunity for escape provided by a second home, especially in a foreign environment. Based on ethnographic analysis, Chaplin (1999) argues that second homes in rural France allow British urban residents to escape from the pressure of work, the everyday routine, and the commodification of post-industrial society to a place that provides a genuine break from urban life in Britain on one hand and commodified tourism products on the other hand. In other words, households look for housing services in a second home that their primary residence lacks; thus, a second home compensates for unmet housing needs in the primary home—the "compensation hypothesis." For example, people living in a high-density urban space such as Spain or Hong Kong are more likely to have a second home for a more spacious living environment (Modenes and Lopez-Colas 2007; Hui and Yu 2008).

Second, while second homes did not originate as investments, investment has become another important motivation for people to own them. Many scholars have argued that purchasing a second home is part of people's life planning and personal or family investment strategies (Coppock 1977; Hall and Muller 2004; Gallent, Mace, and Tewdr-Jones 2005; Smith 2005). Typical second-home owners are middle- or old-aged with a mid- to high-household income (Paris 2006; Francese 2003). Second homes are often purchased with a view of eventual retirement, and there may be a phase of "semiretirement" until the second home becomes unambiguously the first (Coppock 1977, 3). Then the former primary residence represents an asset that can be liquidated through sale or leased to generate an income stream. With growing mobility (both personal and of financial assets) and income in rich countries, there has been a massive expansion of leisure-related investment and consumption (Forrest 2005). Leisure second-home markets overlap seamlessly with housing markets, especially in cities, and the metropolitan second home is a distinctive leisure consumption that may offer potential for capital gains.

Third, with increasing globalization and rising transnationalism and mobility, the share of the population that lives and works in two or more places has also been growing. Improved access to transportation and communication due to globalization facilitates second home ownership (Kaltenborn 1998). Widespread access to the Internet and new ways of working from remote locations are considered driving forces for the next boom of second-home ownership in the United States (Frances 2003). Regional disparities in the economy and the housing market also encourage second-home ownership, especially cross-border second-home ownership, such as Hong Kong residents owning second homes in mainland China (Hui and Yu 2009). At the same time, a second home represents a permanent place in a rapidly changing world, serving as both a reaction to and a rejection of globalization (Kaltenborn 1998). Emotional or familiar attachment to a place is another reason people own second homes—for example, people owning second homes in their childhood environments (Kaltenborn 1997; Hui and Yu 2008).

Despite the rapid growth, the phenomenon of second homes in China is still in its early stages, and research has been sketchy. Increasing social stratification, paid leisure time, change in lifestyle, diminishing urban-rural differences, and the recent housing reforms all have driven the development of this phenomenon (Feng and Liu 2000). Furthermore, second homes can be owned by homeowners as well as renters of their primary homes (Huang and Yi 2010). Whether to have a second home and what kind of tenure to have for their homes are all part of the complex decision-making for the "housing portfolio" that households build; thus they have to be understood together. Both market forces and socialist institutions contribute to the consumption and tenure decision of multiple homes (Huang and Yi 2010). Specifically, the most important reason for people to own second homes was housing allocation from work units (26.6 percent), followed by having an additional home close to the workplace (21.9 percent), unsatisfactory living environment of the first residence (20.7 percent), inheritance from parents or other relatives (14.2 percent), investment (7.1 percent), and housing subsidies from work units during housing reform (9.5 percent) (Feng and Zhou 2004). In Haikou (Hainan Island), which experienced a speculative real estate boom, second homes emerged in a real estate bust and were actively promoted by the local government as a strategy to stabilize the housing market (Wang 2006; Xia 2001). In addition to increasingly mature housing markets, second-home ownership in Chinese cities is also an unintended consequence of socialist housing policies and institutions such as the subsidized sale of public rental housing and associated partial property rights, the continued provision of subsidized housing by work units, the persisting household registration system, and the lack of property tax (Huang and Yi 2011). Thus, the driving forces for second home purchases in Chinese cities are different from those in the West. Yet the vacation-oriented second home is emerging in resort cities like Haikou and Sanyan on Hainan Island (Xu and Bao 2006a; 2006b; Wang 2006). In Beijing, about 13 percent of second homes are used for leisure, recreation, or tourism (Feng and Zhou 2004). While the limited number of studies sheds some light on second homes in China, more research is needed for a better understanding of this.

A Conceptual Framework and Hypotheses

Due to the transitional nature of the housing system in Chinese cities, second-home ownership has to be understood in a different conceptual framework from that of the West. Second-home ownership in Chinese cities shares both similarities with and major differences from its counterpart in the West due to the coexistence of increasingly mature housing markets and unique institutions from the socialist legacy in China. First, after years of housing and economic reform, a housing market is emerging in China, though it is severely constrained by institutional factors. According to the 1 percent survey (the so-called minicensus conducted between censuses) carried out in 2005 by the SSB, only 8.1 percent of urban households were living in public rental housing, and 24.4 percent were living in privatized public housing, while the rest (two-thirds of urban households) were living in various types of private housing. Thus, it should not be surprising that life cycle and afford-ability, the two main factors for second-home ownership in the West, are impor-tant in Chinese cities. Older and married people, larger households, and financially wealthier households seem to be more likely to own a second home—this is called the *market hypothesis.*

Second, despite the official end of public housing provision in 1998 (State Council 1998), large and resourceful work units such as major universities and government ministries continue to provide subsidized housing to their employees. In addition to subsidized rental housing, as in the socialist era, employees in resourceful work units can purchase housing at heavily subsidized prices from their work units. Even if households can afford to purchase or have already purchased housing from the private market, few would reject heavily subsidized housing. Subsidized housing is also convenient, as it is often built close to workplaces and other services such as schools. It is not uncommon for people to live in subsidized housing (owned or rented) and own a second home bought on the private market for occasional use or investment. According to Feng and Zhou (2004), housing allocation from work units is the most important reason people own a second home. The current alloca-tion of subsidized housing more or less follows the socialist allocation system, in which people with political power are more likely to access subsidized housing. Households that can access or have already accessed subsidized housing—because of their high political status, such as high job rank or Chinese Communist Party membership, or because of their resourceful work units—seem to be more likely to own second homes. This is called the *housing subsidy hypothesis.* This extends the market transition debate initiated by Victor Nee (1989) regarding the importance of political or redistributive power to socioeconomic attainment in transitional economy to the consumption of second home.

Third, the *hukou* system, albeit under reform, continues to be an important in-stitution that prevents migrants with *hukou* (urban or rural) registered elsewhere to access subsidized urban housing such as "low-cost rental housing" (*lian zu fang*), "public rental housing" (*gong fang*), "privatized public housing" (*fang gai fang*), "economic housing"(*jingji shiyong fang*), or, recently, "housing with controlled prices and unit sizes" (*liang xian fang*).[2] Many migrants continue to be consid-ered outsiders even though they have lived and worked in cities for years and go

---

[2] There are different kinds of housing with government subsidies. Low-cost rental housing is heavily subsi-dized rental housing provided by the government and work units for the lowest income urban households (State Council 1998, No. 23). Public rental housing is subsidized housing provided also by the government and work units. Its allocation is often based on a set of nonmonetary factors such as job rank, seniority, marital status, and family needs (Huang and Clark 2002; Wang and Murie 1999), thus its tenants may come from different income groups. Privatized public housing is previously public rental housing sold to sitting tenants at lower than market prices. Because of subsidies during the sale, households often have so-called partial property rights, which con-strains them from freely disposing and profiting from the housing. Economic housing is private housing with partial property rights, which is developed with government subsidies (e.g., cheaper land) and sold at government controlled prices (developers are allowed to have only a 3 percent profit rate) to urban low-medium income households. Housing with controlled prices and unit sizes is private housing with full property rights, but with government controlled prices and unit sizes (usually less than 90 m^2 floor space per unit), targeting the so-called sandwiched households who are not qualified for economic housing yet cannot afford commodity housing. In addition to household income, wealth, and existing housing conditions, local household registration is required to access subsidized housing.

back to their hometowns only for major holidays.[3] Constraints such as limited access to medical and educational services also often force migrants to live a marginalized life in cities. Meanwhile, rural migrants continue to have access to collectively owned land in their home villages for housing construction,[4] and urban migrants may be entitled to subsidized housing in their home cities if they qualify. Thus migrants often rent dwellings in the destination city and are somewhat forced to have another home in their hometown for eventual return. If not for the *hukou* system, most migrants would have settled more permanently in a city and would maintain only a home in that city. Under the current system, however, migrants with temporary *hukou* seem more likely to own second homes—this is called the *hukou hypothesis*.

Fourth, public goods vary in quality and are not distributed evenly between neighborhoods. Chinese households increasingly purchase a second home to access better public goods, particularly key public kindergartens and key public schools (zhongdian xuexiao).[5] Good education has traditionally been considered a main path for people to move up the social ladder. With massive numbers of students fighting for limited educational resources, Chinese parents are determined to send their children to the best schools starting from kindergarten to help their eventual entrance to the best university. Yet, official residence and home ownership in the school district are often required for children to attend key schools. Thus households need to purchase a home close to key kindergartens and key schools so that their children can attend schools nearby and they often can avoid paying a large sum of money called an "endorsement fee" (*zan zhu fei*) or "school selection fee" (*ze xiao fei*).[6] While some households have to sell their previous home in order to buy a house near key schools, many convert their previously primary home into a second home, either because they can afford to own two homes or because they are constrained to sell their previous home due to partial property rights. It is also common for households to rent an apartment close to key schools for a few years while owning another home elsewhere (now becoming a second home) because housing near key schools is too expensive for some households, or there may not be decent housing for sale. With everything else the same, households with school-age children seem more likely to own a second home—this is the *school hypothesis*.

In summary, the dynamics for second-home ownership in Chinese cities are shaped by both socioeconomic factors that are consistent with the Western convention and institutional forces that are unique to China, such as the persistent provision of subsidized housing, the discriminatory *hukou* system, and the uneven distribution of key schools. In addition to conventional homeowners owning a

---

[3] According to the 2001 Chinese Urban Labor Survey, migrants' mean duration of stay in cities is 5.26 years, although some have stayed for more than 10 years (Connelly, Roberts, and Zheng 2007).

[4] The housing system in the countryside is different from that in cities. Rural households are entitled to a parcel of collectively owned land for housing construction, mainly for self-consumption (parcel size varies by household size and region). There are no government subsidies for housing development or consumption in rural areas.

[5] Some good public schools in Chinese cities are given the status of "key schools" (*zhongdian xuexiao*), which allow them to recruit better students and receive more resources from the government.

[6] Usually this kind of fee waiver is available only to homeowners in the school district. In some cities such as Beijing, a certain duration of residence or *hukou* registration in the school district (e.g., more than 3 years) is required to be qualified for these fee waivers.

second home, there is the unique phenomenon of renting a primary home and owning a second home, including at least the following scenarios: (1) renting public housing close to the workplace and owning a second home elsewhere in the same city; (2) renting private housing close to key schools and workplace and owning a second home elsewhere in the same city; (3) renting private housing in the destination city and owning a second home in the place of origin. This makes second-home ownership in China different and interesting.

Empirical Analysis

The China General Social Survey (CGSS) is a biannual national survey conducted by the Department of Sociology at Renmin University and the Survey Research Center at Hong Kong University of Science and Technology (HKUST). It aims to "monitor systematically the changing relationship between social structure and quality of life in urban and rural China" (DSRU and SRCHKUST). Based on the 2000 census data, the CGSS sampled about 10,000 households in 26 provinces and cities using a stratified, multistage probability sampling technique. The first survey was conducted in 2003; this chapter refers to the 2005 survey. The focus here is on the urban sample, excluding rural population, suburban farmers who have agricultural *hukou* registered locally, as they both can access collectively owned land for housing construction, and anyone whose occupation is in agriculture. The interviewees are treated as household head for the following housing analysis. The final sample has 5,705 observations. With the exception of table 6.1, which compares urban households with rural households and the nation, the focus is on this subset of the urban sample for the rest of the analyses.

In addition to basic socioeconomic information, the survey also collected information on current housing, such as tenure, floor size, housing structure, year of construction, and housing price or rent. Furthermore, it asked whether the household owns additional homes with partial or full rights elsewhere and the number, floor

TABLE 6.1

Percentage of Households Owning Second Homes

	Urban Households	Urban Households Excluding Suburban/Urban Farmers	Rural Households	All
Do not have second home (%)	88.2	88.5	92.3	89.9
Have second home (%)	11.8	11.5	7.7	10.1
One unit of second home	88.6	88.4	86.3	87.9
Two units of second home	8.9	9.0	11.3	9.6
Three+ units of second home	2.5	2.6	2.4	2.5
Total (%)	100	100	100	100
Total N	6,098	5,705	4,274	10,372

SOURCE: Calculated using CGSS 2005.

size, and value of any additional homes. Thus CGSS 2005 gives us a good opportunity to study the phenomenon of the second home.

Nationwide, about 10 percent of households in China own second homes, and urban households are relatively more likely to own second homes (11.5 percent) than rural households (7.7 percent) (table 6.1). This is much higher than the level in Britain (3 percent); comparable to France (11 percent); but much lower than Sweden (25 percent), Norway (17 percent), and Spain (17 percent) in 1970 (Coppock 1977; Allen, Gallent, and Tewdr-Jones 1999), even though the definitions may be somewhat different. While the majority of second-home owners own only one unit of second home, more than 9 percent of second-home owners own two units of second home (11 percent among rural households), and about 2.5 percent of them own three or more units of second homes. This high level of second-home ownership is astonishing given the fact that a severe housing shortage and crowding prevailed and public rental dominated even in the mid-1990s (Huang 2003; 2004).

Overall, 22.3 percent of urban households rented, 76.7 percent of urban households owned their current dwellings (or primary homes), and 1.1 percent lived in another tenure form in 2005 (table 6.2). However, there are different types of rental (3.8 percent rented work-unit housing, 8.2 percent rented public housing provided by governments such as municipal housing bureaus, 10.3 percent rented private housing from other home owners) and home ownership (12.6 percent owned with partial property rights, 17.8 percent owned private housing inherited from the pre-socialist era or self-built housing, 46.3 percent owned with full property rights). The rate of second-home ownership varied significantly by the tenure of the primary home. Overall, about 22.6 percent of renters and only 8.1 percent of homeowners owned second homes. In other words, renters are much more likely to own second homes than primary-home owners, which seems to be counterintuitive. There are two main reasons for this interesting phenomenon. First, the inclusion of migrants' homes in their place of origin as second homes have contributed to the high probability of renters owning second home. The majority of the 36.7 percent of private renters who owned a second home are migrants. Secondly, the persisting provision of subsidized housing encourages renters to own second homes. For example, 14.7 percent of those who rented work-unit housing and 30.8 percent of those living in public housing with no rent owned a second home; both percentages are much higher than the average for homeowners (8.1). Also interestingly, 6.4 percent of people who purchased housing with subsidies (thus with partial property rights) owned second homes. While supporting the housing subsidy hypothesis, it is somewhat ironic that people living in public housing (rented or owned) owned second homes, which would not be expected in the West.

Considering the tenure of the primary home together with that of the second home, 17.4 percent of urban households rented their primary and only home, 70.4 percent owned their primary and only home, 5.1 percent rented their primary home but owned their second home, and 6.2 percent owned their primary and second homes (figure 6.1). Only the last group is similar to conventional second-home owners in the West; yet, even with this restricted definition of second-home ownership, the rate is still fairly high, especially considering China's recent history of a socialist housing system, which consisted mainly of public rental housing.

TABLE 6.2

Tenure Structure and Second-Home Ownership Among Urban Households, 2005

Tenure of Primary Home	Percentage	Proportion Owning Second Homes
Rent work-unit housing	3.8	14.7
Rent public housing	8.2	8.2
Rent private housing	10.3	36.7
Own private housing (inherited or self-built)	17.8	8.0
Purchased (partial property rights)	12.6	6.4
Purchased (full property rights)	46.3	8.6
No rent (relative/friend's housing)	0.4	10
No rent (public housing)	0.2	30.8
Other	0.5	28.6
Total	100.0	11.5
Rental	22.3	22.6
Ownership	76.7	8.1
Other	1.1	20.8
Total	100.0	11.5
Total sample size (N)	5,705	

SOURCE: Calculated using CGSS 2005.

FIGURE 6.1

Tenure Structure of Primary and Second Homes in Urban China (percent)

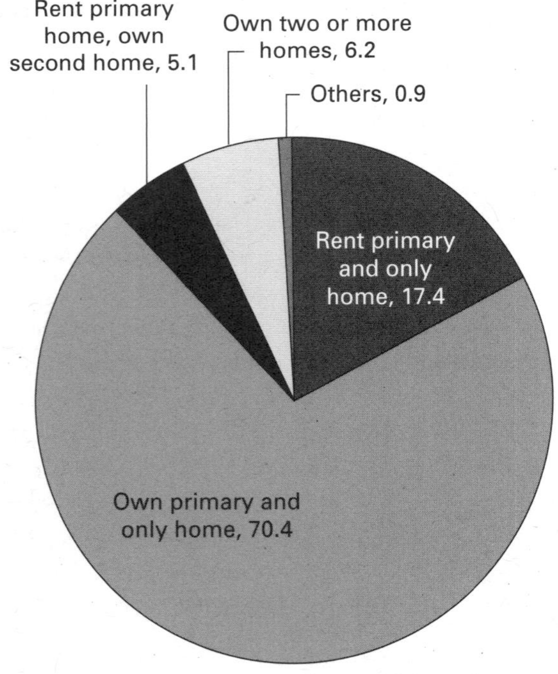

SOURCES: Created using CGSS 2005, and Huang and Yi 2010, figure 2.

TABLE 6.3

Second-Home Ownership by Region and City Type (Urban Households Only)

Region / City Type	Own Second Home (%)	Rent Primary Home, Own Second Home (%)	Own Primary and Second Homes (%)
All	11.5	5.1	6.2
Eastern cities	13.3	5.3	7.8
Central cities	8.6	3.5	5.1
Western cities	10.8	6.5	4.2
Municipalities and provincial capitals	8.8	4.0	4.8
Other cities	13.2	5.9	7.3

SOURCE: Calculated using CGSS 2005.

NOTE: Chi-square test significant at 0.01 level.

There is also a regional difference in second-home ownership. As shown in table 6.3, households in eastern cities are more likely to own a second home (13.3 percent) than those in western (10.8 percent) and central cities (8.6 percent).[7] Conventional second-home ownership—owning both primary and second homes–is also highest in the eastern cities (7.8 percent), followed by the central (5.1 percent) and western cities (4.2 percent). This is probably related to the higher level of household income in eastern cities. Households in western cities are more likely to rent their primary home and own their second home (6.5 percent), followed by eastern (5.3 percent) and central cities (3.5 percent). This shows that the degree of marketization in the housing system is probably not very high in western cities, and the socialist system persists. Households in smaller cities are more likely to own a second home (13.2 percent) than those in municipalities and provincial capitals (8.8 percent), and the former are much more likely to own both the primary and second homes than rent the primary home and own the second home than the latter. This is probably because of relatively cheaper housing in smaller cities.

On average, the second home tends to be larger and more expensive than the primary home. The average floor space of the homes of those who own both primary and second homes is 105 square meters for the second home and 79 square meters for the primary home; about 50 percent of second homes are smaller than primary homes, however, which shows that the floor space of second homes varies more significantly than that of primary homes. The median housing price is 110,000 yuan for second homes and 80,000 yuan for primary homes; about 43 percent of second homes are more expensive than primary homes.

Second-home owners also have different socioeconomic characteristics. As shown in table 6.4, people who own both primary and second homes are about the

---

[7] The boundaries for the Eastern, Central, and Western regions are the same as those defined by the Chinese government, in which the Eastern region includes three municipalities (Beijing, Tianjin, and Shanghai) and nine provinces (Liaoning, Hebei, Shandong, Jiangsu, Zhejiang, Fujian, Guangdong, Guangxi, and Hainan). The Central region includes nine provinces and autonomous regions (Jilin, Heilongjiang, Inner Mongolia, Shanxi, Henan, Hubei, Hunan, Jiangxi, and Anhui), and the rest is the Western region (see map 7.4 in Veeck et al. 2007).

TABLE 6.4

Household Socioeconomic Indicators by Tenure (Urban Households Only)

Socioeconomic Indicator	Rent Primary and Only Home	Own Primary and Only Home	Rent Primary Home, Own Second Home	Own Primary and Second Homes	Total	Total N
Mean age	41.4	46.3	35.1	44.9	44.8	5,657
Household size (number of persons)	3.1	3.4	3.9	3.7	3.4	5,657
Marital status (%)						
Single, live with parents/ relatives	5.8	8.8	7.9	8.7	8.2	464
Single, live alone	14.8	0.9	20.3	3.4	4.5	255
Married, family located here	75.9	89.5	54.5	85.6	85.1	4,813
Married, family located elsewhere	3.5	0.8	17.2	2.3	2.2	125
All	100.0	100.0	100.0	100.0	100.0	
Household income in 2004 (yuan)						
Median	20,000	20,000	24,500	30,000	20,000	5,270
Mean	24,765	26,487	37,484	50,650	28,194	
SD	31,264	38,030	45,896	112,172	45,981	

SOURCE: Calculated using CGSS 2005, and modified based on Huang and Yi 2010, table 2.

NOTE: SD = standard deviation

same as the average owners of one home in terms of age, household size, and marital status; yet they clearly have a much higher income, with a median household income of 30,000 yuan compared to 20,000 yuan. In contrast, people who rent their primary home and own their second home are younger (mean age 35.1) and more likely to be single and living alone or married with family elsewhere, yet surprisingly have the largest households. This is probably due to young migrants who are single but count family members back home as part of their household. They also have a higher household income (median 24,500 yuan) than those who have only one home (rented or owned). The result supports the market hypothesis, as second-home owners are clearly financially better off, though not necessarily older. In addition, households with school-age children (<16 years old)[8] are significantly more likely to own a second home than those without (13.1 percent vs. 10.4 percent),[9] supporting the school hypothesis.

Migrants' temporary *hukou* status has proven to be important to their housing consumption (e.g., Huang and Clark 2002; Wu 2002), yet existing research has focused on primary homes only in that regard. *Hukou* status is also important to the

---

[8] Sixteen is the cutoff point because the school system in Chinese cities allows high school students (16–18 years old) to choose their schools through testing, and students of that age are also old enough to take public transportation, so that living close to school is not as crucial as for families with younger children.

[9] The difference is statistically significant at the 0.01 level.

TABLE 6.5

Second-Home Ownership by *Hukou* Status (Urban Households Only)

Hukou Status	Own Second Home (%)	Rent Primary Home, Own Second Home (%)	Own Primary and Second Home (%)	Total N
Local urban residents	8.6	2.3	6.3	5,084
Urban migrants	31.0	24.4	6.6	316
Rural migrants	44.4	39.7	4.7	232
Other	16.0	12.0	4.0	25
Total	11.4	5.1	6.3	5,657

SOURCE: Calculated using CGSS 2005.

consumption of second homes (table 6.5). With home of origin considered as the second home, both urban and rural migrants (migrants with nonagricultural and agricultural *hukou,* respectively, registered elsewhere) were much more likely to own a second home than local urban residents (31.0 percent and 44.4 percent, respectively, vs. 8.6 percent). Not surprisingly, most migrants who own a second home rent their primary home. This is related to their high mobility and, more important, their temporary *hukou* status in cities, which under the current system constrains their housing access, especially to public and subsidized housing, and thus hinders their long-term settlement in cities. They are somewhat "forced" to own second homes in their place of origin for their eventual return. However, wealthier migrants who could afford it owned both a primary home and a second home. Urban migrants (6.6 percent) were more likely to own both primary and second homes than rural migrants (4.7 percent), but were similar to urban residents (6.3 percent). This supports the *hukou* hypothesis.

Despite three decades of market transition, people's political power continues to be important in housing access and home ownership and the attainment of second-home ownership. According to table 6.6, people with high administrative rank or high technical rank and people with a party membership are more likely to own both primary and second homes than those with no rank or party membership. For example, 11.0 percent of those with an administrative rank of deputy chu (*fu chu ji*) or higher and 9.1 percent of those with an advanced or higher technical rank owned both primary and second homes, compared to only 6.2 percent of those with no administrative rank and 5.3 percent with no technical rank.[10] In addition, 8.9 percent of party members owned primary and second homes, compared to 5.8 percent for those who were not party members. People with a high job rank and party membership seem to still hold privileged positions after almost three decades of reform. Those with no rank and those to whom rank is not applicable (such as people in the private sector) and no party membership are more likely to rent a primary home

---

[10] According to the Law on Civil Servants, civil servants are divided into different administrative ranks. From the highest to the lowest, the ranks include Prime Minister, Ministry level (*bu ji*) cadre, Bureau level (*si ji*) cadre, Department level (*chu ji*) cadre, Division level (*ke ji*) cadre, division members, and ordinary clerks and staff. With the exception of the last two ranks, each rank is further divided into regular (*zheng*) and deputy or vice (*fu*) level cadres.

TABLE 6.6

Second-Home Ownership by Political Status and Work Unit

Political Status and Work Unit	Rent Primary Home, Own Second Home (%)	Own Primary and Second Homes (%)	Total (%)	Total N
Administrative Rank*				
Deputy chu and higher	3.0	11.0	14.0	100
Ke ji and lower	2.3	6.2	8.5	308
No rank	4.4	6.2	10.6	2,960
Not applicable	7.1	5.7	12.8	1,663
Technical Rank*				
Advanced and higher	2.1	9.1	11.2	329
Middle and basic	4.4	7.9	12.3	1,098
No rank	5.6	5.3	10.9	3,604
Party Membership				
Yes	3.5	8.9	12.4	802
No	5.3	5.8	11.1	4,903
Work Unit*				
Party/government/state institution at central or provincial level	3.85	7.69	11.54	182
Party/government/state institution below provincial level	2.28	7.70	9.99	701
SOE in monopoly industry at central or provincial level	3.07	4.29	7.36	163
SOE in monopoly industry below provincial level	3.11	8.56	11.67	257
SOE in nonmonopoly industry	2.24	4.36	6.60	1,560
Private/group enterprise	11.92	6.30	18.22	1,334
Joint venture/foreign company	9.17	7.50	16.67	120
Collectively owned enterprise	2.35	7.38	9.73	637
Total	5.1	6.1	11.2	5,031

SOURCE: Calculated using CGSS 2005.

NOTE: *Chi-square test significant at 0.001 level.

and own a second home. The type of work unit also is important to second-home ownership. People who are affiliated with party, government, or state institutions; state-owned enterprises (SOEs) in a monopoly industry below the provincial level; joint-venture and foreign companies; and private or group enterprises (*siyin he mingyin qiye*) are the most likely (>10 percent), while those in SOEs in nonmonopoly industries are the least likely (6.6 percent) to own a second home.[11] Everyone except people in private or group enterprises and joint-venture or foreign companies, who are more likely to rent a primary home and own a second home, is more likely to

---

[11] Monopoly industries include electricity, gas and water, geological survey and hydrology management, finance/insurance, real estate, medical and physical education, social welfare, education, art and media, movies/TV, research, government/party institution, railway and airline, postal service/telecommunication, oil/gas drilling and refining, and tobacco industries. The rest are nonmonopoly industries. We follow the categorization by Bian and Liu (2005).

own both primary and second homes. In other words, the housing subsidies hypothesis is strongly supported by the data, as people with high political status and those affiliated with resourceful public work units are more likely to own a second home. The fact that people in joint-venture or foreign companies and private or group enterprises are also more likely to own a second home supports the market hypothesis, as they tend to have higher wages.

Conclusions

Besides becoming a nation of homeowners, with more than 80 percent of urban households owning their homes (and almost universal home ownership in the countryside), China is experiencing a rapid increase in second-home ownership, with about 12 percent of urban households (whether they rent or own their primary homes) and 8 percent of urban homeowners owning second homes in 2005. Considering the fact that public rental still dominated and the housing shortage was acute even in the mid-1990s, it is quite astonishing that China has achieved such a high level of second-home ownership within such a short period of time. Interestingly, many second homes are owned by households who are renters of their primary homes, and who are currently living in subsidized housing. In addition to the increasingly mature housing market, unique socialist institutions such as the persistent provision of subsidized housing and the *hukou* system shape the patterns of second home ownership, although different elements of socialist institutions are playing out differently.

With the persistent *hukou* system, migrants continue to be discriminated against in the housing system. Despite their long-term residence in cities, they are not allowed to access subsidized housing and are considered outsiders who will eventually go back to their hometowns. Migrants' peculiar position in cities leads them to rent their primary home at the destination and own a second home at the place of origin. This tenure combination not only discourages long-term settlement in cities but also wastes land and housing resources. Thus, further reform of the *hukou* system is needed. In contrast to the disadvantaged position of migrants in the housing system, privileged urban residents who have access to subsidized housing often own second homes. This further aggravates increasing housing inequality in Chinese cities as low-income households do not have access to affordable housing with ever rising housing prices due in part to the large demand for second homes, while subsidized housing is often allocated to those who can afford second homes. Reform in housing access is needed to ensure that limited housing subsidies go to those in need, not those who can afford second-home ownership.

Finally, as second homes are becoming an important part of the housing system, local governments need to come up with better policies to regulate the provision and consumption of second homes. So far the Chinese government has mainly used financial tools such as higher down payment and mortgage interest rate to regulate the purchase of second homes (CBC 2007), which has not been very successful.[12]

---

[12] While the government changes its policy on mortgages for second homes constantly, in general, households need to pay at least 40 percent of their mortgage for down payment, and the interest rate for a second-home mortgage is often 10 percent higher than that for a primary residence (CBC 2007).

One reason is that many households purchase second homes with cash or savings, thus these financial tools have no impact on them. In addition, second homes are often purchased as a form of investment. With the lack of investment options, the volatile stock market, and high inflation rate on the one hand, and the ever increasing housing price and the rapid urbanization on the other hand, housing investment has become the main method of investment for many households. The lack of property tax further reduces the cost of maintaining second homes. Thus, more comprehensive housing and economic policies—such as offering more sound investment options, controlling housing speculation, regulating the overheated housing market, and collecting property tax on second homes—are needed to mitigate potential negative social and economic consequences to disadvantaged populations and communities.

ACKNOWLEDGMENTS

The research presented in this chapter was funded in part by a Visiting Research Fellowship by Peking University–Lincoln Institute Center for Urban Development and Land Policy in 2009, a research grant in humanities and social sciences by the Ministry of Education in China, and "211" Key Project Funding by Central University of Finance and Economics in China.

REFERENCES

Allen, Chris, Nick Gallent, and Mark Tewdr-Jones. 1999. The limits of policy diffusion: Comparative experiences of second-home ownership in Britain and Sweden. *Environment and Planning: Government and Policy* 17:227–244.

Bian, Yanjie, and Yongli Liu. 2005. Social stratification, home ownership, and quality of living: An analysis of China's fifth census. *Journal of Sociological Research* 117(3):82–98 [in Chinese].

Bielckus, Cynthia L., Alan W. Rogers, and G. P. Wibberley. 1972. Second homes in England and Wales: A study of the distribution and use of rural properties taken over as second residences. London: Invicta Press.

Butler, Richard. 1998. Rural Recreation and Tourism. In *The geography of rural change*, ed. Brian Ilbery. Harlow, Essex, U.K.: Pearson Education.

Central Bank of China (CBC). 2007. A notice about strengthening mortgage management for commercial real estate, No. 359.

Chaplin, Davina. 1999. Consuming work/productive leisure: The consumption patterns of second home environments. *Leisure Studies* 18:41–55.

Cheng, Tiejun, and Mark Selden. 1996. The origins and social consequences of China's *Hukou* system. *China Quarterly* (no. 139):644–668.

Chou, Zhiqun. 2003. Digital link between different housing markets. *Real Estate Times*, Jan. 20.

Clout, Hugh D. 1969. Second home in France. *Journal of Town Planning Institute* 55, October 1969.

Connelly, Rachel, Kenneth Roberts, and Zhenzhen Zheng. 2007. Settlement of rural women migrants in urban China—some of them are not "floating" anymore. Presented at the 4th international Conference on Population Geographies, Hong Kong (July 10–13).

Coppock, John Terence., ed. 1977. *Second homes: Curse or blessing.* Oxford, U.K.: Pergamon Press.

Davies, Richard, and Patrick O'Farrell. 1981. A spatial and temporal analysis of second home ownership in West Wales. *Geoforum* 12(2):161–178.

Davis, Deborah. 2003. From welfare benefit to capitalized asset: The re-commodification of residential space in urban China. In *Chinese Urban Housing Reform*, ed. R. Forrest and J. Lee, 183–196. London: Routledge.

Department of Sociology at Renmin University and Survey Research Center at Hong Kong University of Science and Technology (DSRU and SRCHKUST). China General Social Survey. http://www.chinagss.org.

De Vane, Richard. 1975. Second home ownership: A case study. Cardiff, U.K.: University of Wales Press.

Direct Line. 2005. *Second homes report*. London.

Feng, Jian, and Zhihao Liu. 2000. On the development of China's second residences: Dynamic mechanisms, characteristics, effects, and prospects for planning [*zhongguo dier zhuzhai fazhuan de yanjiu: Dongle jizhi, tezheng, xiaoying yu guihua zhanwang*]. *Geography and Territorial Research* [*dili xue yu guotu yanjiu*] 16(1):30–35.

Feng, Jian, and Yixing Zhou. 2004. Intra-urban migration and correlative spatial behavior in Beijing in the process of suburbanization: Based on 1,000 questionnaires [*jiaoquhua jincheng zhong Beijing chengshi neibu qianju ji xiangguan kongjian xingwei: jiyu qianfeng wenjuan diaocha de fenxi*]. *Geographical Research* [*dili yanjiu*] 23(2):227–242.

Forrest, Ray. 2005. Globalization and the housing asset rich: Geographies, demographies and policy convoys. Paper presented at the APHNR conference. Kobe, Japan (August).

Francese, Peter. 2003. The second home boom. *American Demographics* (June).

Gallent, Nick, Alan Mace, and Mark Tewdr-Jones. 2005. *Second homes: European perspectives and U.K. policies.* Aldershot, U.K.: Ashgate.

Hall, C. Michael 2005. *Tourism: Rethinking the social science of mobility.* Edinburgh: Pearson Education.

Hall, C. Michael, and Dieter K. Muller, eds. 2004. Tourism, mobility, and second homes. Toronto: Channel View.

Hettinger, William S. 2005. Living and working in paradise: Why housing is too expensive and what communities can do about it. Windham, CT: Thames River.

Huang, Youqin. 2003. A room of one's own: Housing consumption and residential crowding in transitional urban China. *Environment and Planning A* 35:591–614.

———. 2004. The road to homeownership: A longitudinal analysis of tenure transition in urban China (1949–1994). *International Journal of Urban and Regional Research* 28(4):774–795.

Huang, Youqin, and William A. V. Clark. 2002. Housing tenure choices in transitional urban China: A multilevel analysis. *Urban Studies* 39(1):7–32.

Huang, Youqin, and Chengdong Yi. 2010. Consumption and tenure choice of multiple homes in transitional urban China. *International Journal of Housing Policy* 1(3):105–131.

———. 2011. Second home ownership in transitional urban China. *Housing Studies* 26(3).

Hui, Eddie Chi Man, and Ka Hung Yu. 2008. Second homes in the Chinese mainland under "one country, two systems": A cross-border perspective. *Habitat International* 33(1):1–130.

Kaltenborn, Bjorn P. 1997. Nature of place attachment: A study among recreation homeowners in southern Norway. *Leisure Sciences* 19:175–189.

———. 1998. The alternate home: Motives for recreation home use. *Norwegian Journal of Geography* 52(3):121–134.

Li, Dongyang. 2002. What does the second home mean? A conversation with Prof. Li Yining [*diertao zhuzhai yiweizhe shemo: yu liyining jiaoshou de duihua*]. *Economic Daily* [*jingji ribao*] (June 14).

Modenes, Juan-Antonio, and Julia Lopez-Colas. 2007. Second homes and compact cities in Spain: Two elements of the same system. *Journal of Economic and Social Geography* 98(3): 325–335.

Nee, Victor. 1989. A theory of market transition: From redistribution to markets in state socialism. *American Sociological Review* 54(5):663–681.

Paris, Chris. 2006. Multiple "homes," dwelling and hyper-mobility and emergent transnational second home ownership. Paper presented at the ENHR conference "Housing in an Expanding Europe: Theory, Policy, Participation and Implementation." Ljubljana, Slovenia (July 2–5).

Robinson, Guy. 1990. *Conflict and change in the countryside: Rural society, economy, and planning in the developed world.* London: Belhaven Press.

Smith, Susan. 2005. Banking on housing? Speculating on the role and relevance of housing wealth in Britain. Paper prepared for *Inquiry into Home Ownership 2010 and Beyond.* York, U.K.: Joseph Rowntree Foundation. www.jrf.org.uk.

State Council. 1998. A notification from the State Council on further deepening the reform of the urban housing system and accelerating housing construction [*guowuyuan guanyu jingyibu shenhua chengzhen zhufang zhidu gaige jiakuai zhufang jianshe de tongzhi*]. State Council Document No. 23. Beijing.

Tress, Gunther. 2002. Development of second home tourism in Denmark. *Scandinavian Journal of Hospitality and Tourism* 2(2):109–121.

Veeck, Gregory, Clifton W. Pannell, Christopher J. Smith, and Youqin Huang. 2007. *China's geography: Globalization and the dynamics of political, economic and social change.* Boulder, CO: Roman and Littlefield.

Wang, Ya Ping, and Alan Murie. 1999. *Housing policy and practice in China.* London/New York: MacMillan.

Wang, Xiaoxiao. 2006. The second home phenomenon in Haikou, China. Master's thesis. University of Waterloo, Ontario, Canada.

Wu, Weiping. 2002. Migrant housing in urban China: Choice and constraints. *Urban Affairs Review* 38(1):90–119.

Xia, Lunan. 2001. The consumption of second homes and new opportunity for Hainan [*dier zhuzhai xiaofei he Hainan de xinjiyu*]. *The New Orient* [*xin dongfang*] 10(2):86–88.

Xu, Wenxiong, and Jigang Bao. 2006a. A preliminary analysis of the spatial distribution of suburban second homes: A case study of Foshan City, Guangdong Province. *Planners* 10(22):71–74 [in Chinese].

———. 2006b. On the spatial distribution and influential factors of vacation-oriented second homes: A case study on Sanya City. *Journal of Yunnan Normal University* 38(5):63–37 [in Chinese].

Zhen, Siqi. 2007. *A microeconomic analysis of housing demand in China* [*zhufang xuqiu de weiguan jingji fenxi—lilun yu shijian*]. Beijing: China Construction Industry Press.

Effects of Local Taxation and Public Spending on Housing Values: Empirical Evidence

JOYCE YANYUN MAN AND SIQI ZHENG

According to Tiebout's (1956) model, consumers "shop" among different communities that offer varying packages of local public services and select as a residence the community that offers the tax-expenditure program best suited to their tastes. His model implies that on a theoretical level a system resembling a market solution may exist that could lead to the efficient provision of public goods and services. However, this hypothesis is based on the assumptions that consumers are fully mobile and have perfect knowledge concerning local revenues and expenditures, that a large number of communities exist for consumers to choose among, that there are no community-based employment restrictions, that there are no externalities associated with local public service provision, and that communities are sized so that they can produce services at the minimum of their average cost curve. In the United States a vast number of studies have examined capitalization of the property tax, because it is the mainstay of local revenue systems in the United States (Oates 1969, 2001; Yinger 1985; Man 1995; Man and Bell 1996).

Unfortunately, the empirical literature yields contradictory results concerning the extent to which property taxes are capitalized. If a property tax change is fully capitalized, the selling value of the asset is reduced by the present discounted value of the tax. Hamilton (1975) argues that public goods financed with property taxes can be provided efficiently and that the property tax is nondistortionary and serves as a benefit tax for public goods and services. However, the "new" view of Mieszkowski (1972) and Aaron (1975) argues that capital owners bear the full burden of a uniform property tax that is progressive, while tax differentials between communities give rise to "excise" effects that may shift forward to higher housing prices or backward to a relatively immobile factor. Wilson (1984) argues that the property tax may act as an excise tax by shifting the burden to the user of the property. Mieszkowski and Zodrow (1989) argue that under the new view, a higher property tax rate in a metropolitan area will reduce the national average rate of return on capital and that there is a tendency toward underprovision of local public services, because local jurisdictions are reluctant to tax mobile capital.

The bid-rent model developed by Yinger (1982) suggests that the amount a household is willing to pay for a unit of housing services in a particular jurisdiction is based on the jurisdiction's level of services and taxes. Yinger (1985) argues that the average tax rate in a metropolitan area is distortionary, but that the variations from this base tax rate will be perfectly capitalized into housing values. A relatively high property tax rate in one jurisdiction will not repel capital, since the rate will be fully capitalized into immobile factors. He draws the conclusion that differences in service levels between jurisdictions will be inexactly capitalized, depending on taste parameters in the utility functions, but that differences in tax rates between communities will be fully capitalized, regardless of the tastes of consumers. If the price of housing is different in different jurisdictions, suppliers will have an incentive to supply houses to jurisdictions with high home values. In the long-run equilibrium, local fiscal variables will be capitalized into house values.

A large number of capitalization studies have centered on the estimation of the degree to which property tax differences are capitalized into property values. If the difference in price between two otherwise identical properties is equal to the present discounted value (PDV) of the tax differential, the full capitalization of the property tax differential occurs.

The seminal capitalization study by Oates (1969) is based on the 1960 census data of 53 municipalities in northeastern New Jersey. Oates finds that a higher tax rate depresses house prices, and that increased school spending increases the price of housing. Using a discount rate of 5 percent and a 40-year time horizon, he finds that tax differentials are fully capitalized. Under a 3 percent discount rate and an infinite house life, the capitalization percentage is 61 percent. In subsequent years, many researchers have tried to measure the degree of capitalization of the property tax. Due to the methodological difficulties and data limitations and other unobservable factors, the empirical capitalization literature has resulted in widely varying results of the rate of capitalization.

This study estimates the rate of capitalization of local taxes and public spending using data for over 200 Chinese cities. In China, all tax rates are determined by the central government, and each provincial and local government is assigned a share of revenue collections within its boundaries. Tax administration is a shared responsibility between the central and local governments. The central government is exclusively entitled to impose taxes, and only the provincial level of government can make decisions with respect to tax rates within the limits set by the central government. Unlike local governments in the United States that rely heavily on property taxes for local public finance, Chinese local governments cannot generate a substantive amount of revenues from land and property taxes and have to rely heavily on taxes that are with the central government, such as the value-added tax (VAT), business tax, income tax from local enterprises, and personal income tax, plus receipts of land leasing and transfers and others.

In this study, we regress the median home value of Chinese cities on local taxes and public spending, as well as other factors identified as influencing the housing price of a jurisdiction. The results from this study make a significant contribution to the capitalization literature. First, previous research on capitalization theory has not yet reached a consensus. Empirical evidence from China will add to the debate on the incidence of local taxes such as property taxes and the extent of capitalization of local fiscal policies. It may provide empirical evidence on the validity of Tiebout's hypothesis in a non-U.S. environment. Second, the empirical studies using U.S. data suffer from the endogeneity problem fundamental to this literature because the median home value and the tax rate term are simultaneously determined due to the residual property tax system and the definition of the effective tax rate often used by researchers, including Oates (1969). It is difficult to determine the direction of causation between tax rates and home values. However, in China the tax rate is exogenous because it is set by the central government and selected by the provincial governments. Local governments in China may make varying efforts to administer and collect tax revenues. Our sample of data is for 220 cities in 31 provinces, allowing for a large amount of sample variation in local tax rate and public spending. Third, local governments in China also administer taxes other than land and property taxes, such as the VAT and business tax and corporate and personal income taxes. The impact of these taxes on housing values may lead to a broad discussion of the degree of substitution between the various inputs at different sectors (industries).

According to Gravelle (1994), when there are other taxes on capital, most notably a corporate income tax, housing, especially owner-occupied housing, is taxed at a very low rate compared to other forms of capital. The property tax actually helps to correct the misallocation of resources resulting from the corporate income tax.

Models and Specification Issues

The current official statistical system does not report city-level median or mean home values. However, the 2007 Large-Sample Urban Household Survey (UHS) contains the current market values of households' homes at the end of 2006. Median home value for every city is calculated based on this micro data set. Since we have only the home value data for 2007, we collect the fiscal variables for 2006 and estimate the following cross-section regression equation:

$$Ln(HV_{i,t}) = \alpha + \beta T_{i,t-lag\_period} + \gamma E_{i,t-lag\_period} + \delta Z_{i,t} + \varepsilon_i \qquad (1)$$

Where HV_i is median home value in city i; T_i is the vector of tax structure variables; E is the vector of local public spending variables; Z_i is the set of other variables that are believed to affect home value variations across cities; and ε_i is the error term.

To mitigate the possible endogeneity problem between home value and taxes and expenditures, we include lagged indicators of local taxes and expenditures on the right-hand side of equation (1). Home value (HV) is of year 2007 ($t = 2007$), and the tax and expending indicators are of year 2006 or 2005 ($lag\_period = 1$ or 2).

Data and Hypotheses

Equation (1) is estimated using cross-sectional data for 2006 for 238 cities of prefecture level or above in China.[1] The data were taken from the 2007 Large-Sample Urban Household Survey conducted by the National Bureau of Statistics of China, *Yearbook of China's Cities*, and *Finance Yearbook of China*. Table 7.1 shows the descriptive statistics of the variables used in this study.

The Urban Household Survey (UHS) is conducted annually by the Urban Survey Department of the National Bureau of Statistics of China (NBSC). The sample size is about 50,000. In 2007, the bureau conducted a large-scale survey that covered all of the 255 prefecture-level cities in China and had a sample size of 300,000 households. Chinese cities have a three-tier submunicipal administrative structure: The first tier is district, or *qu*; the second tier is street block, or *jiedao* (*JD*); and the third tier is street neighborhood, or *juweihui* (*JWH*). Beijing, for example, had 18 Qu, 130 JDs, and 2,625 JWHs in 2006. The 2007 UHS employed the three-stage stratified sampling method. First, JDs in each city were sorted by their identification (ID) numbers and sampled at fixed distances. Next, JWHs in each selected JD were sorted by their ID number and sampled at fixed distances. Finally, 20–40 households were randomly sampled in each selected JWH. The selected household reported its annual income, household head's education attainment, and the size and current market value of the housing unit. The current market value was estimated by the interviewer using a simple market comparison approach.

The dependent variable is measured as city median home value (per housing unit) in logarithm in equation (1). The median home in the average city has a value of 179,000 yuan. The most expensive city has a median home value of 690,000 yuan.

The explanatory variables fall into three categories: (1) taxes and other revenues; (2) public expenditures; and (3) economic and demographic characteristics, industrial composition, housing market attributes, and city and region dummies.

The total fiscal revenue is disaggregated into VAT, business tax, corporate income tax, personal income tax, and other taxes and revenues. Local public expenditure is disaggregated into education expenditure, infrastructure expenditure, and other expenditures. Tax variables are measured as per capita tax revenue or the ratio of the tax revenue to GDP as a measure of the average tax rate. Public expenditure variables are measured as per capita expenditure. In 2006, the average city yielded a fiscal revenue of 6,844 yuan per capita and expended 10,549 yuan per capita. Of the taxes, the business tax took the largest share (22.8 percent), and the individual income tax had the smallest share (3.9 percent). On average, 22.4 percent of the total fiscal expenditure was spent on education.

A measure of various effective tax rates, per se, would be ideal. However, any attempt to use statutory tax rate schedules in constructing a measure of effective rates across Chinese cities is problematic because of the substantial lack of uniformity of enforcement practices and variations in rate structures of some taxes across

---

[1] There were 255 prefecture-level cities in China in 2006. Some key variables are missing for 17 cities. Therefore, the final regressions have 238 cities. After dropping observations with missing data, the sample size is 229 Chinese perfecture-level cities.

Descriptive Statistics of City-Specific Variables

Variable	Variable Name	Maximum	Minimum	Mean	SD
Dependent Variable					
Median home value (in thousand yuan)[a]	HV	690	50	175.9	108.8
Explanatory Variables					
(1) Taxes and other revenues					
Fiscal revenue per capita (in thousand yuan)[b]	REV_PC	44.923	0.375	6.844	6.086
Fiscal revenue as a ratio to GDP	REV_RATIO	0.820	0.029	0.142	0.097
VAT per capita (in thousand yuan)[b]	VAT_PC	8.924	0.079	1.302	1.409
VAT as a ratio to GDP	VAT_RATIO	0.242	0.003	0.027	0.025
Business tax per capita (in thousand yuan)[b]	BTAX_PC	10.195	0.070	1.561	1.505
Business tax as a ratio to GDP	BTAX_RATIO	0.116	0.003	0.031	0.020
Corporate income tax per capita (in thousand yuan)[b]	CITAX_PC	5.632	0.015	0.578	0.806
Corporate income tax as a ratio to GDP (in yuan)[b]	CITAX_RATIO	0.061	0.001	0.010	0.009
Individual income tax per capita (in thousand yuan)[b]	HITAX_PC	2.707	0.016	0.267	0.335
Individual income tax as a ratio to GDP (in thousand yuan)[b]	HITAX_RATIO	0.020	0.001	0.005	0.004
Other revenue per capita (fiscal revenue per capita minus the above four categories, in thousand yuan)[b]	OREV_PC	24.233	0.195	3.136	2.766
Other revenue as a ratio to GDP	OREV_RATIO	0.414	0.012	0.069	0.053
(2) Public expenditures					
Fiscal expenditure per capita (in thousand yuan)[b]	EXP_PC	40.216	1.022	10.549	7.129
Education expenditure per capita (in thousand yuan)[b]	EDUEXP_PC	9.702	0.052	2.368	1.908
Infrastructure expenditure per capita (in thousand yuan)[b]	INFRAEXP_PC	11.405	0.004	0.963	1.242
Other expenditure per capita (fiscal expenditure per capita minus the above two categories; in thousand yuan)[b]	OEXP_PC	43.229	0.945	9.982	6.713

(continued)

TABLE 7.1 (*continued*)

Variable	Variable Name	Maximum	Minimum	Mean	SD
(3) Economic and demographic characteristics, industrial composition, housing market attributes, city/region dummies					
Median annual household income (in thousand yuan)[a]	HINC	80	14.4	30.55	5.19
City gross domestic product (in trillion yuan)[c]	GDP	10.26	0.02	0.18	1.07
City nonagriculture population (in millions)[c]	POP	13.68	0.17	3.52	2.42
Average years to schooling (years)[a]	EDU	13.54	10.09	12.04	0.60
Primary industry's share in GDP (%)[c]	IND1	31.67	0.12	4.67	6.85
Secondary industry's share in GDP (%)[c]	IND2	89.72	20.93	51.05	12.50
Share of commodity housing in total housing stock (%)[a]	COMHOUSE	73	1	31	15
Median housing unit size (square meters)[a]	HSIZE	161.51	55.55	88.43	17.89
Dummy variable (1=Beijing; 0=other)	BEIJING	1	0	—	—
Dummy variable (1=Shanghai; 0=other)	SHANGHAI	1	0	—	—
Dummy variable (1=city in eastern region; 0=other)	EAST	1	0	0.432	—

SOURCES: [a]National Bureau of Statistics of China, *China Statistical Yearbook*, 2007; [b] Ministry of Finance of China, *Finance Yearbook of China*, 2007; and [c] China Research Society of Urban Development, *Yearbook of China's Cities*, 2007.

NOTE: SD=standard deviation.

regions in China. As an alternative, revenues from various taxes as a share of GDP in each city are used as tax rate proxies.

In variable group (3), we include each city's economic and demographic characteristics, such as median annual household income, GDP, population, human capital level (average years of schooling), and shares of primary and secondary industries in each city's GDP. We also include two housing market variables: share of commodity housing in total housing stock, and median housing unit size. The cities with larger shares of commodity housing are expected to have higher home values because commodity housing is newer and more expensive than average housing stock. The cities with larger houses on average should also have higher home values. The regression results are discussed in the following section.

Empirical Results

Table 7.2 presents the regression estimation of the property value equation for the sample of this study. Our explanatory variables can explain over 60 percent of home value variation across cities.

According to regressions results from equation (1) in table 7.3, the variable of our primary interest, the per capita expenditure, has a positive and statistically significant coefficient estimate, indicating that the level and quality of public goods and services are reflected in the home value of a city in China. A 10 percent increase in per capital public spending leads to a nearly 4 percent increase in residential home

TABLE 7.2

Capitalization of Fiscal Variables in Home Values: Aggregate Tax and Expenditure Indicators

Explanatory Variable	Model (1) Coefficient (t-statistics)	Model (2) Coefficient (t-statistics)
Constant	−5.909 (−6.6)***	−5.956 (−6.7)***
$Ln(HSIZE)$	0.512 (3.7)***	0.522 (3.8)***
$Ln(HINC)$	0.520 (4.9)***	0.505 (4.8)***
$Ln(REV\_RATIO_{2006})$	−0.002 (−0.0)	
$Ln(EXP\_PC_{2006})$	0.338 (5.4)***	
$Ln(REV\_RATIO_{2005})$		−0.073 (−1.5)
$Ln(EXP\_PC_{2005})$		0.373 (6.5)***
$Ln(POP)$	0.228 (5.4)***	0.223 (5.3)***
EDU	−0.031 (−0.8)	−0.032 (−0.9)
IND1	−0.008 (−1.7)*	−0.009 (−2.0)**
IND2	−0.002 (−1.1)	−0.003 (−1.5)
COMHOUSE	0.312 (2.1)**	0.302 (2.0)**
EAST	0.185 (3.7)***	0.192 (3.9)***
BEIJING	0.068 (0.2)	0.067 (0.2)
SHANGHAI	−0.136 (-0.4)	−0.117 (−0.4)
R-square	0.654	0.655
No. of observations	229	229

NOTES: Dependent variable is the median housing value in year 2007 in logarithm, that is, Log(HV2007). The t values are in parentheses: * = significant at 10%; ** = significant at 5%; *** = significant at 1%.

TABLE 7.3

Capitalization of Fiscal Variables in Home Values: Disaggregate Tax and Expenditure Indicators

Explanatory Variable	Model (3) Coefficient (t-statistics)	Model (4) Coefficient (t-statistics)
Constant	−3.845 (−4.4)***	−4.198 (−4.9)***
$Ln(HSIZE)$	0.472 (3.6)***	0.458 (3.6)***
$Ln(HINC)$	0.331 (3.2)***	0.358 (3.6)***
$Ln(VAT\_RATIO_{2006})$	−0.040 (−0.8)	
$Ln(BTAX\_RATIO_{2006})$	0.232 (3.7)***	
$Ln(CITAX\_RATIO_{2006})$	0.162 (3.8)***	
$Ln(HITAX\_RATIO_{2006})$	−0.150 (−2.7)***	
$Ln(OTAX\_RATIO_{2006})$	−0.289 (4.7)***	
$Ln(VAT\_RATIO_{2005})$		−0.074 (−1.5)
$Ln(BTAX\_RATIO_{2005})$		0.311 (5.0)***
$Ln(CITAX\_RATIO_{2005})$		0.153 (3.5)***
$Ln(HITAX\_RATIO_{2005})$		−0.152 (−2.7)***
$Ln(OTAX\_RATIO_{2005})$		−0.281 (4.6)***
$Ln(EDUEXP\_PC_{2006})$	0.066 (0.9)	
$Ln(INFEXP\_PC_{2006})$	0.033 (2.0)**	
$Ln(OEXP\_PC_{2006})$	0.259 (2.7)***	
$Ln(EDUEXP\_PC_{2005})$		0.012 (0.2)
$Ln(INFEXP\_PC_{2005})$		0.034 (1.8)*
$Ln(OEXP\_PC_{2005})$		0.340 (4.1)***
$Ln(POP)$	0.195 (4.7)***	0.208 (5.3)***
EDU	−0.023 (−0.7)	−0.027 (-0.8)
IND1	−0.006 (−1.3)	−0.006 (−1.3)
IND2	0.000 (0.1)	0.001 (0.4)
COMHOUSE	0.167 (1.2)	0.128 (0.9)
EAST	0.184 (3.9)***	0.198 (4.4)***
BEIJING	−0.111 (−0.4)	−0.213 (−0.7)
SHANGHAI	−0.225 (−0.7)	−0.267 (−0.9)
R-square	0.724	0.714
No. of observations	229	229

NOTES: Dependent variable is the median housing value in year 2007 in logarithm, that is, Log(HV2007). The t values are in parentheses: *=significant at 10%; **=significant at 5%; ***=significant at 1%.

value, everything else being constant. This result suggests that Chinese consumers do take into account the provision of local public goods and services in their location choices. A city with a higher per capita public expenditure results in a higher value of houses. In China subnational government spending accounts for nearly 70 percent of total public spending, and there exists a vast disparity in quality and quantities of public goods and services, including public housing, social security, public health, education, and civil services among others. This may demonstrate that with rapid urbanization and increasing household mobility, the differences in services among cities in China are capitalized into home values. It provides empirical evidence that even in an environment where the set of assumptions of the Tiebout model are unrealistic or too restrictive, the Tiebout hypothesis is relevant in China. It supports the Tiebout hypothesis by demonstrating that consumers or households in China do consider the available programs of public services in their choices of locality of residence. So other things being equal (including tax rates), the communities that offer a more attractive package of public goods and services result in higher gross rents and therefore higher property values. Thus, the outputs of public services influence the attractiveness of a community to potential residents and thereby affect local property values. This result confirms Yinger's (1982) theory that individual families desiring to consume higher levels of public output would presumably tend to bid up property values in communities with high-quality programs of pubic services, affecting locational decisions of consumers and households.

The total local revenue as a share of GDP in a city has a negative sign but is statistically not significantly different from zero at the 10 percent level. This result may be caused by the possible competing effects of multitax structures and rates used by the local governments in China. Unlike the United States, where local property tax accounts for roughly 75 percent of revenues on average, the tax on the value of land and structure as a property tax in China accounts for a small share of tax revenue. There is no tax on the value of owner-occupied residential housing. As a result, the property tax in China does not fully reflect the average cost of local public goods and services. Consequently, a package of local taxes used in the financing of public goods and services in a Chinese city is included in the estimation equation of the residential housing value to better measure the differential impacts of varying taxes.

The income elasticity of the housing demand is about 0.3–0.5, which is consistent with Zheng (2007), who estimates the elasticity using micro household data in Chinese cities. Larger homes have higher values. All else being equal, a 1 percent increase in housing unit size results in a 0.5 percent increase in home value. Larger cities in terms of nonagriculture population have higher home values. All else being equal, a 10 percent population growth causes a 1.5 percent home value appreciation. Cities with larger shares of tertiary industry also have more expensive homes. Consistent with our intuition, cities with larger shares of commodity housing have significantly higher home prices.

Table 7.3 presents the estimation results of the residential housing value equation with varying local tax structures and rates and different public service programs. The tax variable estimates suggest that the taxes on proceeds or capital gains of property sales through business taxes and enterprise income taxes have statistically significant positive effects on residential housing value. Taxes on household income through the personal income tax and other local taxes and fees—via the urban real estate tax and the taxes on land use and appreciation and non-owner-occupied property—have a statistically significant negative effect on house value. It may well be that, with everything else constant, the higher taxes on business capital as a profit and during the transaction stage cause the flight of capital to the housing sector, providing incentives to supply more capital to housing construction and the consequent conversion of more nonresidential land to residential land. With a high demand for housing due to urbanization and rapid income growth, median house values increase. According to Gravelle (1994), when there are other taxes on capital, most notably corporate income taxes, housing, especially owner-occupied housing, is taxed at a very low rate compared to other forms of capital.

The property tax actually helps to correct the misallocation of resources resulting from the corporate income tax.

Not surprisingly, the tax on personal income reduces the median house value of a community. It may be that the personal income tax burden on households depresses the purchasing power of consumers, leading to lower property values in the community because of the demand side effect.

Other local taxes, including those on real estate in urban areas, result in a statistically significant negative effect on property values. This result is consistent with the empirical results of many previous researchers, suggesting that the differences in local taxes are capitalized in the value of residential housing.

Conclusions

This chapter analyzes the effects of local taxes and local public spending on the price of residential housing in Chinese cities in 2007. After controlling for possible simultaneity problems, this cross-sectional study finds that local property values have a significant positive relationship with local public spending but a negative correlation with taxes on land and property and personal income in Chinese cities.

These results are consistent with the Tiebout model, in which households take into account local public services and tax liability in choosing a community of residence. People do appear willing to pay higher prices for residential housing in a community that provides a high level and quality of public services or in a community that provides the same public services with lower tax rates on land and property. This study also indicates that the Chinese local public finance that tax other forms of capital more heavily than owner-occupied housing results in incentives to supply capital to the residential sector and may lead to the misallocation of resources. It supports the observation of Gravelle (1994) that preferential treatment of housing accounts for the distortions arising from the misallocation of capital. It may indicate that the property tax financing of local public expenditure programs in China may correct for the misallocation of resources resulting from the business income tax, business taxes, and value-added tax that constitute the bulk of local taxes.

This study contributes to the capitalization literature in a country where local tax and expenditure structures are quite different from those in the United States. It provides empirical evidence that even in an environment where the Tiebout assumptions do not apply, consumers and households take into account the local public expenditure programs and local tax burdens in their choice of a community of residence, as the Tiebout model suggests. However, more research is warranted to test the incidence of local taxes.

REFERENCES

Aaron, Henry J. 1975. *Who pays the property tax?* Washington, DC: Brookings Institution.
China Research Society of Urban Development. 2007. *Yearbook of China's Cities*. Beijing, China.
Gravelle, Jane G. 1994. *The economic effects of taxing capital income*. Cambridge, MA: MIT Press.

Hamilton, Bruce. 1975. Capitalization of intra-jurisdictional differences in local tax prices. *American Economic Review* 66 (December):743–753.

Man, Joyce Y. 1995. The incidence of differential commercial property taxes: Empirical evidence. *National Tax Journal* 48(4):479–482.

Man, Joyce Y., and Michael Bell. 1996. The impact of the local sales tax on the value of owner-occupied housing. *Journal of Urban Economics* 39:114–130.

Mieszkowski, Peter M. 1972. The property tax: An excise tax or a profit tax? *Journal of Public Economics* 1 (April):73–96.

Mieszkowski, Peter, and George R. Zodrow. 1989. Taxation and the Tiebout model: The differential effects of head taxes, taxes on land rents, and property taxes. *Journal of Economic Literature* 27:1098–1146.

Ministry of Finance of China. 2007. *Finance Yearbook of China.* Beijing, China.

National Bureau of Statistics of China. 2007. *China Statistical Yearbook.* Beijing: China Statistics Press.

Oates, Wallace E. 1969. The effects of property taxes and local public spending on property values: An empirical study of tax capitalization and the Tiebout hypothesis. *Journal of Political Economy* 77 (Nov./Dec.):957–971.

———, ed. 2001. *Property taxation and local government finance.* Cambridge, MA: Lincoln Institute of Land Policy.

Tiebout, Charles M. 1956. A pure theory of local expenditures. *Journal of Political Economy* 64(5):416–424.

Wilson, John D. 1984. The excise tax effects of the property tax. *Journal of Public Economics* 24 (August):309–329.

Yinger, J. Milton. 1985. Ethnicity. *Annual Review of Sociology* 11:151–180.

Yinger, John. 1982. Capitalization and the theory of local public finance. *Journal of Political Economy* 90(5):917–943.

Low-Income Housing Policy and Challenges

8

Housing Finance in China

YONGHENG DENG AND PENG FEI

Evolution of the Mortgage Markets

The residential mortgage market is a newly emerging sector of the capital market in China. It has been evolving rapidly with the housing system reforms carried out over the past decade and is gaining strength as a financial engine for the booming residential housing development and general economic growth in China. The Chinese government's efforts to transfer residential property ownership from state-owned enterprises (SOEs) to private households created the mortgage lending business and propelled the development of the mortgage market from near negligible levels in 1997 to over US$450 billion 10 years later.

Table 8.1 presents the annual growth of the mortgage market in China from 1998 to 2007. Despite the impressive 62 percent compound annual growth rate, China's outstanding mortgage balance accounted for only 12.9 percent of GDP in 2007 compared to 80 percent for the United States.[1]

A Dual-Channel Housing Finance System

The Chinese mortgage market developed as a by-product of the housing reform that was initiated in the 1990s and has accelerated since 1998. Since then, massive privatization of state-owned housing and the establishment of a commodity residential housing market have helped lay the foundation for private capital formation and wealth accumulation.[2] This, in turn, has contributed to the development

---

[1] In 2002, right before the global boom of the property market, the outstanding mortgage balance as a percentage of GDP was 58 percent for the United States, 65 percent for Singapore, 50 percent for Hong Kong, 38 percent for South Korea, and 7 percent for China.

[2] After the privatization of state-owned housing, SOEs no longer provided housing directly to employees as a benefit, and the ownership rate of housing increased quickly. At the end of 2003, the rate reached 80 percent.

TABLE 8.1

Outstanding Balance of Mortgage Loans, 1998–2007

	1998	1999	2000	2001	2002	2003	2004	2005	2006	2007
Mortgage loans (billions of yuan)	43	136	332	560	827	1,330	1,800	2,084	2,480	3,314
Annual growth (billions of yuan)	30	93	196	228	267	503	470	284	396	834
Annual growth rate (%)	124	216	144	69	48	61	35	15.8	19.0	33.6
Mortgage as % of total bank loans	0.5	1.4	3.0	5.0	6.3	8.4	10.1	10.7	11.0	12.7
Mortgage as % of GDP	0.5	1.7	3.7	5.1	6.9	9.8	11.3	11.4	11.8	12.9

SOURCE: People's Bank of China.

of the market for residential mortgage lending.[3] Table 8.2 summarizes the major events of China's housing reform from 1949 to 1999.

After the housing reforms, China set up a housing finance system with Chinese characteristics: The system is operated through both the policy-driven and the market-oriented housing finance channels. Policy-driven finance occurs mainly through the Housing Provident Fund (HPF), which is a mandatory housing savings scheme, while market-oriented housing finance is obtained via mortgage loans from commercial banks (called commercial mortgages[4] or bank loans). This dual-channel housing finance system is illustrated in figure 8.1.

Compared to HPFs in other countries, China's HPF system has some unique characteristics. The HPF in China is a mandatory housing savings scheme. All employees in urban areas are required to contribute a certain portion of their salary to the HPF, and employers are required to match the employee's contribution. The total contribution is deposited monthly into a special HPF account at a commercial bank for each employee by the employer. The account is closed only if the account holder leaves the city, retires, or dies. SOE work units play an important role in managing the HPF. They deposit the savings on behalf of employees, service the loans, and arrange for withdrawals.[5] A specialized entity, a Housing Provident Fund management center, is usually set up in each city and is responsible for the daily management of the HPF. The center is under the supervision of the municipal government, which is also responsible for making relevant HPF policies.

Housing reform and new demand for housing (mainly from urbanization, population growth, and housing upgrades) is mostly fulfilled by the commodity residential housing market.

[3] SOEs do not provide mortgage loans to their employees.

[4] It should be noted that China's commercial mortgage (bank loan) is different from the commercial mortgage in the U.S. market, where *commercial mortgage* refers to collateralized lending to property developers or corporations. In China the term simply means that the mortgagee is a commercial bank, whereas in a noncommercial mortgage loan the mortgagee is the HPF center. So in China, commercial mortgage loans include mortgage loans issued to individual property buyers and developers for both residential and business purposes by commercial banks.

[5] See Wang (2001) for a more detailed discussion.

TABLE 8.2

Chronology of Major Housing Reform Events, 1949–1999

Socialist housing system (before housing reform)	1949	• People's Republic of China was founded. • Land and residential property were nationalized.
	1960	Housing was part of compensation for workers in SOEs.
Housing reform (phase 1): ownership recognition	1978	Commodity residential housing market emerged for high-income foreigners and nonstate employees.
	1986	China Construction Bank began to issue residential mortgage loans.
	1988	Citizens could hold and transfer legal rights to occupy land and buildings for a specified period (70 years for residential units, 30–50 years for commercial properties).
Housing reform (phase 2): private housing market development	1991	Housing Provident Funds (CPFs) were first established in Shanghai.
	1992	Government encouraged citizens to purchase their residences at subsidized prices.
	1995	• Government launched a housing reform program to provide housing, especially for low-income households. • Efforts were taken to ensure funding for constructing and remodeling of residential housing.
Development of mortgage market	1998	• Welfare housing ceased. SOEs were required to stop building new housing units. • Workers' housing benefit was converted to cash compensation. • Certain areas were allocated to develop economical residential buildings for low-income households. • People's Bank of China issued regulations on mortgage lending, including prudential standards such as a maximum loan-to-value ratio of 70 percent (later changed to 80 percent) and mandatory income verification.
	1999	State Council issued "Ordinance of Housing Provident Funds."

Currently, China's HPFs are still very localized in terms of policies, administration, and fund usage. Cities are allowed to have their own policies or rules on fund contributions, withdrawals, and mortgage applications, as long as these rules do not contradict the policies made by the central government. Thus, the contribution rate may vary by city. The central government requires a minimum contribution of 5 percent of the salary from the employee, and the employer must match that amount. However, cities with a good economic performance are allowed to increase the minimum contribution rate. In 1999, the minimum contribution rate was set at 8 percent and 7 percent in Beijing and Shanghai, respectively. Enterprises in good economic condition are also encouraged to set up a supplemental account for their

FIGURE 8.1

The Housing Finance System Framework

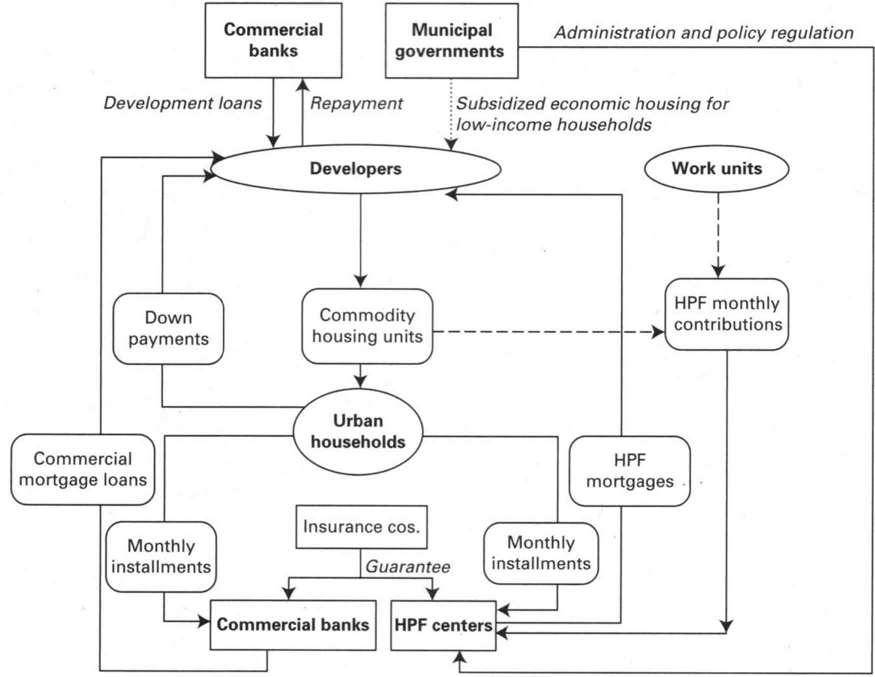

employees in some cities, such as Shanghai. Currently, the contribution rate of the supplemental account in Shanghai varies between 1 percent and 9 percent.

The HPF provides low-cost mortgage loans to its members, who can use the funds for home purchase, repairs, and construction activities (see table 8.3). HPFs set up mortgage loan ceilings, which vary by city. For example, the maximum loan amount per household per incident in Shanghai was originally 100,000 yuan; it was increased to 200,000 yuan in August 2005.[6]

From its inception in 1991 to 10 years afterward, however, the HPF was available only to urban employees who had a permit for permanent residency in the city; it excluded workers from rural areas and self-employed individuals. By the end of 2004, although the total outstanding balance of the HPFs was 740 billion yuan and about 61.38 million urban employees participated in the HPF scheme, according to the statistics published by the National Bureau of Statistics, only 58.4 percent of urban employees were covered by HPFs. To change this situation, in 2005, the Ministry of Construction, the Ministry of Finance, and the People's Bank of China (PBoC) jointly issued "Guidelines on the Issues of Management of HPFs," which broadened the coverage of HPFs to include workers from rural areas and the self-employed.

---

[6] On 21 July 2005, the People's Bank of China announced a foreign exchange rate reform after almost nine years of pegging the yuan to the U.S. dollar at US$1 = 8.30 yuan. According to the bank, the exchange rate on 22 April 2009 was US$1 = 6.83 yuan.

TABLE 8.3

Rate Spreads Between HPF and Commercial (Bank) Mortgage Loans

Loan Term		HPF Mortgage Loans		Commercial Mortgage Loans		Interest Payment Difference in Yuan (based on loan amount)			
Year	Month	Annual Int. Rate (%)	Monthly Int. Rate (%)	Annual Int. Rate (%)	Monthly Int. Rate (%)	10,000	50,000	100,000	150,000
1	12	3.33	2.775	5.31	4.425	198.00	990.00	1,980.00	2,970.00
2	24	3.33	2.775	5.40	4.500	221.62	1,108.10	2,216.20	3,324.30
3	36	3.33	2.775	5.40	4.500	332.62	1,663.10	3,326.20	4,989.30
4	48	3.33	2.775	5.76	4.800	525.44	2,627.20	5,254.40	7,881.60
5	60	3.33	2.775	5.76	4.800	663.41	3,317.05	6,634.10	9,951.15
6	72	3.87	3.225	5.94	4.950	690.16	3,450.80	6,901.60	10,352.40
7	84	3.87	3.225	5.94	4.950	815.44	4,077.20	8,154.40	12,231.60
8	96	3.87	3.225	5.94	4.950	944.01	4,720.05	9,440.10	14,160.15
9	108	3.87	3.225	5.94	4.950	1,075.84	5,379.20	10,758.40	16,137.60
10	120	3.87	3.225	5.94	4.950	1,210.92	6,054.60	12,109.20	18,163.80
11	132	3.87	3.225	5.94	4.950	1,349.20	6,746.00	13,492.00	20,238.00
12	144	3.87	3.225	5.94	4.950	1,490.66	7,453.30	14,906.60	22,359.90
13	156	3.87	3.225	5.94	4.950	1,635.26	8,176.30	16,352.60	24,528.90
14	168	3.87	3.225	5.94	4.950	1,782.96	8,914.80	17,829.60	26,744.40
15	180	3.87	3.225	5.94	4.950	1,933.71	9,668.55	19,337.10	29,005.65

SOURCE: Based on the interest rate adjustment of the People's Bank of China, 23 December 2008.

In general, an HPF loan alone is not sufficient for most households to purchase a house. As a result, the demand for loans from residential home buyers cannot be met. Hybrid mortgages, which combine the maximum amount of HPF funds and mortgage loans (bank loans) were rapidly developed by many commercial banks in China. Most urban home buyers apply the maximum mortgage loan (up to 80 percent of the loan-to-value ratio) to finance the purchase and use HPF funds to cover part of the down payment. As a result, residential mortgage loans currently dominant the market share of China's residential loan market. According to a PBoC report, HPF loans accounted for only 12 percent of total residential loans balance in 2002.

The Primary Market of Commercial Mortgage Lending

In 1986, the China Construction Bank (CCB) was the first to offer mortgage loans in China. For the first 12 years, prior to the beginning of the housing reform in 1998, the mortgage market grew very slowly. In May 1998, in order to support housing reform and increase the availability of affordable housing for the general public, the PBoC published residential mortgage lending regulations. The regulations established basic mortgage lending standards, including a maximum loan-to-value ratio of 70 percent (later changed to 80 percent) and mandatory income verification. PBoC also regulated the preferential mortgage interest rate and set the mortgage rate 10 basis points below commercial loans with the same term. Today all mortgages in China are adjustable rate mortgages (ARMs). Once PBoC announces a rate adjustment, the new rate will be applied to all existing mortgage loans (with terms longer than one year) starting from the beginning of the following year.

Since 1998, the economic deflation has forced PBoC to lower the mortgage interest rate five times. In February 2002, the mortgage interest rate hit a record low. At the same time, stable and strong GDP growth and government support for the residential property industry established a favorable macro environment for the primary mortgage lending market. A historically low interest rate since 1999 and the sluggish performance of the stock market since June 2002 have attracted many investors to invest in the real estate market, which pushed up the price of property in some areas (see figure 8.2).

Under these favorable conditions, China's mortgage market has experienced unprecedented growth. From 1998 to 2003, the outstanding balance of property development and residential mortgage loans grew by an average annual rate of 49 percent, compared to 15 percent growth for total bank lending. In 2005, the central bank reported that the total value of outstanding residential mortgages had reached 1.65 trillion yuan (US$199 billion), equivalent to 23 percent of banks' medium- to long-term lending and 9 percent of total lending, while in 1998, total residential mortgages were 43 billion yuan (US$5 billion), which accounted for only 0.5 percent of total bank lending.

During the period from 2001 to 2004, housing prices and land prices in almost every major city showed a remarkable increase of about 25 percent. Especially in some big cities, such as Shanghai, which account for about 12.1 percent of China's mortgage market, the housing selling price has risen more than 70 percent since 2000. The combination of rapidly increasing housing prices and the enormous outstanding mortgage balance have raised concerns about a "bubble" in the housing market. To curb the rapid growth of housing prices, on 16 March 2005, the central bank (PBoC) announced a floor lending rate of 5.51 percent for housing loans over five years (an increase of 20 basis points from the previous rate of 5.31 percent) and also lowered the loan-to-value rate back to 70 percent from 80 percent. The major policies related to China's mortgage market are summarized in table 8.4.

Types of Mortgage Loans

Currently, there are three categories of mortgages in China: residential mortgage loans (bank loans), HPF loans, and hybrid mortgage loans. HPF loans refer to loans granted by the bank with the authorization of the HPF management center, using the HPF program's accumulated deposits as the source of funding. HPF loans can be applied only to residential housing. Hybrid mortgage loans use both HPFs and commercial bank loans as sources of financing.

However, bank mortgage loans in China can be classified as residential mortgage loans and business mortgage loans. The latter mainly refers to loans granted to developers to purchase or develop business properties such as office buildings and retail shops. Since the mortgagor will use the business property as collateral, which is much riskier than typical collateral for residential property, commercial banks typically tighten the lending criteria for business mortgage loans. The business mortgage term will be less than 10 years, while a residential mortgage term could be 30

Interest Rates, Stock Market Returns, and the Property Market

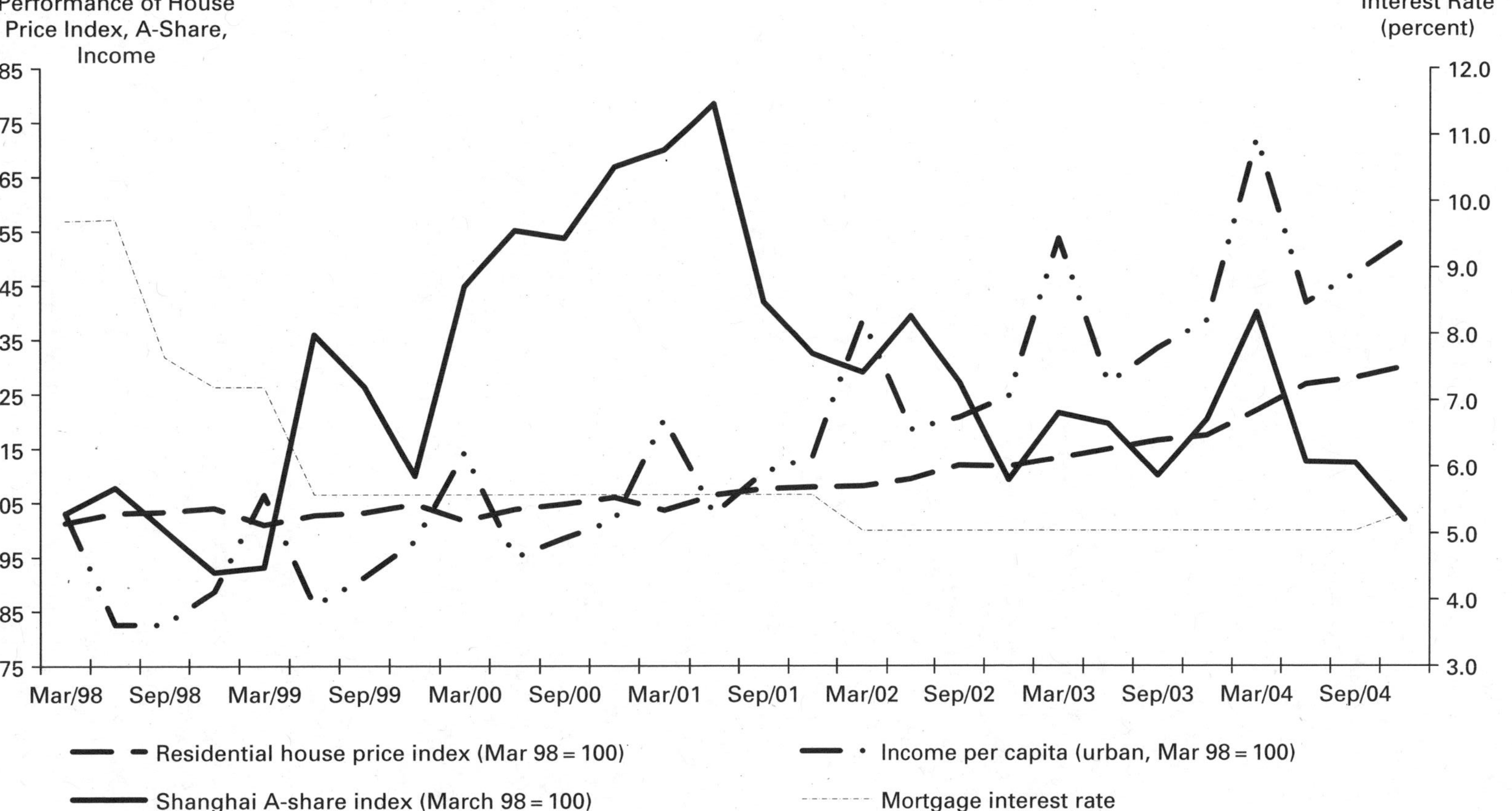

NOTES: The Shanghai A-share market is the most important stock market in mainland China in the number of listed companies, number of listed shares, total market value, tradable market value, securities turnover in value, stock turnover in value, and T-bond turnover in value. The residential housing price index is taken from the monthly statistical report of the National Bureau of Statistics of China.

Chronology of China's Mortgage Market Policy Changes

1998	PBoC initiated mortgage lending as a key part of urban housing reform; geographical restrictions on the mortgage market were eliminated (previously, people could apply for mortgage loans only in a few big cities); the preferential mortgage loan interest rate was regulated.
1999	The restriction on the loan-to-value was loosened from 70 percent to 80 percent; mortgage loan maturity could be extended from 20 to 30 years.
2002	In February the mortgage rate became the lowest in history, and the Housing Provident Fund rate was 4.05 percent; in August, the PBoC first warned of a bubble in the real estate market.
2003	In February, the PBoC again warned of a bubble in the property market and expressed concern about an excessively growing mortgage market in some big cities; in June, the PBoC issued a circular further strengthening the administration of banking loans for the real estate industry (Circular No. 121); restrictions were placed on loans to real estate developers whose equity ratio was less than 30 percent and on mortgage loans to presale housing.
2004	The China Development and Reform Commission listed the real estate industry as the key target of macroeconomic control.
2005	Banking loans to the real estate industry decreased by 16 percent, but real estate investment increased 28.1 percent year on year; the supreme court of the PRC issued a regulation that owner-occupied houses could not be foreclosed, even if the mortgage borrower defaulted; CCB issued the first mortgage-backed security (MBS) products.
2007	China's central bank raised the required down payment ratio for buying a second house to 40 percent.

years. The loan-to-value ratio for business mortgage loans in China is less than 60 percent, compared to residential mortgage loans of 70 percent. In addition, the policies for business mortgage loans are not as favorable as those for residential mortgages. Currently, the market size of business mortgages is quite small. In March 2003, it was reported that in Shanghai outstanding mortgage loans were 121.6 billion yuan, of which only 4.2 billion yuan was business mortgage loans.

Major Players in China's Mortgage Market

Before the 1994 banking reforms, China's banking industry was mainly monopolized by the big four state-owned commercial banks (SOCBs), which had obtained a credit guarantee from the state. As part of the banking reform efforts to create a more unified and efficient banking system, China's SOCBs were reorganized into commercial entities. Under the new system, each SOCB is held accountable for its profitability. These four banks, the Industrial and Commercial Bank of China (ICBC), Bank of China (BOC), China Construction Bank (CCB), and Agriculture Bank of China (ABC), are supervised by the People's Bank of China—the central bank of China—and report directly to the State Council. In addition to the SOCBs, by the end of 2002, there were 80 foreign commercial banks, 112 city commercial banks,

TABLE 8.5

Big Four State-Owned Commercial Banks

Bank	Brief Description
Industrial and Commercial Bank of China (ICBC)	ICBC was established in 1984 to manage short-term industrial and commercial lending. It is approved to accept deposits and remittances, make loans, and conduct foreign exchange transactions.
China Construction Bank (CCB)	CCB was the conduit for capital allocations to state enterprises and was supervised initially by the Ministry of Finance, PBoC, and the State Capital Construction Commission. It is responsible for overseeing state investment projects and providing loans for capital construction. It also conducts foreign exchange transactions, markets overseas investments, and issues bonds.
Agriculture Bank of China (ABC)	ABC serves as the primary lender to the agricultural sector and is responsible for examining and approving state funds to support the agricultural industry. Additionally, it purchases agricultural products for the state and supervises the rural credit cooperatives.
Bank of China (BOC)	BOC is China's primary foreign exchange bank and functions as the overseas agent of the PBoC. It handles international accounts and deposits; foreign exchanges; international syndicated loans; and other services such as trusts, investments, leasing, and business consultancy.

11 shareholding commercial banks, and 3 state policy banks in China's banking system (The Economist, 2004).

A brief description of the historic function of each of the SOCBs is provided in table 8.5. The four state-owned banks, especially CCB and ICBC, are also the key players in China's mortgage market, given their advantages in size, long-term relationship with property developers, and broad geographical coverage through a national network.

Historically, CCB was responsible for overseeing state infrastructure investment and providing loans for real estate construction. It holds a 70 percent market share of the trustee business for Housing Provident Funds. The CCB is the first commercial bank authorized by the central bank to do a pilot project on mortgage-backed securities (MBSs) in China.

ICBC is the largest mortgage market share holder (31.2 percent in 2002) and also the largest lender in China and has a good relationship with developers. It had total assets of 5.3 trillion yuan at the end of 2003. Its profits were 74.7 billion yuan (US$9 billion) in 2004, which was up by 18 percent from 2003. It has a 20 percent market share of the trustee business of Housing Provident Funds.[7]

---

[7] In practice a Housing Provident Fund center will entrust a bank to manage its funds and issue the mortgage loans that offer the bank the best opportunity to access the potential borrower and issue combined mortgage loans to him/her.

TABLE 8.6

Market Shares and Key Players in the Mortgage Market, 2001–2002

Bank	Mortgage Loans (in Yuan billions)		Mortgage Market Share (%)		Mortgage Loans as % of Total Loans		YOY Growth Rate in 2002 (%)	
	2001	2002	2001	2002	2001	2002	Mortgages	Total Loans
BOC	53	98	9.5	11.9	4.5	7.1	84.6	16.4
ICBC	186	258	33.2	31.2	7.0	8.8	38.7	10.5
CCB	171	235	30.6	28.4	11.4	13.5	37.0	15.8
ABC	81	130	14.5	15.8	4.9	6.8	61.1	16.2
China Merchants	9	12	1.5	1.9	6.1	6.8	78.5	49.4
Shanghai Pudong Development Bank	6	8	6.3	6.3	6.3	6.3	72.6	72.5
Bank of Shanghai	6	10	1.1	1.2	11.3	13.3	111.8	32.5
Shenzhen Development Bank	3	3	0.6	0.4	4.7	3.7	12.3	67.3
Sector	560	827	100.0	100.0	4.6	5.9	47.7	15.9

SOURCE: Banks' annual reports.

Table 8.6 illustrates the market share of key players. We can see that in 2002 the four state-owned banks had a 87.3 percent market share in China's mortgage lending market, in which ICBC and CCB predominately accounted for 59.6 percent.

Risk Features and Performance of Mortgage Financing

The borrowers' motivations for prepayment and default in China are quite different from those observed in the United States and other developed countries.

Prepayment Risk

Since all mortgage loans issued in China are adjustable rate mortgages without a cap, there are no refinance-driven prepayments reported in the mortgage market. So far the financial "call option" has virtually no value to Chinese mortgage borrowers. This contradicts the conventional wisdom in the existing mortgage literature, where the call option is considered a dominant factor driving prepayments in the U.S. residential mortgage market.[8]

However, Chinese borrowers are quite sensitive to increases in mortgage rates. In October 2004, to curb speculative house purchasing, the PBoC announced that it would raise mortgage rates by 27 basis points for the first time in nine years. On

---

[8] See, for example, Kau et al. (1990) and Deng, Quigley, and Van Order (2000) for theoretical and empirical studies of the mortgage prepayment and default analysis in option theory framework. Quigley (1987) and Stanton and Wallace (1995) analyze the impact of interest rates on adjustable rate mortgage termination and valuation. Cunningham and Capone (1990) and Calhoun and Deng (2002) provide empirical evidence of the association between the call option value and the ARM prepayment behavior in the U.S. market.

16 March 2005 the central bank announced further measures to tighten housing credit. The interest rate on loans longer than five years was raised by 20 basis points, to 5.51 percent. Facing the continuous increase of mortgage interest rates, and given the low deposit rate and limited available investment vehicles in China, many borrowers chose to pay off their mortgage loans before maturity.

Default Risk

The number of default cases in China is quite small. The average rate of non-performing mortgage loans was only 1.5 percent in 2004.[9] There are three major reasons for default in China:

Mortgage fraud. There are three parties involved in the origination of mortgage loans: commercial banks, home buyers, and property developers. Mortgage loans issued by commercial banks will be directed to a developer except for the down payment, which is paid by the home buyer. However, some developers ask their employees or friends to buy houses for them and get the mortgage loans directly from banks with no intention to repay. The ICBC estimates that almost 80 percent of its nonperforming residential mortgage loans are caused by mortgage fraud. In early April 2005 the Bank of China reported that a Beijing real estate developer had allegedly defrauded the bank of $78 million using forged home-purchase contracts. Since the residential mortgage interest rate is much lower than the business loan interest rate and the approval process of residential mortgage loans is also much simpler than that of business loans, some developers in China have taken advantage of the favored treatment of residential mortgage lending. Mortgage fraud has been the key reason for defaults in Chinese mortgage loans.

Presale disputes. Presale (or *forward sale*) refers to the sale of properties either "off plan" or under construction. This practice, which allows developers to recoup their capital some 10 months earlier, is popular in the residential housing market in China. On average, presale units are 10 to 15 percent cheaper than finished properties. Statistics reported by the Ministry of Construction show that over 80 percent of residential properties in China's major cities are presold. Presale has important effects on both developers and buyers in China's housing market. For developers, a presale is a key financing tool, because there are almost no other channels for developers in China to access capital. On the other side, it is widely believed that a presale will inspire speculative activities of buyers. Using Hong Kong's real estate data from the 1990s, Wong et al. (2006) found that presale activities have significant effects on the volatility of spot pieces in the real estate market. In addition, empirical evidence showed that many home buyers in China used commercial bank mortgage loans as insurance to protect themselves from presale risks (Deng and Liu 2009).

There have been increasing reports of home buyers refusing to pay off their mortgages due to disputes with real estate developers regarding the quality and delivery time of their housing. These cases are mostly related to residential properties whose developers fail to deliver the housing in accord with presale contracts. In such cases, the lender takes the loss if the recovered net value is less than the outstanding loan

---

[9] See Bank of China (2005).

balance. In fact, many Chinese borrowers use the mortgage as an instrument for sharing the presale risks with the bank. If the home buyers (mortgage borrowers) are satisfied with the properties delivered by the developers, some might choose to pay off the debts as soon as they can. In case the developer fails to satisfy the home buyer on the date of delivery, the borrowers have the option of defaulting on the mortgage loan. In other words, the mortgage borrower has a put option to sell a poorly constructed house to the bank at a price set by the remaining balance of the loan.

Deterioration of affordability. Affordability of borrowers is also a major determinant of mortgage default in China. Due to unexpected unemployment or overestimation of household income, when the financial resources of a borrower deteriorates, the default risk increases.

Foreclosure

Generally speaking, the legal framework of a mortgage foreclosure is based on the related articles in the Guaranty Law (1996) and the Civil Procedure Law of the PRC. Article 53 of the Guaranty Law states, "A mortgagee who is not compensated upon the expiration of the term for performance of the debt may, through agreement with the mortgagor, be compensated from the money received from converting the things mortgaged into cash or from auctioning and selling of the things mortgaged, and if no agreement is reached, the mortgagee may file a suit in a people's court." This seems to offer the banks a convenient reason for foreclosure, in which they can directly foreclose on a property and sell it through auction or other method if the borrower agrees. However, in practice, most banks need to appeal to the court to enforce a foreclosure. During the appeal period, the process is regulated by the Civil Procedure Law.

At the end of 2004, the People's Supreme Court issued a ruling on the civil procedures of mortgage foreclosures. The rule removed banks' right to sell a repossessed home if it is the owner's sole residence. Under the new ruling, which took effect on January 1, 2005, banks have the right to repossess but not to sell the property. This new policy changes not only the ex-ante loan-screening process, but also the ex-post bargaining between bank and borrower. When borrowers are delinquent in their mortgage payments, lenders have the option to foreclose on the property or suggest a solution by lowering the interest payment or the mortgage amount (Wang, Young, and Zhou 2002; Chen and Deng 2003). However, according to the new People's Supreme Court ruling, a mortgage lender will have a limited option of foreclosure, which surely increases the default risk faced by the banks.

Early Evidence of Residential Mortgage Market Performance

Despite the rapid growth of the residential mortgage market and the potential of a developing MBS market in China, empirical studies on the performance of this newly developed, important sector of the financial market have been rare, which can be largely attributed to the immature regulatory environment and sparse mortgage data. Deng, Zheng, and Ling (2005) provided the first rigorous empirical study of the performance of residential mortgages in China, based on a unique micro data set of loan histories collected by a major residential mortgage lender.

Their research has found that the financial call option is currently unavailable to mortgage borrowers due to imperfect market conditions, while the financial put option, measured by the contemporaneous equity-to-market value of the property, is in general "out-of-money" to the borrowers because of the steady increases of property values in the housing market during the sampling period. Option theory apparently fails to explain the prepayment and default behavior in the current residential mortgage market.

On the other hand, other socioeconomic factors unrelated to financial options, such as borrower characteristics, play a major role in explaining prepayment and default behavior in China. Borrowers choose to pay off mortgage debts in a bear market and when the yield curve is flat. The current extremely low deposit rate in China makes saving no longer a rational option for long-term investment for many people. The stock market provides Chinese households with a viable means of benefiting from a higher return on investment in the capital market. Therefore, the stock market's fluctuations have a significant impact on mortgage borrowers' prepayment and default decisions.

Many Chinese borrowers tend to be "uncertainty averse"—that is, when the unemployment rate rises, they tend to reallocate their investment portfolio to safe assets by paying off their mortgage debt. This phenomenon is inconsistent with the borrower behaviors observed in the residential mortgage markets in the United States and other countries.

The reform of housing and the housing finance system in China have brought swift changes in many related policies and regulations, which influence households' decisions. Changes of policy have proved to be one of the critical determinants in the model for mortgage prepayment risk.

Borrower characteristics have been found to be significant in determining borrower prepayment behavior and hence may be used as an effective tool for screening loan applicants and identifying the potential high-risk borrowers. These findings have important policy implications. Medium-high- to high-income borrowers, as well as white-collar workers, are more likely to prepay their mortgage debts. Younger households and blue-collar workers are less likely to prepay. Therefore, adopting risk-based pricing in residential mortgage lending in China not only will improve the efficiency of the market, but also will enhance the credit available to the most needy households—that is, younger households, blue-collar workers, lower-income households—and help them become homeowners.

Finally, many residential housing units are transacted in the forward housing market via the preselling system. Deng and Liu (2009) find that the risk premium of a mortgage borrower's default and prepayment between the forward and spot housing markets in China can be as high as 250 basis points.

Emergence of the Secondary Mortgage Market

With the rapid growth of residential mortgage lending in China, commercial banks have been eager to improve the liquidity of mortgage loans. At the end of 2004, the PBoC submitted the proposal for a pilot project on MBSs to the State Council. In February 2005, the proposal was approved, and CCB was the first bank to implement

MBSs in China. To support the pilot project, the PBoC built up a coordination mechanism across 10 related departments and commissions and issued "The Regulation on the Pilot Issuance of MBSs" with the China Banking Regulatory Commission.

In December 2005, the first MBS in China was issued by CCB. The total size was about 3.01 billion yuan (US$0.45 billion). To ensure its success, CCB especially selected three branches, in Shanghai, Jiangsu, and Fujian, which are all economically well-developed provinces near the east coast, to implement the pilot project. The deal structure of CCB's MBS mainly adopts the trust mode. The China International Trust Investment Company (CITIC) is the special purpose trust (SPT) of securitization and serves as the channel of "bankruptcy remoteness" and "true sale." The trustee has no access to cash, and the principal and interest paid by the debtor are directly transferred by the service provider to the trust account opened in the trustee bank. Entrusted by the trustee, the transaction manager, according to the transaction contract, issues instructions to the trustee bank to operate the capital, pay related taxes and fees, and pay the investors the principal and interest through the China Government Securities Depository Trust & Clearing Co. Ltd. The decision-making right should be exercised at the investors' meeting.

Instead of using a third-party financial guaranty firm as a credit enhancement, CCB chose an internal credit enhancement with a senior-subordinated structure similar to the classic collateral mortgage obligation (CMO). The senior class is total 2.92 billion yuan, and CCB holds the junior-subordinated class, which is 90 million yuan. The right of junior tranches of investors to receive principle and interest is subordinated to the rights of the senior tranches. Moreover, the senior class of CCB's MBS includes three tranches—A, B, and C—which are awarded the credit rating AAA, A, and BBB, respectively, by China Chengxin International Co. Ltd. and Moody's jointly. The first tranche, A, which has the shortest maturity, is repaid entirely prior to any repayment of the other tranches; the second, B, prior to any repayment of the third, C, and so on. However, there is no accrual tranche "Z-bond," which is commonly the last tranche in classic CMO structure, in CCB's MBS. The tranche A and tranche B MBSs can be traded directly in the Countryside Interbank Bond Market, but tranche C can be traded only under the regulations by the PBoC. The subordinated tranche held by CCB cannot be traded.

The principal and interest of CCB's MBS are paid monthly. Since the underlying loans are all floating-rate mortgage loans, the coupon rate of the MBS also adopts the floating interest rate, which is determined by the benchmark interest rate and the interest rate spread, and updated semiannually. The weighted average annual percent rate (APR) of the underlying mortgage loans is 5.31 percent, and the weighted average life is 205 months. Currently, the senior tranche has 3 percent of credit support through the subordinate tranche; hence, the first 3 percent loss in the underlying mortgage pools should be absorbed by the subordinate tranche. Considering that the average rate of nonperforming mortgage loans in CCB is only 1.2 percent, the 3 percent credit support should cover the existing nonperforming loan risk for senior tranche investors.

The major legal problems of MBS can be handled in compliance with trust and contract laws, and other supporting laws and regulations are under formulation. According to CCB, related government authorities attach high importance to the

MBS, and a number of ministries have jointly set up a pilot issuance coordination group to study the policies and business innovations related to credit asset-backed securities (ABSs) and clearly define the requirements for formulating and enacting various ABS supporting systems, laws, and regulations. The "Management Rules on Credit Asset-Backed Securities Pilot" released recently provides a system guarantee for the standardized operation of the MBS business.

REFERENCES

Bank of China. 2005. *2004 China real estate financial report.* Beijing: Bank of China Real Estate Financial Analysis Group.

Calhoun, A., and Yongheng Deng. 2002. A dynamic analysis of fixed- and adjustable-rate mortgage terminations. *Journal of Real Estate Finance and Economics* 24(1–2):9–33.

Chen, Jun, and Yongheng Deng. 2003. Commercial mortgage workout strategy and conditional default probability: Evidence from special serviced CMBS loans. Working Paper No. 2003-1008. Los Angeles: University of Southern California, Lusk Center for Real Estate.

Cunningham, Donald, and Charles Capone. 1990. The relative termination experience of adjustable to fixed-rate mortgage. *Journal of Finance* 45(5):1687–1703.

Deng, Yongheng, and Peng Liu. 2009. Forward housing market and its impact on mortgage prepayment and default risks in China. *Journal of Real Estate Finance and Economics* 38(3): 214–240.

Deng, Yongheng, John M. Quigley, and Robert Van Order. 2000. Mortgage terminations, heterogeneity and the exercise of mortgage options. *Econometrica* 68(2):275–307.

Deng, Yongheng, Diehang Zheng, and Changfeng Ling. 2005. An early assessment of residential mortgage performance in China. *Journal of Real Estate Finance and Economics* 31(2):117–136.

The Economist. 2004. Finance and economics: Root and branch, China's banks. Nov 6, 373(8400): 88.

Kau, James B., Donald C. Keenan, Walter J. Muller, and James F. Epperson. 1990. The valuation and analysis of adjustable rate mortgages. *Management Science* 36(12):1417–1431.

Quigley, John M. 1987. Interest rate variations, mortgage prepayments and household mobility. *Review of Economics and Statistics* 69:636–643.

Stanton, Richard, and Nancy Wallace. 1995. ARM wrestling: Valuing adjustable rate mortgages indexed to the eleventh district cost of funds. *Real Estate Economics* 23:311–345.

Wang, Ko, Leslie Young, and Yuqing Zhou. 2002. Non-discriminating foreclosure and voluntary liquidating costs. *Review of Financial Studies* 15(3):959–985.

Wang, Ya Ping 2001. Urban housing reform and finance in China: A case study of Beijing. *Urban Affairs Review* 36(5):620–645.

Wong, Kelvin S. K., Edward C. Y. Yiu, M. Tse, and Kwong Wing Chau. 2006. Do the forward sales of real estate stabilize spot prices? *Journal of Real Estate Finance and Economics* 32(3):289–304.

Urban Expansion, Land Conversion, and Affordable Housing: The Case of Zhengzhou

9

SHLOMO ANGEL, MIDORI VALDIVIA, AND REBECCA M. LUTZY

WITH

MAI HARIU, JONATHAN KAUFMAN, DENNIS MARKATOS, JONA REPISHTI, NICOLE RIGGS, ARITETSOMA UKUEBERUWA, YAN ZHANG, AND YUEYUAN ZHENG

Chinese cities are quickly surpassing population and urban land area projections from prior decades. Between 2000 and 2020, for example, China's urban population is expected to grow by 66 percent. And if expansion of the land occupied by cities proceeds at the same rate observed from 1990 to 2000, it could grow by as much as 133 percent between 2000 and 2030, double the rate of urban population growth.[1]

In 2000, the urban population of China was 454 million and comprised 36 percent of the population of the country (United Nations 2007). By 2030, this population is expected to rise to 1 billion, with more than two-thirds of China's population residing in urban areas (Woetzel et al. 2008). According to recent UN estimates, China's urban population is now growing by 15 million people every year, and its urban area is growing by some 43,200 square kilometers each year. Using built-up area density calculations from a sample of nine Chinese cities, we estimated that in 2000 the land area of China's cities was some 48,000 square kilometers and amounted to 3.4 percent of the arable land in the country. Given the observed decline of average urban densities—by an average of 3.6 percent per year in the sample between 1990 and 2000 and at least 1.7 percent per year both in China and in a global sample of cities between 1990 and 2000—the land area of China's cities may now be growing by as much as 5.74 percent per year. At this rate, it can be expected to reach 15,013,000 square kilometers by 2020 (Angel et al. 2005). At that point, it would amount to some 107.7 percent of the arable land in the country.

---

[1] This exponential growth projection by the authors is based on the 5.7 percent annual growth rate observed between 1990 and 2000 in a sample of nine Chinese cities (Angel et al. 2005).

Yet arable land constitutes less than 15 percent of China's land area (Liy 2006). Since China has one of the lowest ratios of arable land per person in the world,[2] the Chinese government mandated strict quotas on the conversion of arable land to urban land in the name of protecting its food security and independence (Lichtenberg and Ding 2007). The quotas have had a significant impact on the shape and character of urban expansion, resulting in fragmented development on the urban fringe, the destruction of highly affordable housing in urban villages both within cities and on the fringe of cities, and land supply bottlenecks that have led to steep increases in urban land prices in recent years (Bertaud 2007a).[3] Although the central government recognizes that China's cities are its engine of economic success, concern is mounting over the exorbitant urban land prices that threaten to slow economic development. The government has proactively mandated the production of new affordable housing by the private sector.[4] Despite these measures, the National Development and Reform Commission has admitted to failure in curbing home prices.[5]

The Chinese government thus faces a serious predicament: How does it ensure national food security without compromising the prospects of urban-based economic development and without becoming an accomplice to an unmanageable housing crisis? The government cannot solve these challenges at the theoretical level or by appeal to ideology. Any resolution must be grounded in a more detailed analysis of the real-world interactions between urban population growth, the contribution of conversion quotas to future food security, the pattern of urban expansion in the face of these conversion quotas, and the delivery system of affordable housing in Chinese cities. This challenge requires a pragmatic solution that stakeholders can apply throughout China's urban system.

This chapter focuses on the key issues surrounding this urban growth challenge in one intermediate-size city—Zhengzhou, the capital of Henan Province. A city of 3.22 million people, its growth and expansion in recent years are typical of the rapid urbanization process currently sweeping China. A former capital of China, Zhengzhou is a transportation hub and a cultural center (Zhengzhou Municipality). Located just south of the Yellow River, this fast-growing industrial city sits at the intersection of two major railways, which connect Beijing in the north to Guangzhou in the south, and Xi'an in the west to Shanghai in the east (Zhengzhou

---

[2] In 2000, there were 739 square meters of arable land and permanent crops per person in China. Among the 48 largest countries that had populations in excess of 20 million and contained 87 percent of the world's population in 2000, China had the fourth-lowest ration of arable land area per person, after Egypt, Japan, and South Korea. The weighted average arable land per capita in those 48 countries was 2,245 square meters, three times that of China (World Bank 2007).

[3] Bertaud (2007a) states further that the enclaves of agricultural land within the urban built-up areas results in less agricultural productivity due to the lack of access to irrigation systems and rejection of lower-paid employment opportunities by rural migrants.

[4] Initiatives include Ministry of Construction regulations stipulating that residential units with an area of 90 square meters or less should occupy 70 percent of the floor area of newly built residential housing (called the 90–70 regulation), mandating that municipalities earmark 10 percent of proceeds from land sales to low-rent housing, and levying taxes on land appreciation of 30–60 percent. Xinhua News Agency 2007. House funding for the low-income tops the agenda, August 31; Hongxiao, Chang. 2007. China's affordable housing push: Easier said than done. *Caijing English Newsletter*, August 20.

[5] Xinhua News Agency 2007. Policies fail to curb soaring home prices, August 30.

Municipality). In 1983, the Zhengzhou Administrative Area was given jurisdiction over six districts and five county-level cities with a total area of 7,446 square kilometers. The administrative area of Zhengzhou City proper is 1,062 square kilometers, of which some 280 square kilometers constitute the built-up area of the city (Zhengzhou Municipality).

A team of 10 graduate students from the Woodrow Wilson School of Public and International Affairs of Princeton University focused on the issues surrounding urban expansion and its impact on affordable housing in China in a policy workshop led by Dr. Shlomo Angel in the fall of 2007. The team visited China in October–November 2007 and conducted interviews in Beijing, as well as extensive fieldwork and interviews in Zhengzhou, focusing on four main topics:

- The physical expansion of the built-up area of Zhengzhou.
- Agriculture and income-generation on the urban fringe in light of restrictions on the conversion of arable land to urban use.
- The low-income housing delivery system.
- The critical role of urban villages in the provision of affordable housing to the lowest-income households.

Urban Expansion in Zhengzhou, 1992–2006

First, satellite imagery for the urbanized area of Zhengzhou in four time periods—1988, 1992, 2001, and 2007—was examined. The spatial data in the images were classified into three land use categories—built-up area, arable land, and other land use—and combined with population data (see figure 9.1). The black indicates built-up areas.

Zhengzhou has changed significantly during the past 15 years. Analysis shows that while the annual rate of population increase was 3.6 percent to 3.22 million people in 2007, the built-up area of Zhengzhou increased at an annual rate of

FIGURE 9.1

The Built-Up Area of Zhengzhou, 1992 and 2001

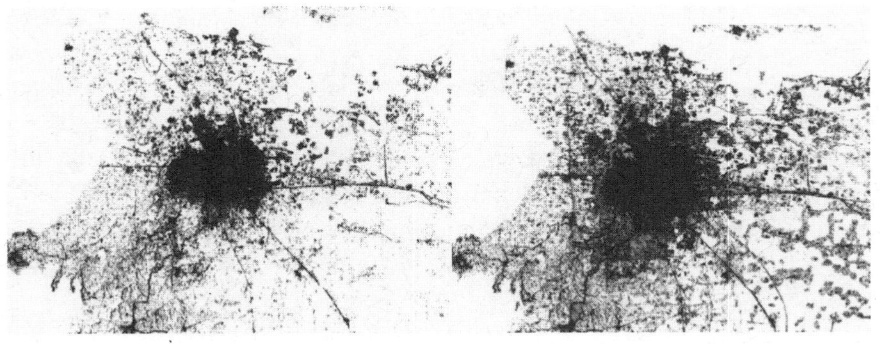

SOURCE: Angel, Sheppard, and Civco, 2005.

FIGURE 9.2

Urban Land and Population Trends in Zhengzhou City

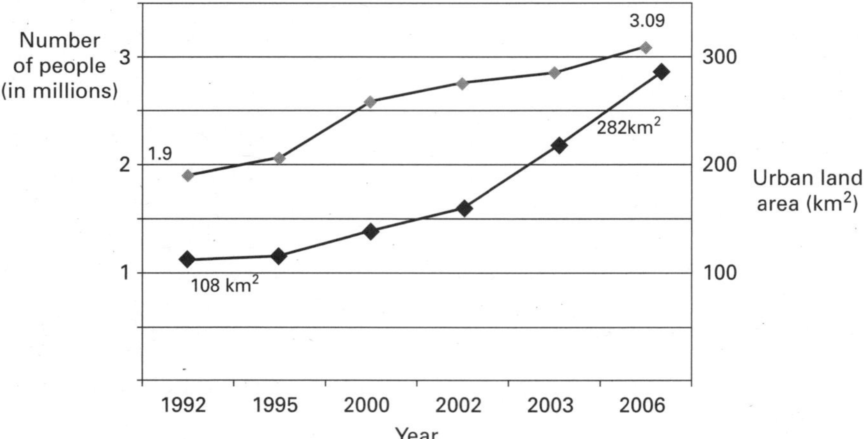

SOURCE: Zhengzhou Municipality, General Information on Zhengzhou, http://torchrelay.beijing2008.cn/en/journey/zhengzhou/news/n214325673.shtml (in Chinese).

7.1 percent, almost double the rate of its population increase.[6] Figure 9.2 shows the growth of people as well as the urban land area.

Analysis of the figure shows that the gross density of the built-up area of Zhengzhou city declined from 1992 until 2006, from 174 to 110 persons per hectare, at an annual rate of 3.4 percent.

By comparing these numbers to projections of population, density, and built-up area, we estimate that by 2020 Zhengzhou City's population will have increased to 3.5 million (Office of Zhengzhou Water Resources Group.)[7] Its density will decline by 1.7–3.0 percent, from 100 to 73–87 persons per hectare, and its built-up area will increase to 400–480 square kilometers.[8]

Our projection and the municipality's projections of the built-up area are not far apart. The municipality's 2020 master plan projects the population to be 5.5 million, the density to remain at 110 persons per hectare, and the built-up area to increase to 500 square kilometers. If, however, the municipality's population projections and our density projections are correct, the built-up area of Zhengzhou City may reach 630–750 square kilometers by 2020, a figure much higher than the master plan's projections.

Recently, after approval by the Henan provincial government, the municipality submitted its 2020 plan to the central government for approval. However, the central government has been slow to approve plans that call for considerable urban expansion. According to Zhengzhou urban planners, a Beijing municipality had its plan quickly approved last year, when it committed itself to practically zero urban

---

[6] These figures are based on GIS analysis of satellite images for 1988, 1992, and 2001. The 2006 figures are from personal communication with the Zhengzhou Planning Bureau and do not include an arable land estimate.

[7] Compared to the Zhengzhou master plan and UN Population Division estimates, the Office of Water Resources numbers are our central estimate.

[8] 1.7 percent is the average annual density increase in world cities described in Angel et al. (2005). The upper boundary in this scenario is 5 percent, which is Zhengzhou's average annual decrease in density between 1995 and 2006.

expansion in the coming years. These planners felt that the Zhengzhou municipality could not follow in Beijing's footsteps. Its 2010 plan, submitted in 1998, grossly underestimated both population growth and urban expansion: It estimated its 2010 population at 2.3 million and its area at 189 square kilometers. Both were surpassed by 2003.

A significant portion of the growth in the built-up area of Zhengzhou arises from the urbanization of rural villages. From an institutional perspective, land use in China is strictly differentiated into two categories. Municipalities own all *urban* land, and portions of it are leased (through official auctions[9]) to various entities for construction (Peterson 2006). Communes and villages own all *rural* land. Villages may distribute plots for residential use by villagers and other plots for various productive land uses. Rural land is transformed into urban land only when a municipality purchases the land from a rural commune, compensates the farmer, and provides the land with urban infrastructure.[10]

In reality, the boundary between urban and rural land use is fuzzy; cities are surrounded by broad regions of "urban" or "urbanizing" villages, referred to as *desakota* in the geographic literature (Heikkila 2003).[11] These urban villages are characterized by an increase in nonagricultural activities; by the fluidity and mobility of their populations; and by highly mixed land uses, with agriculture, small-scale industry, rental housing, and other uses located side by side (McGee 1991). Many of these villages are already completely encompassed by municipally owned urban land without a change in ownership status from communal ownership to municipal ownership. Figure 9.3 shows a traditional entrance for an urban village in the City of Zhengzhou.

Based on observations in 20 villages outside the city of Zhengzhou and interviews in 16 of them, these villages are now undergoing rapid urbanization, albeit without the ownership of their land being transferred to the municipality.[12] A patchwork of nonagricultural land uses was apparent in these villages: industrial and commercial centers; new roads and bus lines; and local factories and small-scale industry established by outsiders and locals. Also evident were an increase in the importance of rental housing as a significant source of income for villagers and an influx of outsiders, including factory workers, construction workers, and college students.[13]

Through comparisons of satellite imagery and data collected by recording GPS points at locations with increasingly urbanizing characteristics, we estimate that

---

[9] Previously, land sales had little transparency. The Ministry of Land and Resources found that more than 95 percent of all transfers had been done through private negotiation in the mid-1990s, losing revenue for municipal governments. In 2002, the central government ordered all municipal land transfers to go through public competition. Public bidding and auction transfers rose from 15 percent to 33 percent by 2003.

[10] Whether proper compensation is given is still a controversial issue. In addition, illegal land grabs by municipalities are a highly charged human interest story of the Chinese print media.

[11] The name *desakota*, coined by T. G. McGee, is derived from a combination of the words for "village" and "city" in Bahasa, Indonesia.

[12] A village was considered to be a part of the functional urban area of Zhengzhou if (1) a substantial fraction of villagers had transitioned to nonagricultural commercial and industrial livelihoods; and (2) there was a substantial amount of nontraditional, new housing construction in the village that could be rented to workers and students. In contrast, McGee classified urban areas primarily based on (1) the contribution of nonagricultural activities to the area GDP; and (2) the percentage of the labor force involved in nonagricultural activities.

[13] Field interviews from various urban villages in the Zhengzhou urban fringe, October–November 2007.

FIGURE 9.3

Entrance to Urban Village in Zhengzhou, 2007

SOURCE: Yueyuan Zheng, Princeton University.

up to 15 percent of the built-up area of the 1,100-square-kilometer Zhengzhou City district may be composed of scattered urban villages outside the built-up area of the city proper. A more precise figure requires a more rigorous study than we were able to undertake.

According to published reports, in 1990 the built-up area of the city completely surrounded 39 urban villages. By 2002 the number had grown to 114, and as many as 75 more are now gradually being encircled by the expanding city (Net East News 2007). Due to restrictions on the conversion of cultivated land to urban land, the municipality now plans to obtain most of the land needed for urban expansion by destroying and redeveloping the built-up areas of urban villages. Figure 9.4 shows a familiar site in Zhengzhou, the redevelopment of an urban village.

While the municipality is committed to the construction of new affordable housing, it remains largely oblivious to the sad fact that the destruction of urban villages and their redevelopment will seriously exacerbate housing affordability, as these villages provide most of the low-cost housing to low-income groups. Restrictions on the conversion of cultivated land and the patchwork redevelopment of villages are also likely to lead to fragmented urban expansion, increasing the cost of infrastructure provision. Ultimately, noncompact, leapfrogging urban expansion is likely to result in higher transport costs, as well as higher levels of traffic congestion and air pollution.

FIGURE 9.4

Private Redevelopment of an Urban Village in Zhengzhou, 2007

SOURCE: Jona Repshiti, Princeton University.

Agricultural Productivity on the Urban Fringe of Zhengzhou

A review of China's farmland preservation policies from 1994 to the present underscores the underlying tensions between the growing demand for urban land to make room for the urban-based economic boom and the traditional concern with famines, food shortages, and food security.[14] The Chinese government has given a high priority to agricultural land preservation in its food security policies, among them the Basic Farmland Protection Regulation of 1994, the 1998 Land Management Law, and the New Land Administration Act of 1999 (Lichtenberg and Ding 2007).

Henan Province, in which Zhengzhou is situated, is one of China's principal agricultural regions, providing 24.5 percent of China's total wheat crop and 50 percent of the frozen and processed foods distributed within China (He and Yu'an 2005). Along the meandering edge of Zhengzhou City and in between the built-up areas on its periphery, rural villagers still practice mainly subsistence farming, selling only a small portion of their produce to local markets in the city. The collectives on the outskirts of Zhengzhou City are divided into villages, with approximately 100–200 families belonging to each. Each family is entitled to a 200-square-meter

---

[14] Lester Brown's 1994 work, *Who Will Feed China?*, largely inspired the Chinese government to adopt a nationwide plan for food self-sufficiency in the same year. Various actors, including the U.S. Embassy in Beijing, have alluded to this as a top concern of other governments. For example, see U.S. Embassy in Beijing. Can China feed itself in the 21st century? Land use patterns may provide some answers, June 1996.

residential plot and to half a *mu* (333 m^2) of farmland per family member. Families usually grow leafy greens and vegetables such as cabbage and tubers on this land and are responsible for farming a portion of a large communal wheat plot, from which they typically reap an annual income of some 700–1,000 yuan (US$95–135).[15]

Ten farming families on the periphery of Zhengzhou were interviewed about the size of their plots, their yields, and their sources of farm and nonfarm income. Based on our fieldwork, interviews with agricultural economists at Henan Agricultural University, and data on farm crop output per hectare in Henan Province in 2006, we estimate that typical income per mu of cultivated land on the periphery of the city may be on the order of 15 percent (for vegetables) and 75 percent (for wheat and corn) of the average income per mu of cultivated land in Henan Province as a whole. Figure 9.5 shows an example of farming near an urban village.

The reduced productivity is attributable, at least in part, to the use of plots for subsistence farming of vegetables and the emergence of new income-earning opportunities: the construction of rental housing on villagers' residential plots; the leasing or selling of communal lands directly to commercial developers; and the employment of rural youth in the nearby city. For example, a typical building on a villager's residential plot may have 24 rooms for rent on three floors, yielding a monthly income of 1,200–1,800 yuan (US$170–250), considerably more than household income from agriculture.[16]

FIGURE 9.5

Subsistence Farming in the Built-Up Area of Zhengzhou City, 2007

SOURCE: Aritetsoma Ukueberuwa, Princeton University.

---

[15] Field interviews, October–November 2007.
[16] Ibid.

Thus, the protection of communal farmland on the fringe of Zhengzhou City from urban development may be futile.[17] Because of its low productivity, it fails to serve the national interest in food security and only contributes to inefficient development on the periphery of China's cities (Bertaud 2007a).

Chinese cities fragment significantly more rural land on their fringes than cities in the rest of the world. We define the urban footprint of cities as the sum of their built-up area and fringe open space not more than 100 meters away from the built-up area. The urban footprint of nine Chinese cities in 2000 averaged 2.4 of their average built-up area. In 111 cities in the rest of the world in 2000 it averaged only 1.9 of their average built-up area. In other words, Chinese cities fragment open space equivalent to 140 percent of their built-up areas. If we assume that cities in China now occupy some 75,000 square kilometers, they also fragment 106,000 square kilometers of cultivated land, some 8 percent of all cultivated land, and make it less productive.

Assuming that arable land area is currently at its peak and consumption rates remain fairly stable, China's major cities will continue to encroach into surrounding rural and agricultural lands. If land conversion quotas are removed, we project that arable land in China will decline from 1,381,000 square kilometers to 1,279,000 square kilometers, a decline of 7.4 percent, from 2000 to 2020.[18]

Land productivity in China is among the highest in the world. According to the UN Food and Agricultural Organization (FAO), its wheat yield, for example, measured in tons per square kilometers, is now the highest in the world. Its corn yield is the second-highest, after the United States (FAO 2007). China will need to increase its land productivity, through the use of improved agricultural technology, seeds, and fertilizers. It will also need to increase the amount of land in cultivation away from urban areas to replace the projected 7.4 percent loss of arable land.

Although the Chinese government does not currently share this view, it is more sensible to focus on increasing the productivity of the available arable land and on bringing additional land into cultivation than to limit urban expansion in the name of ensuring food security. In the short term, Zhengzhou and other cities facing the same predicament may also benefit from following the pragmatic approach of Shanghai and Tianjin in securing adequate lands for urban expansion. The municipalities of both cities were permitted to purchase and develop arable land in Xinyan Province in northwestern China in exchange for converting arable lands on their periphery to urban use in excess of their land conversion quotas.[19] That initiative cannot remain the exception and must become the foundation of a new agricultural policy.

Agricultural economists at Henan Agricultural University estimate that the development of one mu of land into arable land in Xinyan Province costs 12,000 yuan, or US$2.40 per square meter. In comparison, in 2007 one mu of urban land with infrastructure in Zhengzhou (and several other cities) was auctioned for 4.5

---

[17] Several studies show also that China's total grain production has been declining since 1997 (Lichtenberg and Ding 2007; Rural Development Institute 1999).

[18] This figure was calculated by applying the rate of arable land consumption since 1980 from the World Development Indicators of the World Bank. April 2008. http://data.worldbank.org/indicator.

[19] Interview with agricultural economists at Henan Agricultural University, November 2007.

million yuan, or for 6,400 yuan (US$890) per square meter,[20] 375 times the cost of adding one mu to the total stock of arable land in the country.

Therefore, a strong case can be made for massive urban-to-rural transfers aimed at increasing the amount and productivity of agricultural land in the country, with the principal goal of ensuring China's food security, and the secondary goal of freeing urban areas from the current distortions of the urban development process. These land conversion distortions are more apparent when we focus on the effects of land conversion quotas on the housing market in Zhengzhou.

The Housing Delivery System in Zhengzhou

As noted earlier, the Chinese government is concerned that rapid increases in housing demand, coupled with increased construction costs and land prices, have created a housing affordability crisis in the country.[21] The central government recognizes the challenge despite the recent global economic downturn. As recently as January 2008, the housing and finance ministries, as well as the central bank and the National Development and Reform Commission stated that prices are still "not affordable for ordinary people" (Poon and Shaw 2009; Xinzhen 2009).

To understand the nature of residential affordability, our fieldwork in Zhengzhou addressed two fundamental questions about the city's housing delivery system: (1) Under what conditions are residents housed, and who are the suppliers of housing, assuming that all households are housed in one way or another? (2) To what extent are the available housing options affordable to households in *all* income groups? Observations show that *basic* housing conditions in Zhengzhou at the present time are surprisingly adequate and acceptable, as follows:

- All households in Zhengzhou are properly housed; there is no evidence of homelessness.
- There are no shantytowns, and all housing is constructed with permanent building materials and supplied with indoor water and sanitation as well as electricity.[22]
- There does not seem to be significant overcrowding, and the amount of floor area per person appears to be on the increase (Bertaud 2007b).

In other words, there is no housing "deficit," and there are no slums in Zhengzhou. This finding, in and of itself, is very significant. We must infer from our field observations that the contention of the UN Human Settlements Programme that 38 percent of the urban population in China lives in slums is wrong, even if we accept its definition of a slum dwelling as a dwelling with at least one of four shelter deprivations: unimproved water, unimproved sanitation, impermanent structures,

---

[20] According to developers and planners interviewed in Zhengzhou, November 2007.

[21] Since 2003, the central government has been focused on pursuing "macrocontrol" policies, appropriately called "cooling initiatives" (Xinzhen 2007).

[22] The housing conditions of migrant workers whose temporary housing is part of the wage package are the major exception.

and overcrowding (UN Habitat 2003).[23] None of these deprivations were found in Zhengzhou in observable quantities.

At the very least, the housing delivery system in Zhengzhou has been able to supply adequate, or minimal, shelter for all. This does not imply, of course, that the available housing meets people's expectations, that there are no households forced to share units or bathrooms, that there is adequate floor space to ensure minimal privacy, that there are no shortages of residential infrastructure, that buildings are solid enough and have proper fire escapes, or that neighborhoods are safe and have adequate amenities.[24] In the long term, the impact of recent job losses for migrants within urban China remains unclear (BBC News Asia 2008).

Since everyone is housed, the housing delivery system in Zhengzhou apparently produces dwellings that are affordable to *all* income groups. How can this be so? Table 9.1 calculates the monthly housing budget for a variety of household income levels to begin the affordability analysis.

The housing delivery system in Zhengzhou produces both dwellings for owner occupation and dwellings for rental occupation. Our fieldwork noted six types of dwellings for owner occupation.[25] These are typically bought with cash, but mortgage financing is available on good terms. Figure 9.6 shows the general housing typology for Zhengzhou.

Currently, no median-income household could afford any of the units presently offered on the market. For example, if a median-income household could afford to pay 30 percent of its income (308 yuan per month) on housing and it had savings amounting to a third of the value of a unit for a down payment, it could obtain a 30-year mortgage at an annual fixed-interest rate of 6.15 percent. With this loan it could only afford to buy a unit with a value of 73,000 yuan (US$10,100). Most dwelling units for sale in Zhengzhou are bought by pulling together cash from savings, but the amount of savings available to households in different income groups is hard to

TABLE 9.1

Calculating the Housing Budget for a Variety of Zhengzhou Households

	Annual Income	Monthly Income	Housing Budget (30% of annual income)
Median household income	12,330 yuan 1,712 USD	1,030 yuan 143 USD	308 yuan or 43 USD
Lowest income decile household	5,201 yuan 722 USD	435 yuan 60 USD	130 yuan or 18 USD
Highest income decile household	23,800 yuan 3,304 USD	1,980 yuan 275 USD	595 yuan or 83 USD

SOURCE: *Zhengzhou Statistical Yearbook*, 2006.

NOTES: US$1 = RMB 7.2027; this was calculated using currency rates from November, 2006.

---

[23] This was also confirmed during our fieldwork in Zhengzhou, where we observed almost zero homelessness.

[24] In fact, the Zhengzhou Planning Bureau cited concerns over the safety of urban village housing, and in our fieldwork interviews with self-financed property developers in these villages, owners used neighbors' building standards as their own.

[25] Field interviews and observations, October–November 2007.

Housing Typology for Owner Occupation in Zhengzhou

Luxury Housing

Price: Up to 4.5 million yuan (US$320,000)
Floor area: Range with maximum at 300 m^2
Affordability: 185 times median annual household income
Description: New single-family dwellings built by private developers, produced and quickly sold in limited numbers. Recently, they have become less available as new directives from the central government focus on affordable housing.

Market-Rate Housing

Price: 120,000–600,000 yuan (US$17,000–43,000)
Floor area: 30–120 m^2
Affordability: 10–25 times median annual household income
Description: New housing built by private developers. Smaller units are a newer phenomenon and are sold furnished.

Secondhand Housing

Price: 180,000–1,210,000 yuan (US$25,000–85,000)
Floor area: 60–120 m^2
Affordability: 16–50 times the annual median household income
Description: Older apartments, with smaller, less expensive units. Secondhand residences comprise the most housing sold by real estate agents.

Economic and Suitable Housing

Price: 105,000–290,000 yuan (US$15,000–40,000)
Floor area: 60–120 m^2
Affordability: 9–23 times the annual median household income
Description: New "affordable" apartments built by private developers with municipal subsidies or on municipal land.

Developer-Built Housing on Village Land

Price: 100,000–170,000 yuan (US$14,000–24,000)
Floor area: 60–100 m^2
Affordability: 8–14 times the annual median household income
Description: New apartments built by developers on land obtained from villagers in semiofficially sanctioned arrangements.

Secondhand Enterprise (*Danwei*) Housing

Price: 100,000–300,000 yuan (US$14,000–42,000)
Floor area: 50–100 m^2
Affordability: 8–24 times the annual median household income
Description: Built from the 1950s to 1980s by public enterprises and work units, *danwei* housing has recently been privatized and sold to inhabitants at discounted prices.

SOURCE: All information was collected from field interviews in Zhengzhou, October–November 2007.

determine. Another example: If a median-income household had saved 30 percent of its income at 6 percent per annum for the past 15 years, it would have accumulated some 90,000 yuan (US$12,500), and, coupled with a mortgage loan of 50,000 yuan, that would allow them entry into the bottom end of the housing market.

Clearly, a significant portion of the dwelling units for sale as of late 2007—including the "economic and suitable" housing produced with municipal assistance—are not affordable for the majority of Zhengzhou residents.[26] In addition, households without an urban *hukou*[27] are not eligible for the "economic and suitable" housing even though unofficial estimates put these migrants at 22.6 percent of China's total urban population (*The Economist* 2007). There is, indeed, a housing affordability crisis that affects the emerging urban middle class. Although the growing number of urban middle-class households are starting to see higher incomes, which translate to high expectations, most cannot afford to buy the housing now offered by the market. Given the data, it seems that only households in the highest decile of the income distribution can acquire units in the housing market.

In addition to owner-occupied dwellings, the housing delivery system in Zhengzhou produces four types of rental units. As a whole, these housing types are considerably more affordable than units for sale. Figure 9.7 shows a basic typology of rental housing units found in Zhengzhou.

Our analysis shows that urban villages within and outside the built-up area of the city provide the majority of the low-income housing stock in Zhengzhou. The most prevalent type of lodging for rent is a room with a shared bathroom on the same floor. Though such conditions meets residents' basic housing needs at an affordable cost, renters in urban villages often lack urban residence permits (*hukou*) and are thus deprived of hospital, school, and other essential social services. Proponents of urban village destruction and redevelopment frequently cite fire safety and public health concerns within these villages (Wu 2004).[28]

The municipal government has drafted an ambitious plan that aims to tear down all urban villages within the third ring road by 2020, and it is now proceeding at an aggressive pace to implement this plan.[29] Yet our fieldwork identified several urban villages in good condition that are en route to destruction. The municipality calculates that the destruction and redevelopment of urban villages will provide sufficient land for the city's development needs for the next 10 years, thus presenting a viable alternative to the conversion of cultivated land (Fulong et al. 2007). However, there has been no attempt to calculate the amount of affordable housing that will be permanently eliminated by this plan, nor have there been any attempts to explore alternative affordable housing production options.

---

[26] While it is envisioned that by 2010, "economic and suitable" housing will constitute 12.5 percent of new residential construction, the supply of that housing stock is not nearly enough today. In 2006, only .06 percent of total residential investment was spent on it (Zhengzhou Real Estate Statistics 2005).

[27] For general information about the *hukou*, see Chan and Zhang (1999). The *hukou* system and rural-urban migration in China: Process and changes. *The China Quarterly.* 160:818–855

[28] Interviews with the Zhengzhou Planning Bureau, October–November 2007.

[29] This plan is not dissimilar to efforts in other Chinese municipalities. For more information about how these redevelopment schemes tie in to urban land development in China, see Wu, Xu, and Yeh (2007).

FIGURE 9.7

Housing Typology for Rental Occupation

Private Apartment Rentals
Price: Rent for 500–1,000 yuan (US$70–139) per month
Floor area: 10–12 m^2 for rooms; 40–80 m^2 for units
Affordability: These units are not affordable for below-median-income
households
Description: Individual rooms in private apartments.

Rooms or Units in *Danwei* Housing

Price: Rent for 100–800 yuan (US$14–110) per month
Floor area: 10–100 m^2
Affordability: Affordable for households at all income levels
Description: Rooms and apartments rented by owners of
dwellings in *danwei* housing.

Rooms or Units in Urban Villages
Price: Rent for 50–400 yuan (US$7–55) per month
Floor area: 10–40 m^2
Affordability: Affordable for households at all income levels
Description: Walk-up blocks of apartments, up to 7 stories, with rooms and small
apartments.

Temporary Rentals

Price: Included in wages
Description: This includes construction worker housing where
rent and government-provided units are included in wages. It is
not uncommon for developers to provide basic housing for
workers during the months-long construction phase.

SOURCE: Field interviews in urban villages, October–November 2007.

Land conversion quotas play a significant role in the destruction of the most affordable housing—rental housing in urban villages—given the central government pressure to preserve land quotas. Moreover, the municipality does not perceive rental housing in urban villages as worth preserving, preferring to tear it down in the name of building "affordable" housing that fails to serve the majority of Zhengzhou residents. Buildings in these villages are typically clustered close together along narrow roads, with floor-area ratios as high as 7.0, three to four times as high as typical ratios in commercial housing projects.[30] Since commercial developers build at considerably lower floor-to-area ratios, as many as six or seven affordable rental units are potentially destroyed for one so-called affordable unit.[31]

---

[30] Field observation and interviews, October–November 2007.
[31] Observations and site visits to new development sites in Zhengzhou confirm this claim. Bertaud (2007b) highlights the phenomenon of low floor to area ratios in Chinese cities.

Dwelling tenants and owners feel the short-term consequences of urban village destruction. However, the real effect of land conversion quotas on housing affordability in Zhengzhou (as well as other Chinese cities) has yet to be felt. As government planners insist that enough land exists for urban expansion, land conversion constraints create serious land supply bottlenecks. These bottlenecks have resulted in land hoarding in expectation of further land shortages. According to municipal planners, in 2005, for example, the amount of land purchased but not developed amounted to 53.8 percent of all land purchased that year. Conversion quotas have also resulted in steep increases in urban land prices. As noted earlier, land in Zhengzhou City and other Chinese cities was auctioned at 6,400 yuan (US$890) per square meter in 2007.[32] There is no question that these quotas have now created a land market in which housing is unaffordable for anyone, except those at the peak of the urban income distribution, for years to come. What does this imply for the future of affordable housing? Although China's GDP growth has calmed, the country's urbanization trends do not waver. As incomes continue to rise, a strong housing market demand will dominate the landscape for years to come (Zhiming and Xu 2009).

The cost of land plays a crucial role in the ultimate price tag of these dwellings. Since urban units are sold on expensive land (i.e., land acquisition costs are high), affordability is a lofty goal even at the onset of the development process. Presently, median-income households cannot afford any housing built on market-priced land.

- At current land prices, if land accounted for 30 percent of the selling price of apartments and if developers built units in high-rise apartments with a floor-area ratio of 2.0, a 90-square-meter apartment would cost 960,000 yuan (US$133,000), or 77 annual median household incomes.
- At current land prices, if land accounted for 30 percent of the selling price of apartments and if developers built units in high-rise apartments with a floor-area ratio of 3.0, a 70-square-meter apartment would cost 500,000 yuan (US$69,000), or 40 annual median household incomes.
- At current land prices, if land accounted for 50 percent of the selling price of apartments, and if developers built units in high-rise apartments with a floor-area ratio of 3.0, a 50-square-meter apartment would still cost as much as 350,000 yuan (US$49,000), or 29 annual median household incomes.

In other words, the majority of urban households cannot afford housing built on land bought at the current market prices. Several explanations exist as to why urban land prices have increased sharply, but this chapter's limited scope prevents lengthy discussion of the matter. Simply put, compensations paid to farmers for the transfer of their lands to the municipality may be high, municipal infrastructure standards are high, and the time it takes to effect a land transfer and prepare land for urbanization is long.[33]

---

[32] Field interviews with Zhengzhou Planning Bureau, October–November 2007.
[33] Field interviews in Zhengzhou, October–November 2007.

More important, demand for land far exceeds supply; supply is limited due to conversion quotas, and supply elasticity is low, which means rapid increases in demand cannot be quickly accommodated. This suggests that even if land conversion quotas were relaxed and municipalities could acquire more land for urban expansion, land prices are not likely to come down for a long time. In the short term, releasing more land into the urban market is likely to result in more hoarding in expectation of future shortages than in real land price reductions.

Toward a Shift in National Land Policy

Given this rather alarming scenario, the inevitable two-part recommendation from our analysis is a radical one:

1. Land conversion quotas should be eliminated, and there should be no restriction on the conversion of cultivated land to urban land.
2. The institutional distinction between urban and rural land should be eliminated, and villagers should be able to sell land directly to developers.

Eliminating Land Conversion Quotas

Emphasis on national food security should focus on increasing both the productivity and the amount of arable land. The removal of land conversion quotas will not damage China's future food security. Cultivated lands in and around cities are not productive and are well below the average productivity of land in properly cultivated agricultural areas. The productivity of agricultural land can be improved by a new emphasis on rural development: on improving the lot of farmers through better water management, flood protection, modern machinery, better seeds, better cultivation methods, agricultural waste recycling, and the judicious use of pesticides and insecticides.

In addition, the innovative initiative of rural land development projects in Xinyan, for example, can bring pastureland into intensive cultivation, with the aim of maintaining a fixed amount of cultivated land in the country as a whole over the years. These rural initiatives, which should be actively supported by cities, will do much more for national food security and for addressing the present inequities between rural and urban areas than distorting the process of urban expansion by the imposition of land conversion quotas.

Conversion quotas are quantitative targets, and, as such, they do not and cannot protect the sensitive lands in the vicinity of cities: wetlands, sensitive natural habitats, and other areas that should remain undeveloped. Pragmatic environmental protection of the periphery of cities will require the active protection of specific, well-defined swaths of open space through the creation of a system of parks and nature conservancies that are in the public domain and on which no urban development unit is allowed.

Pushing aside the ineffectiveness of the land conversion policy, the quotas, as noted, have a serious unintended consequence: the destruction of the most affordable housing in Zhengzhou and other Chinese cities. Furthermore, the limited land market managed by the municipality is too small and too rigid to supply all the land needed for the rapid urban expansion expected in the future. China's urban-based economic growth hinges on providing adequate land for housing, as well as for industrial and commercial enterprises both big and small. While removing the conversion quotas will no doubt help reduce the upward pressure on land prices, municipal "urban" land supply is inelastic; once land prices reach a peak, they are not likely to come down anytime soon.

Eliminating the Distinction Between Municipal and Village Land

In contrast, opening up the rural land market for urban development will create an alternative market that is not bound by the peak prices of the existing municipal land market. In this market, land prices are likely to remain much lower and housing much more affordable.

Opening up the land market on the urban fringe will result in more compact urban development, reduced open-space fragmentation, and a smaller urban footprint. Built-up area densities, while declining, will still be high enough to sustain transit-friendly urban development. Even if densities decline to 75 persons per hectare by 2020, as we project, they will still be considerably higher than the 50 persons per hectare required to sustain regular and frequent bus transport.

This initiative will require extending urban land use planning beyond the limited land under the jurisdiction of the municipality. In particular, it will require the early planning of the primary infrastructure grid in all outward directions where urbanization is taking place.[34] Urban land use planning must not be limited to areas where the municipality would prefer development to take place, but allowed in all areas where urbanization—evident in the gradual formation of urban villages—is already taking place.

It is important to emphasize that allowing direct land transactions between villagers and developers will also require a radical reform of the municipal finance system. A considerable portion of municipal budgets now depends on an irregular stream of profits and losses from the land conversion process, transactions that are far from transparent. The municipalities use land lease profits as off-budget revenue, revenue that is unreported to the central government.[35] According to some estimates, land sales and leases have accounted for up to 60 percent of the annual revenue of some Chinese cities (Farrell, Devan, and Woetzel 2008). Municipal budgets will need to be reformed with the introduction of appropriate new taxes on land development— such as property taxes, sales taxes, value-added taxes, or capital gains taxes—in lieu of profits from the appropriation of lands from village communes, their subdivision and servicing, and their auctioning to private developers (Peterson 2006; Su and Zhao 2006).

Villages and developers on the periphery of Zhengzhou now already participate in informal transactions, and these activities are likely to gather momentum in the future in light of the exorbitant prices of lands auctioned by the municipality. Pragmatic

---

[34] This is the grid of arterial roads that will carry future public transportation.

[35] The following reports give a comprehensive overview: Peterson, George E. 2006. Land leasing and land sale as an infrastructure financing option. Policy Research Working Paper No. 4043. Washington, DC: World Bank, November. Su, Ming, and Quanhou Zhao. 2006. The fiscal framework and urban infrastructure in China. Policy Research Working Paper No. 4051. Washington, DC: World Bank, November.

county, municipal, and provincial governments have not been particularly diligent in preventing land transactions on the urban periphery. We witnessed several instances in which developers bought or leased land from village communes, and, as noted earlier, the municipal planners estimated that developers building on village lands now provide up to 20 percent of new residential floor space. On a visit to a building site of a developer currently constructing four seven-story apartment buildings on the urban fringe, we observed 80-square-meter units selling for 136,000 yuan (US$19,000) or 1,700 yuan (US$235) per square meter. Although we have not been able to ascertain how much this developer paid villagers for the land, if land cost amounted to 15 percent of the sale price of units (we believe it to be less than that), and the floor-area ratio was 3.0, then the cost of land to the developer would have been on the order of 765 yuan (US$106) per square meter, one-eighth the cost of land auctioned by the municipality.[36]

Minimally serviced rural land on the fringe of Zhengzhou City constitutes a different land market, and the prices there are not dependent on prices of auctioned municipal land with a high level of infrastructure. It is likely, therefore, that opening up this land market for unrestricted urban development will not result in quick land price inflation. In contrast, simply abandoning the land conversion quotas while maintaining the monopoly of municipalities on urban land will not result in the desired reduction in land prices, a reduction that is absolutely necessary to ensure the steady flow of affordable housing in the years to come.

Admittedly, these conclusions call for a radical change in China's basic policy framework, a change that—much as it is desirable and necessary—is not likely to take place in the near future. In the short term we envision a continuing housing affordability crisis that cannot be ameliorated by marginal changes in policy such as requiring developers to construct smaller units, reducing building and infrastructure standards, increasing permissible floor-area ratios, providing direct demand-side subsidies to deserving households from central government budgets, or providing supply-side subsidies to developers in the form of free or below-market municipal lands. In fact, the burdens of a national housing policy implemented with local funds linked to the fundamental tensions between land leases, municipal revenue, and "economic and suitable" housing policies may only exacerbate the affordable housing crisis in Zhengzhou. None of these policies—important as they are in a housing market that is free of the distortions plaguing urban land markets in Chinese cities—will work to make housing affordable to the large majority of the urban population, both present and future, neither to the middle class nor to poor unregistered migrants.

Urban villages in and around Chinese cities provide the pragmatic solution to affordable housing for poor and very poor families, potentially freeing governments at all levels from the responsibility to subsidize housing and freeing the private sector to construct housing that is entirely oriented to satisfy the needs of the rich and prosperous few while ignoring the needs of the masses. Municipal plans and initiatives bent on the destruction of these villages and their replacement by officially

---

[36] Fieldwork, October–November 2007.

affordable housing that, in reality, is affordable only to a thin sliver of better-off households, are unconscionable. Steps must be taken immediately to stop this indiscriminate destruction. Instead, China should refocus attention on the important role of urban villages in the provision of housing to the lowest-income urban households. If government intervention in these villages is to take place at all, it should focus on infrastructure improvements; fire safety; and the provision of basic amenities like health care, social services, parks, and playgrounds.

Chinese cities have managed to provide adequate shelter for all in recent years within a pragmatic, albeit unplanned, housing delivery system, thus largely avoiding some of the housing ills besetting the cities of other developing countries. As China continues to make massive strides to urbanize its society and economy, it can do so by opening its peripheral land markets to urban development and by allowing its urban villagers to flourish and survive, while ensuring its food security through effective increases in the productivity of its arable lands. With minor adjustments to its current pragmatic approach to affordable housing, China can continue to urbanize while at the same time continuing to deliver adequate shelter for all in the years to come.

ACKNOWLEDGMENTS

The contributors to this chapter participated in a policy workshop at the Woodrow Wilson School of Public and International Affairs at Princeton University in the fall of 2007, which focused on housing and urban development in China. The group is indebted to Mr. Wang Peng, the director of the Zhengzhou Urban Planning Bureau, for hosting us in Zhengzhou; to Roger Ye Jun, the head of the Planning Department at the bureau, who greatly facilitated our fieldwork in Zhengzhou; and to Lucy Gitlin, who assisted us in the fieldwork.

REFERENCES

Angel, Shlomo, Stephen C. Sheppard, and Daniel Civco. 2005. The dynamics of global urban expansion. Washington, DC: World Bank, Department of Transport and Urban Development.

BBC News, Asia Pacific. 2008. Chinese job losses prompt exodus. November 6. http://news.bbc.co.uk/2/hi/asia-pacific/7713594.stm.

Bertaud, Alain. 2007a. Urbanization in China: Land use efficiency issues. Washington, DC: World Bank, August 30.

———. 2007b. Presentation at the Workshop on Middle- and Low-Income Housing in China. Beijing, China. Sponsored by Development Research Center of the State Council, World Bank and the International Finance Corporation. (July 19).

Chan, Kam Wing, and Li Zhang. 1999. The *Hukou* system and rural-urban migration in China: Process and changes. *China Quarterly* 160:818–855.

China Statistics Press. 2006. *Zhengzhou Statistical Yearbook*. Beijing

China's migrant workers: No place to call home. 2007. *The Economist* (June 7). http://www.economist.com/node/9302841?story_id=9302841.

CIA Factbook. https://www.cia.gov/library/publications/the-world-factbook/geos/ch.html.

Deng, Frederic F., and Youqin Huang. 2004. Uneven land reform and urban sprawl in China: The case of Beijing. *Progress in Planning* 61:211–236.

Ding, Chengri. 2007. Policy and praxis of land acquisition in China. *Land Use Policy* (24) 1:1–13.

FAO. 2007. ProdStat. Production of maize and rank in world; Production of fruits and rank in the World. http://faostat.fao.org/site/339/default.aspx.

Farrell, Diana, Janamitra Devan, and Jonathan Woetzel. 2008. Where big is best. *Newsweek International*, May 17.

Heikkila, E. J. 2003. Fuzzy urban sets: Theory and application to desakota regions in China. *Environment and Planning* 30:239–254.

Jie, He, and Zhang Yu'an. 2005. Zhengzhou presents huge business potential. *China Daily*, May 17.

Lichtenberg, Erik, and Chengri Ding. 2007. Assessing farmland protection policy in China. In *Urbanization in China: Critical issues in an era of rapid growth*, eds. Yan Song and Chengri Ding. Cambridge, MA: Lincoln Institute of Land Policy.

Liy, Yingling. 2006. Shrinking arable land jeopardizes China's food security. *World Watch*. April 18, 2006. http://www.worldwatch.org/node/3912.

McGee, T. G. 1991. The emergence of Desakota regions in Asia. In *The extended metropolis: Settlement transition in Asia*, ed. Norton Ginsburg, Bruce Koppel, and T. G. McGee. Honolulu, HI: University of Hawai'i Press.

Municipality of Tianjin. 2006. Per capita floor space of urban residential buildings. *Tianjin Facts and Figures*.

Net East News. 2007. ViC redevelopment should go hand in hand with development of cheap rental housing, November 30.

Office of Zhengzhou Water Resources Group. n.d. The master plan for a water saving society of Zhengzhou. http://www.hnzzjs.com/jssh/sdjh_3.asp.

Peterson, George E. 2006. Land leasing and land sale as an infrastructure financing option. Policy Research Working Paper No. 4043. Washington, DC: World Bank.

Poon, Terence, and Joy Shaw. 2009. China tries to boost real estate market. *Wall Street Journal*, January 6. http://chinadigitaltimes.net/2009/01/china-tries-to-boost-real-estate-market/.

Rural Development Institute. China land management. http://www.rdiland.org/PDF/PDF_Reports/RDI_098.pdf.

Song, Yan, Yves Zenou, and Chengri Ding. 2008. Let's not throw out the baby with the bathwater: The role of urban villages in housing rural migrants in China. *Urban Studies* 45(2):313–330.

Su, Ming, and Quanhou Zhao. 2006. The fiscal framework and urban infrastructure in China. World Bank Policy Research Working Paper No. 4051(November). Washington, DC: World Bank.

United Nations. 2007. World urbanization prospects: The 2007 revision population database. New York: United Nations Population Division. http://esa.un.org/unup/.

United Nations, UN-Habitat. 2003. The challenge of slums: Global report on human settlements. http://www.unhabitat.org/pmss/listItemDetails.aspx?publicationID=1156.

U.S. Embassy in Beijing 1996. Can China feed itself in the 21st century? Land use patterns may provide some answers.

Woetzel, Jonathan, Lenny Mendonca, Janamitra Devan, Stefano Negri, et al. 2008. Preparing for China's urban billion. McKinsey Global Institute, McKinsey & Company. http://www.mckinsey.com/mgi/publications/china_urban_summary_of_findings.asp.

World Bank. World development indicators. http://data.worldbank.org/data-catalog/world-development-indicators/wdi-2007.

Wu, Fulong, Jiang Xu, and Anthony Gar-On Yeh. 2007. *Urban development in post-reform China: State, market and space*. London: Routledge.

Wu, W. P. 2004. Sources of migrant housing disadvantages in urban China. *Environment and Planning A* 26:1285–1304.

Xinzhen, Lan. 2007. Reality check on real estate. *Beijing Review*. March 15. http://www.bjreview.com/business/txt/2007-03/12/content_58877_3.htm.

———. 2009. New hope for the housing market. *Beijing Review*. January 22. http://english.beijingreview.com.cn/quotes/txt/2009–01/23/content_175818.htm.

Zhengzhou Municipality. 2008. General information on Zhengzhou. http://torchrelay.beijing2008.cn/en/journey/zhengzhou/news/n214325673.shtml [in Chinese].

Zhengzhou Real Estate Statistics. 2005. Updated 2006. http://www.stats.gov.cn/english/.

Zhiming, Xin, and Wang Xu. 2009. China's economy grows by 9 percent in 2008. *China Daily*. January 22. http://www.chinadaily.com.cn/bizchina/200901/22/content_7420790.htm.

Assimilation of Villages Within Cities

10

YAN SONG

Since China's economic reforms and other "open door" policies in the late 1970s, Chinese cities have been flourishing. The nation is experiencing rapid urbanization triggered by economic growth and the migration of the rural population to urban areas. The urbanization rate in China increased from 19.6 percent in 1980 to 42.2 percent in 2007, and it is expected to reach approximately 70 percent by 2050 (Song and Ding 2007). As a result, China's urban landscapes have changed dramatically. Modern cities are being built with generic skyscrapers and wide streets.

Amid the modern urban landscape, dense settlements of uniform structures, five to seven floors high, on small streets can be spotted in many Chinese cities. These compressed settlements were previously farming villages; thus, they are called "villages within cities" (Cheng Zhong Cun).

These urbanizing villages were formed when expanded modern city districts encroached upon rural settlements. For example, in 2000 in the city of Shenzhen, whose official population was listed at around 9 million, there were 241 urbanizing villages with a land area of approximately 43.9 square kilometers and approximately 2.15 million total inhabitants (author's survey). The emergence and fast growth of urbanizing villages is an outcome of China's rapid urbanization, its associated rural-to-urban migration, and China's land policies. China's urbanization has induced a massive rural migration since the late 1970s; the majority of rural migrants are living in urbanizing villages. According to official estimates, there were about 70 million rural migrants working and living in urban areas at the end of 2000 (Song, Zenou, and Ding 2008). China's land policies have enabled the native farmers in the urbanizing villages to construct inexpensive housing units and rent those units to the migrants. Through these villages, indigenous farmers are becoming wealthy

A version of this chapter has been submitted to the *Journal of Regional Science and Urban Economics* and is currently under review.

landlords by building and leasing extra rooms (Mobrand 2006). Rural migrants are able to find shelter while being excluded from the more expensive urban housing system.

Much has been written on China's urbanizing villages. Articles have focused on understanding the villages, criticizing the redevelopment policies that affect villages (Zhang, Zhao, and Tian 2003), and exploring the reasons rural migrants choose to live in these villages (Wu 2002, 2004; Song, Zenou, and Ding 2008). As urbanizing villages are woven into the modern urban landscape by surrounding residential and commercial developments, an interesting question is whether these villages are becoming assimilated into the urban landscape.

How Urbanizing Villages Began

China's Urbanization

The level of urbanization in China has increased rapidly, from 17.9 percent in 1978 to 39.1 percent in 2002, with an annual growth rate two times higher than the world average in the same period. Statistics also show that there were 660 cities and 20,600 administrative towns in China, with a total population of 502 million at the end of 2002. As Chinese cities expanded beyond their administrative districts, rural territories have been surrounded and absorbed by urban developments. Many rural villages are thus turned into villages within cities.

In 2000, about 63 percent of migrants living and working in urban areas were employed in industry, construction, and service sectors, the majority being self-employed or employed by privately owned enterprises (Chan, Liu, and Yang 1999). The massive rural migration since the late 1970s can be broadly attributed to the following factors: the pushing forces from rural areas to transform surplus rural labor unleashed by a set of rural reform programs in 1978; and the pulling forces from urban areas due to rapid industrialization and the resulting increased income disparity between rural and urban residents (Zhao 1999).

One corollary of the massive rural migration is the enormous demand for inexpensive and accessible housing units in urban areas. Despite the reduced constraints on rural labor mobility since the late 1970s and recent improvements in migration control, rural migrants still encounter great difficulty in acquiring urban household registration (*hukou*) and permanent residence status in urban areas. Due to incomplete reforms of the urban social service system, nearly all migrants are considered temporary in urban areas and thus do not have access to many urban amenities.

As a result, it remains difficult for rural migrants to access urban housing (Wu 2002, 2004; Song, Zenou, and Ding 2008). The first source of this difficulty is the restructuring of the urban housing market. Because the reforms are oriented toward privatization and commercialization of housing, new units of commercial housing are built essentially for profit by real estate developers. These units are generally expensive and thus not affordable for migrants in low-paying jobs. Second, more affordable units provided by the urban housing provision system generally require a local urban *hukou* and thus are not available to rural migrants. Therefore, scholars conclude that recent reforms in urban housing provision have overlooked the needs of rural migrants to access urban housing (Song, Zenou, and Ding 2008).

China's Land Policy

The phenomenon of villages within cities as residential locations for rural migrants cannot be fully understood without reference to China's land policy. There are two main types of land ownership in China: state ownership of administratively allocated urban land whose land use rights can be transferred and leased to users in exchange for payment, and collective ownership of rural land by rural communities. All members of a rural community are entitled to an equal share of the collectively owned land, acting as de facto land owners with unrestricted tenure (Ding and Song 2005). Rural land can be categorized by function into land for farming and land for housing (*zhai ji di*). In most cases of urban expansion, the city government acquires land for farming only from rural communities to avoid the cost of compensation for farmers' housing and relocation. After acquisition of land by a city government, the native farmers still possess property rights on the remaining rural land and can use the land as long as they keep their rural *hukou*.

This system of land ownership contributes to the formation of villages within cities in several ways. First, collective land ownership, which grants native villagers free or less costly access to land, also allows them to develop housing projects at much lower costs than those of the real estate developers in cities. Second, to avoid the larger amount of monetary compensation for farmers' housing and relocation, city governments do not usually acquire land for housing. Thus, native farmers have the opportunity to redevelop the free land beyond their own housing needs and increase their income by leasing out housing units to rural migrants (Tang and Chung 2002). Third, when land for farming is acquired by a city government, the native farmers can collect the necessary capital for housing redevelopment projects in response to the demand for inexpensive housing by rural migrants. The guaranteed financial capacity comes from the monetary compensation for the farmland, off-farm income, or loans from family or friends.

The Gap Between Urban and Rural Management Systems

As mentioned above, the governance of a village within a city is under the rural administrative system. Therefore, the design and construction of buildings and the plan for the neighborhoods are not constrained by the application, inspection, and approval procedures in urban areas that specify construction standards such as building height, floor-area ratio, width of corridors, existence of stairways and exits, proportion of public space, and distances between buildings for the purpose of public safety. By making use of this difference between rural and urban land management systems, indigenous farmers are thus able to maximize their profits by constructing substandard housing units.

Redevelopment Policies of Urbanizing Villages

Because design, construction, and planning are not constrained by the approval procedures in urban areas, the physical environment in many villages is usually in poor condition. Buildings are overcrowded. Public stairways and hallways inside buildings are extremely narrow. Public facilities are inadequate and poorly maintained. Roadways do not meet the basic requirements of transportation and fire control standards. Distances between buildings are well below standard and do not meet fire control standards. Garbage is scattered about. Inadequate urban infrastructure and high housing and population densities have together caused congestion, environmental pollution, and inadequate waste disposal (Zhang, Zhao, and Tian 2003). Furthermore, land uses in these villages are extremely disorganized.

Consequently, villages within cities were generally perceived as undesirable places by urban authorities. Urban policies were eventually adopted to demolish many urbanizing villages and redevelop them into modern, commercialized urban housing districts. These policies have not been effective, however, for several reasons. First, there is still a great demand by rural migrants for cheap housing. Second, the local governments lack resources to relocate the village residents after redevelopment. Third, and most important, the strong negotiation power of the indigenous farmers is a substantial barrier to redeveloping many urbanizing villages. The farmers often ask for large compensation packages (for example, a certain number of the new housing units after redevelopment), which makes the redevelopment project less profitable at a density level that is acceptable by the local planning authority. For example, in the redevelopment of Yunong village (figure 10.1), about 40 percent of new units were used to compensate the indigenous farmers. The Floor Area Ration (FAR) has been doubled in order for the real estate developer to make a profit.

Incrementally, local governments began to realize the contribution of urbanizing villages in housing rural migrants. Song, Zenou, and Ding (2008) identified the factors that would increase the probability of rural migrants choosing to live in urbanizing villages. Their findings suggest that housing for rural migrants is related to the rural-urban dichotomy in land policy and housing provision. Rural migrants in search of urban housing are constrained in several aspects. First, most rural migrant laborers take low-income jobs, which limit their capacity to consume urban housing units in the commercial housing market. Second, rural migrants are excluded from the urban housing market because of institutional restrictions associated with the urban *hukou* system. Despite reduced constraints on rural labor mobility since the late 1970s and recent improvements in supporting migration control, rural migrants still encounter great difficulty in acquiring permanent residence status in urban areas. The lack of urban *hukou* has greatly limited rural migrants' access to urban housing since there is a rural-urban dichotomy in China's land policy and housing provision policies. Quercia and Song (2007) show that there are three major affordable housing programs in China's urban housing provision system: economy housing, low-cost renting, and the Housing Provident Fund (HPF) (also known as *jing ji shi yong fang, lian zufang,* and *gong ji jin,* respectively). They show that the housing program discriminates against those who do not have local urban *hukou*; that although the low-cost renting program is accessible

Redevelopment Plan for Yunong Village

SOURCE: www.nddaily.com, May 2005.

to rural migrants, its effectiveness in meeting their housing needs is limited by its scarcity; and that the utility of the HPF to rural migrants is limited because it is an employment-based housing finance system and many rural migrants are self-employed or employed by small businesses that do not contribute to the HPF. These results show that urbanizing villages in Shenzhen play an important role in providing shelter for the people who are constrained institutionally and financially from having access to other types of urban housing.

Recognizing the contribution of the urban villages, the comprehensive plan for Shenzhen 2020 has set forth the redevelopment of villages within cities as one of its major goals and has called for different redevelopment strategies for various types of villages. For those villages with extremely dilapidated structures and public safety hazards, the plan calls for complete redevelopment; for those villages with acceptable environment, the plan calls for redevelopment by adding more public facilities and services to the villages.

Value of the Villages to Urban Residents

Villages within cities have existed for more than a decade, and redevelopment efforts have been carried out for almost 10 years in Shenzhen. In determining whether these villages have been assimilated into cities, it is helpful to determine how they are valued by city residents.

Data from Shenzhen was used for the analysis. Shenzhen is a direct product of the economic reforms in China since 1978. Special economic zones (SEZs) were established in Shenzhen in 1980 as an experiment to attract foreign capital, technology, and people with management skills. By 2001, the city had a population of more than 9 million, the highest GDP per capita in China, the highest per capita disposable income of urban residents in China, and the highest value in total exports in China. Because of expected higher income opportunities, rural migrants were attracted to Shenzhen from all over China (Bruton, Bruton, and Li 2005).

Housing Prices for Owned Units

A hedonic price model was performed to estimate the effect of villages on housing prices based on a data set collected from Nanzhan District in the city of Shenzhen. Data on sale transaction records was collected from the Shenzhen Municipal Bureau of Land Resources and Housing Management. The data set contains 940 housing sale transactions in the study area.

A standard hedonic price model is specified. As a semilog is a common form of such a model, the dependent variable is specified as the log of sale price:

$$\log(P_i) = \beta_0 + \beta_i X_i + e \tag{1}$$

where $\log(P_i)$ is the dependent variable (LOGPRICE), β_0 is the constant, β_i $(i = 14)$ are coefficients, and X_i $(i = 14)$ are all independent variables, listed in table 10.1. Distance to the nearest urbanizing village (VILLAGE) is included to explore the effect of villages within cities on residential property values. In addition, the following categories of control variables are included: physical property features, public services, location variables, and amenity and disamenity features (see table 10.1 for definitions). Summary statistics for the dependent variable and all independent variables are also provided in table 10.1.

The results of our analysis, including the t-statistics and coefficients of each variable, are provided in table 10.2. The R-square indicates that we were able to explain 84 percent of the variation in our sample of sale prices. Most of the coefficients have expected signs. The estimated effect of an urbanizing village on property values is our primary interest. The positive sign of VILLAGE indicates that housing prices increase with distance from the nearest urbanizing village. To estimate the value of a premium (or discounted) sales price for a condominium with an original sales price of 1,360,000 yuan (the mean sales value in our sample) from a one-unit change in one

TABLE 10.1

Urbanizing Villages and Housing Prices: Summary Statistics

Variable Name (description)	Unit of Measure	Mean	SD	Min.	Max.
Dependent Variable					
LOGPRICE (log of total sale price in yuan)	Yuan(= $0.15)	4.70	0.62	2.71	6.68
Independent Variables					
Physical property features					
FLOORSPACE (building area)	Square meters	106.69	43.68	20.00	278.00
AGE (age of the building)	Years	9.58	13.66	1.00	28.00
FLOOR (the floor the unit is on)	NA	8.51	6.29	1.00	32.00
FAR (floor-area ratio)	NA	3.53	1.89	0.60	16.30
Public services					
HOSPITAL (distance to the nearest hospital)	Meters	923.61	477.09	16.59	2,397.29
SCHOOL (distance to the nearest school)	Meters	472.83	226.93	15.46	1,334.02
COLLEGE (distance to the nearest college)	Meters	2,521.76	1,402.14	115.96	6,613.03
Location measures					
INDUSTRY (distance to the nearest industrial zone)	Meters	1,182.68	711.16	38.84	3,518.18
SCIPARK (distance to the science park)	Meters	1,289.58	735.77	81.50	4,099.66
COMMERCIAL (distance to the nearest commercial center)	Meters	682.50	795.22	36.54	5,406.62
SUBWAY (distance to the nearest subway station)	Meters	974.21	842.73	48.13	6,183.61
Amenities and disamenities					
PUBLIC (overall accessibility to public open space)	NA	534.47	135.78	306.22	872.46
ONMAJRD (if within 100 meters of a major highway)	Binary	0.20	0.40	0.00	1.00
Urbanizing villages					
VILLAGE (distance to the nearest urbanizing village)	Meters	439.13	494.78	0.00	2,663.47

NOTE: SD = standard deviation.

of the independent variables while holding all other predictors constant, we compute changes in the sales price resulting from a one-unit change and the associated price premium in the last two columns of table 10.2. From this procedure, we show that price discount associated with being 1 meter (3.28 feet) closer to the nearest urbanizing village, while holding other attributes constant, is 155.86 yuan (approximately US$23) for a typical condominium unit in Nanzhan District in Shenzhen.

TABLE 10.2

Urbanizing Villages and Housing Prices: Regression Results

Variable	Parameter Estimate	Standard Error	t value	Pr>t	e^β	Premium (at 1,360,000 yuan)
Intercept	3.77612	0.11452	32.97	0.0000		
Physical property features						
FLOORSPACE (building area in square meters)	0.01126	0.00032	35.01	0.0000	1.011325	15,401.65
AGE (age of the building in years)	−0.03484	0.00490	−7.11	0.0000	0.965761	−46,564.66
FLOOR (the floor the unit is on)	0.00549	0.00219	2.52	0.0130	1.005505	7,486.52
FAR (floor-area ratio)	−0.01137	0.00738	−2.54	0.0124	0.988693	−15,377.51
Public services						
HOSPITAL (distance to the nearest hospital)	−0.00001	0.00003	−1.96	0.0500	0.999995	−6.90
SCHOOL (distance to the nearest school)	−0.00001	0.00006	−0.22	0.8260	NA	NA
COLLEGE (distance to the nearest college)	−0.00003	0.00001	−2.39	0.0170	0.999974	−35.36
Location measures						
INDUSTRY (distance to the nearest industrial zone)	0.00010	0.00003	3.59	0.0000	1.000101	136.82
SCIPARK (distance to the science park)	−0.00002	0.00002	−1.00	0.3200	NA	NA
COMMERCIAL (distance to the nearest commercial center)	−0.00007	0.00003	−2.35	0.0190	0.999934	−89.21
SUBWAY (distance to the nearest subway station)	−0.00005	0.00003	−2.37	0.0180	0.999949	−69.36
Amenities and disamenities						
PUBLIC (overall accessibility to public open space)	0.00001	0.00000	6.72	0.0000	1.000152	206.87
ONMAJRD (if within 100 meters of a major highway)	−0.02129	0.03640	−1.97	0.0500	0.97894	−28,641.70
Urbanizing villages						
VILLAGE (distance to the nearest urbanizing village)	0.00011	0.00003	3.83	0.0000	1.000115	155.86

Total number of observations = 951
R2 = 0.84

A Survey of Urban Residents

To further identify causes of this price discount, we carried out a survey of a random sample of 305 urban residents who own housing units in Nanzhan District. These residents were selected from a random sample of condominium developments included in our regression analysis.

Individual data were collected through face-to-face interviews. A total of 238 valid responses were generated, resulting in a response rate of 79 percent. In a questionnaire, we asked each urban resident to evaluate urbanizing villages. The survey results show that approximately 69 percent of the respondents believe the villages bring more disadvantages than advantages, 21 percent support the villages and believe they bring benefits, 7 percent believe the villages bring about the same benefits as costs, and the rest do not have an opinion. We also asked the respondents to provide and to rank reasons for favoring or disapproving the urbanizing villages nearby. The three most important reasons for favoring the villages were: (1) convenient shopping opportunities for daily goods; (2) availability of inexpensive goods and services; and (3) availability of a high level of social interactions. On the other hand, the reasons for disliking the villages included: (1) cluttered physical environment; (2) perceived high crime incidence; (3) noise nuisance; and (4) floating population.

Conclusions

In this study, we explored how villages within cities affect the urban housing market. Our main findings suggest that urbanizing villages, taken as a whole, are considered disamenities by most urban residents who own housing units nearby. Preliminarily, these results show that the villages within cities are not yet assimilated.

More important, these findings indicate that although significant efforts have been made to improve the physical environment of the villages, there is still a perceived disamenity effect associated with villages, especially by urban owners. In the short run, urban villages seem to be a realistic and effective solution for providing affordable housing to rural migrants. In the long run, however, the concentration of rural migrants in these villages, particularly those with lower incomes, may be the prelude to a new form of residential segregation in urban China. Strategies aimed at serving rural migrants should promote the dispersion of poverty and not encourage the concentration of these groups in small geographic areas. There is thus a dilemma for policy makers related to urban villages. On one hand, programs aimed at eliminating urbanizing villages and improving the physical environment of urbanizing villages would likely be largely ineffectual and even harmful to China's economy. Without the complementary consideration of rehousing current rural migrants, the renewal of villages within cities is obviously a planning action at the expense of those migrants. Neglecting rural migrants in urban areas would, in our view, ignite social unrest. On the other hand, the concentration of migrants and the urban poor would form a source of disamenity in the urban landscape. A more effective redevelopment strategy, accompanied by the current physical environment improvement program, should be comprehensive enough to incorporate community development (Fan 2001) and economic development strategies.

REFERENCES

Bruton, Michael J., Sheila G. Bruton, and Yu Li. 2005. Shenzhen: Coping with uncertainties in planning. *Habitat International* 29(2):227–243.

Chan, Kam Wing, Ta Liu, and Yunyan Yang. 1999. *Hukou* and non-*hukou* migrations in China: Comparisons and contrasts. *International Journal of Population Geography* 5:425–448.

Ding, Chengri, and Yan, Song, eds. 2005. *Emerging land and housing markets in China*. Cambridge, MA: Lincoln Institute of Land Policy.

Fan, C. Cindy. 2001. Migration and labor-market returns in urban China: Results from a recent survey in Guangzhou. *Environment and Planning A* 33(3):479–508.

Mobrand, Erik. 2006. Politics of cityward migration: An overview of China in comparative perspective. *Habitat International* 30(2):261–274.

Quercia, Roberto, and Yan Song. 2007. Housing rural migrants in urban China: Lessons from the United States. In *Urbanization in China: Critical issues in an era of rapid growth*, ed. Yan Song and Chengri Ding. Cambridge, MA: Lincoln Institute of Land Policy.

Song, Yan, and Chengri Ding, eds. 2007. *Urbanization in China: Critical issues in an era of rapid growth*. Cambridge, MA: Lincoln Institute of Land Policy.

Song, Yan, Yves Zenou, and Chengri Ding. 2008. Let's not throw the baby out with the bath water: The role of urban villages in housing rural migrants in China. *Urban Studies* 45(2):313–330.

Tang, Wing-Shing, and Him Chung. 2002. Rural-urban transition in China: Illegal land use and construction. *Asia Pacific Viewpoint* 43(1):43–62.

Wu, Weiping. 2002. Migrant housing in urban China: Choices and constraints. *Urban Affairs Review* 38(1):90–119.

———. 2004. Sources of migrant housing disadvantage in urban China. *Environment and Planning A* 36:1285–1304.

Zhang, Li, Simon X. B. Zhao, and J. P. Tian. 2003. Self-help in housing and chengzhongcun in China's urbanization. *International Journal of Urban and Regional Research* 27(4):912–937.

Zhao, Yaohui. 1999. Leaving the countryside: Rural-to-urban migration decisions in China. *American Economic Review* 89(2):281–286.

Comparative Studies of Housing Policy and Implications for China

Public Housing in China and the United States: A Policy Primer

LANLAN XU AND DAVID A. REINGOLD

In December 2008 the Chinese State Council announced a new real estate stimulus package emphasizing low-income housing and home ownership as part of a 4 trillion yuan (US$584 billion) economic stimulus plan. The government has estimated that the real estate initiative will benefit 7.5 million low-income urban families and 2.4 million under-housed households within three years. Rural homes in substandard condition will also be renovated.

This latest effort builds on China's affordable housing policies from the early 1980s, which put an end to the housing provision system under which houses were distributed through work units as a type of social welfare. The government hopes to establish through the current reform initiative a diversified multilevel urban housing provision system with three major components: (1) commercially built private housing at market prices for the high-income group; (2) commercially built subsidized affordable housing for the middle- and low-income groups; and (3) social housing for rent to the very low-income group.

As a result of these reforms, new housing units are developed through the private market and commercial housing enterprises and are built essentially for profit by real estate developers, making them generally unaffordable for middle- to low-income groups (Ding and Song 2005). Acknowledging the housing needs of moderate- and low-income families, the state introduced a multilayered housing supply system in 1998. Within this framework there are three programs: (1) a compulsory housing savings system known as Housing Provident Funds (*gongji jin*); (2) the development of subsidized affordable housing ("economic and comfortable housing"—*jingjishiyongfang* and *anju* projects); and (3) low-cost or subsidized rental housing (*lianzu fang*).

The Housing Provident Fund (HPF) was implemented in cities throughout China in 1994. This is a policy-based financing system under which the state, work units, and individual buyers join together to provide funds for housing development.

Because HPF is employment-based, those who are unemployed or laid off are excluded from the system. The large number of rural migrants employed by small businesses or self-employed are also excluded from the HPF program unless they can contribute to it directly.

The development of jingjishiyongfang and anju projects (akin to affordable housing initiatives in the United States) began in 1998. This affordable housing policy involves government subsidies and profit caps for developers. The subsidies include the administrative allocation of state-owned land at no cost and the reduction of 21 different taxes, development costs, and fees paid to local government. Developer profits are limited to 3 percent. The program is designed for middle- and low-income households in the urban housing sector, since one of its requirements specifies that applicants must have the local *hukou,* or household registration permit. The program is less applicable in meeting the housing needs of rural migrants in urban areas. Nevertheless, there are several pilot cases in which local governments have relaxed the requirement of local *hukou* and thus made the affordable housing units accessible by the rural migrants. For example, in Nanchang in 2005, the requirement that applicants for such housing have a local residence permit was replaced with the requirement that they work or pay taxes in the city for three consecutive years. Because affordable housing is generally located in peripheral areas, vacancy rates are high. This situation is worsened in the current economic downturn. There are proposals to convert part of the affordable housing stock to low-income housing.

The government was quite ambitious with the jingjishiyongfang and anju projects and planned to make this type of housing accessible to most urban residents (70–80 percent). In the first few years after the State Council published the circular "Further Deepening Urban Housing Reform and Accelerating Housing Construction" in July 1998, the development of jingjishiyongfang and anju projects boomed. Figure 11.1 and table 11.1 indicate that the total floor space of both the newly

TABLE 11.1

Housing Construction in China, 1998–2007

	Total Residential Buildings Started (10,000 m²)	Economic and Comfortable Housing Started (10,000 m²)	Ratio (%)
1998	16,637.5	3,466.4	21
1999	18,797.94	3,970.36	21
2000	24,401.15	5,313.32	22
2001	30,532.72	5,795.97	19
2002	34,719.35	5,279.68	15
2003	43,853.88	5,330.58	12
2004	47,949.01	4,257.49	9
2005	55,185.07	3,513.45	6
2006	64,403.8	4,379.03	7
2007	78,795.51	4,810.26	6

SOURCE: National Bureau of Statistics of China, *China Statistical Yearbook,* 1998–2007.

FIGURE 11.1

Construction and Sales of Affordable Housing

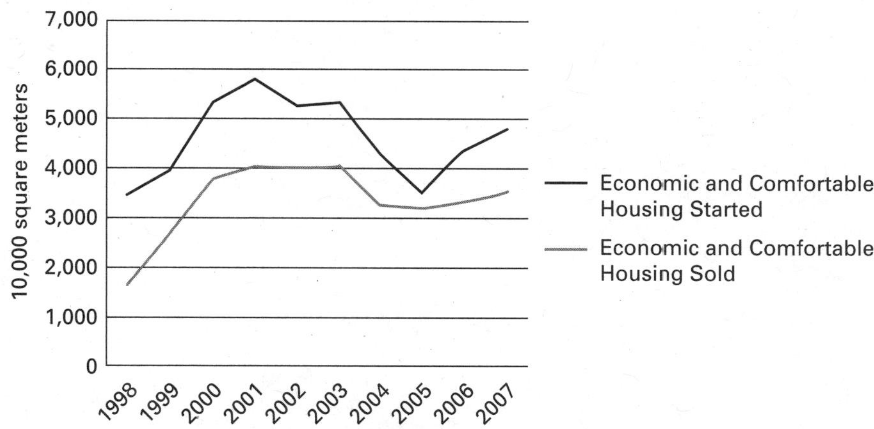

SOURCE: National Bureau of Statistics of China, *China Statistical Yearbook*, 1998–2007.

started and the sold housing of this type grew rapidly between 1998 and 2000. However, it quickly turned out that although this housing is heavily subsidized and the selling price per square meter is only about 60 percent of the market value, the low-income groups that were the target of this policy still could not afford to buy. Due to the ambiguity of the definition of the middle- and low-income groups, the allocation and management of the jingjishiyongfang have been fraught with scandals. There have been numerous news reports about high-level local officials and people driving expensive cars living in those housing units. The state quickly shifted policy direction to promote market-rate commercial housing as the main housing option for the majority of the middle-income population. In 2004 the "Management Rules of Affordable Housing" was promulgated, including more stringent regulations. For example, the floor area of jingjishiyongfang now is limited to 60 square meters, compared to between 60 and 80 square meters in 1998, and the housing can be provided to low-income families only. As shown in table 11.1 and figure 11.1, the proportion of newly constructed jingjishiyongfang and anju projects fell from 22 percent in 2000 to 6 percent in 2007, and sales declined accordingly. Table 11.2 depicts the trend of the relative price of jingjishiyongfang to other residential buildings in the same time period. The average selling price for jingjishiyongfang was about 56 percent of the average selling price of all residential buildings in 1998. This ratio peaked at 63 percent in 2003, and has been declining since then, reaching a historical low of 48 percent in 2007. People who were eligible for jingjishiyongfang only paid less than half of the market price in 2007, a significant discount for low-income people.

China's low-rent homes program was formally established in 1999 by the National Reform and Development Commission. Under government regulation, the price of low-rent housing is to cover housing maintenance and management costs and should be affordable to urban low-income families. There are two main forms of low-cost rental units. The first is converted former work-unit apartments. This

TABLE 11.2

Average Selling Price of Residential Buildings

	All Residential Buildings (yuan/m^2)	Economic and Comfortable Housing (yuan/m^2)	Ratio (percentage)
1998	1,854	1,035	56
1999	1,857	1,093	59
2000	1,948	1,202	62
2001	2,017	1,240	61
2002	2,092	1,283	61
2003	2,197	1,380	63
2004	2,608	1,482	57
2005	2,937	1,655	56
2006	3,119	1,729	55
2007	3,645	1,754	48

SOURCE: National Bureau of Statistics of China, *China Statistical Yearbook*, 1988–2007.

type of housing is the primary vehicle for serving the housing needs of China's low-income population. Temporary exemptions of property and business taxes can be applied to these units, which are leased at prices prescribed by the government. The second type, new low-rent housing units, is being constructed by local governments in several cities, mostly at the urban fringe to avoid the high cost of land in city centers. Guangzhou was at the forefront of providing social housing for the poor among the official urban residents (Wang 2000). However, the low-cost rental units have poor access to employment sites, so people are not as willing to move into them (Xiao 2006). An extreme case happened in Mingdemen District, the only low-rental housing district in Xi'an City. The district has six blocks with 246 low-rental units (14,000 square meters). Although the units were constructed in 2001, by the end of 2007 five blocks were still empty (*China Youth Daily* 2007). The program for low-cost rental units requires a direct commitment of public investment, but the lack of available funds from most local governments explains the program's limited extent to date. Since the allocation of funds is not yet institutionalized, the implementation of these programs remains ad hoc. The construction of low-rent housing is a big part of the government's $584 billion economic stimulus plan.

China's proposed expansion of low-rent (or public) housing raises a number of pressing questions about the implementation of this effort. Specifically, how will intergovernmental relations affect implementation? That is, how well will the central government, regional governments, and municipal governments work together to achieve this collective goal? Will this new initiative affect the country's rural-urban migration patterns and the ability of urban municipalities to absorb new migrants, and how will that be managed? Will these efforts inflame ethnic and regional conflict and stigmatize segments of the population?

While these questions will be answered in time with the expansion and implementation of low-income housing in China, the United States confronted a number of these issues in the 1950s and 1960s (and is still dealing with the consequences of its efforts) following its dramatic expansion of housing assistance to the poor (i.e., social housing). Certainly, China's plan and experience are unique and at a scale not seen before in many other countries. However, the U.S. experience provides insights into the potential implementation problems the Chinese will likely experience. Attention to these issues in advance will help to minimize the unintended consequences that frequently flow from low-income housing policy. To that end, this chapter describes current efforts to dramatically expand public housing provisions in China, while drawing lessons from the U.S. experience to help understand the potential challenges of implementation.

Low-Income Housing Policy: A Brief Literature Review

Research on Chinese housing reform is generally more concerned with the success and failure of housing reform progress and gives more focus to the economic impact or consequences of these efforts. Very little research has viewed housing reform from a social policy perspective, focusing on the winners and losers of these efforts and the unanticipated outcomes that may result.

What are the implications of the recent housing reform policies for disadvantaged groups? A number of empirical studies set out to examine the nature of the emerging urban poor and their accessibility to housing. Wang (2000) identifies two major groups of urban poor in Chinese cities: the poor among the official urban residents[1] and the poor rural-to-urban migrants. Wang concludes that while the housing problems of the official urban poor have been recognized, there is no formal policy in relation to housing provision for the unofficial poor.

The influx of migrants and the demand for inexpensive housing have created a unique urban form—villages within cities, also referred to as "urbanizing villages" (*cheng zhong cun*). The physical environment in many urbanizing villages in Chinese cities is in poor condition, with overcrowded buildings, narrow public stairways and pathways, and unhygienic public spaces. However, basic living standards are met through the provision of fundamental utilities such as water, electricity, phone lines, and natural gas. Furthermore, many of these urbanized villages are located near busy downtown financial districts and are accessible to employment centers. In 2005 there were about 100 "urban villages" in Tianjin, 231 in Beijing, and 139 in Guangzhou (Yu 2005). These are typically regarded with suspicion by both city officials and urban residents (Zhou et al. 2005).

Migrant housing patterns in urban China are linked with the country's unique institutional factors, particularly the circulating nature of migration, the existing household registration system, and the transitioning state of the urban housing market. Internal migration in contemporary China takes place in two forms:

---

[1] The bulk of the official urban poor are the so-called *xiagang* workers. Xiagang refers to a public-sector employee who has lost a permanent job but still receives a monthly benefit or a proportion of his wage from the employer. Xiagang means unemployment but is different from immediate redundancy since the employer may ask the person back to the post or find other jobs for him. Xiagang is also a special arrangement for long-established employees, most of whom were employed before urban employment reform; it is not applicable to the short-term contracted workers. Although the xiagang workers are not counted in the official documents as unemployed (because their relationship with the employer was not cut entirely), they are in fact unemployed people.

through permanent migration (*qianyi*) with formal changes of household registration (*hukou*), and through temporary movement (officially called "floating population," or *liudong renkou*) without official changes of *hukou* from the origin to the destination. The latter group, which makes up the bulk of China's internal migration, is expected to eventually return to their rural home places. The notion of temporary migrants is peculiar in China's contemporary context because it denotes not necessarily a time frame but an official designation (Chan 1996; Ma and Xiang 1998). Temporary migrants have restricted access to the urban social services enjoyed by local residents, and thus tend to invest little income to improve their housing conditions.

Among the studies investigating differential housing outcomes across groups, Wu (2004) models tenure choice in a sample that includes migrants (both with and without local *hukou*) and urban natives in Beijing and Shanghai. She finds that having local *hukou* (i.e., being a nonmigrant) substantially increases the odds of being a homeowner. Huang and Clark's (2002) research supports this result—when other relevant factors are controlled, households without permanent residency are 78 percent less likely to own homes than those with local residency in their national sample. Similarly, Li's (2000) study in Guangzhou finds that institutional factors severely limit urban home ownership opportunities for rural migrants. Wu (2006) also shows that having a rural *hukou* increases mobility rates and that migrants who have been able to find housing in public-sector rentals have lower mobility rates. Wu (2002) finds that renting from private individuals who own (or control use rights to) housing is the dominant housing option for migrants, but that a substantial minority occupies employer-provided dormitories and work sheds. In summary, the principal policy prescription that emerges from the China housing choice and mobility literature is to eliminate any residual housing market barriers migrants face as a result of their *hukou* status.

However, using data from a survey of 800 low-status migrants in Tianjin, Li, Duda, and Peng (2007) find that many migrants do not exercise housing "choice" but, rather, undergo housing "sorting" that follows from occupational choices. They conclude that the need to eliminate institutional barriers that limit access to certain kinds of housing is desirable but inadequate and may not respond to the concerns of migrants themselves. Housing policy that obstructs migrants' ability to obtain and change employment would probably not succeed. They suggest implementing regulation of the employer-provided housing pool as a first step in addressing the housing needs of urban migrants. Moreover, using statistics from the 2000 census, Jiang (2006) finds that migrants do not necessarily live in poorer housing conditions than nonmigrants in urban areas; some housing facilities for the floating population are even better than those of local urban residents.

In sum, the current research recognizes the difficulty low-income groups face amid the success of the recent housing reforms. Although offering different policy recommendations, most scholars call upon the government to focus on the housing problems low-income people face to further the housing reform.

Policy and Management of Low-Income Housing

Although the central government specified social housing as one important component of the new housing system, the provision of low-rent homes developed very slowly in the first few years after the policy was introduced in 1998, especially in comparison to the booming private real estate sector. By 2003, the practice of social housing was still at an experimental stage, with only a few provinces producing local regulations aimed at implementing this policy. The provision of low-income housing accelerated after "Measures for the Management of Social Housing for Urban Low-Income Households" (Department of Minimum Living Standards 2004) was published in 2004. According to the statistics published by the Ministry of Construction, among all 656 cities, 586 cities had set up low-income housing systems by the end of June 2007. This represented an 11.4 percent increase from the end of 2006. In 2007, 7.94 billion yuan was allocated, surpassing all previous governmental investments in low-income housing. However, it was estimated that approximately 10 million low-income households were still living in houses smaller than 10 square meters per person. Meeting the housing needs of these people poses a great challenge to local governments.

"Measures for the Guarantee of Low-rent Homes" (Department of Minimum Living Standards 2007) —discussed and adopted at the 139th executive meeting of the Ministry of Construction on 26 September 2007 and signed by the National Development and Reform Commission, Ministry of Supervision, Ministry of Civil Affairs, Ministry of Finance, Ministry of Land and Resources, People's Bank of China, State Administration of Taxation, and National Bureau of Statistics—came into force as of 1 December 2007. These are guiding rules for the current practice of social housing provision in China.

The sources of funds for the guarantee of low-rent homes include the following:

- Annual budget allocated to low-rent homes fund.
- The balance of Housing Providence Funds after drawing the loan risk reserve and management fee.
- The low-rent home guarantee fund arranged in the net proceeds of land transfer, the rate not to be less than 10 percent of land transfer net proceeds.
- The government's income from rent of low-rent homes.
- Donations and funds raised by other means.

The sources of low-rent homes mainly include the following:

- Homes newly built and purchased by the government.
- Vacated public homes.
- Donated homes.
- Other homes acquired by other means.

Social housing provision is seen as an important part of the social protection system by the central government. Most cities link social housing provision with the local minimum living standard (see appendix) and have provided help only to families falling below the poverty level. Households with per capita income above the poverty level but living in poor conditions are not included.

The provision and management of low-rent homes are decentralized and vary according to municipality. The common qualification criteria are

- monthly per capita income below the municipal poverty level;
- less living floor space per person than the threshold defined by the municipal government;
- possession of local *hukou* by all household members; and
- legal or foster relationship between family members.

Because of the high demand for social housing, applicants are queued and their position on a waiting list is determined by the score their application receives. Applicants are given a higher score if they live in poor housing conditions, hold city *hukou* for a longer time, live with parents or grandparents, are married for a longer time, and are on the waiting list for a longer time than other applicants.

Applications are submitted to a subdistrict office or township government. However, the application and supporting documents are primarily verified by neighborhood committees since the committee members are presumably most familiar with the social and economic status of the applicants. According to the recommendations of the neighborhood committee, within 30 days the subdistrict office or township government must assess whether the applicants meet the criteria, publicize their findings, and forward their recommendations along with the application packages to the Bureau of Construction or Public Housing Management Office on the city, district, or county level. Within 15 days of receiving the application, the Bureau of Construction or Public Housing Management Office must form their opinion on whether the applicants are eligible for public assistance and forward the eligible applications to the Bureau of Civil Affairs on the same municipal level for recommendations. The Bureau of Civil Affairs also has 15 days to check the eligibility of the applications and provide feedback to the Bureau of Construction or Public Housing Management Office, which then publishes the names of the applicants that meet the criteria in the media for 15 days. Those applicants who do not receive any valid objections from the public are officially registered as recipients of low-income housing. The final decision on each application should be sent to the applicant in a letter and publicized.

The current practice of low-income housing provision takes two forms: direct provision of low-rent homes and monetary subsidies. For convenience in operation, most local authorities prefer a monetary subsidy rather than a direct provision of low-rent public housing. Rent subsidies are thought to avoid the concentration of the poor into specific areas. Direct housing allocation is usually targeted to elderly or disabled people, households that are living below the local minimum living standards, or other households that are in desperate need of assistance. Those households are required to pay 5 percent of their income as rent in Shanghai (Wang 2004). When direct allocation is necessary, old empty public housing or difficult-to-sell commercial housing bought by local housing authorities is usually used. Low-rent homes specifically built by the municipal governments are rare to date.

In Shanghai, for example, households meeting the criteria can apply to the District Social Housing Office (*lianzuban*) for support. If a household was assessed and qualified for support, rent allowances would be provided to cover the cost of the difference between the maximum floor space limit for housing support and the current per capita floor space used by the family. Rent levels are set according to the location in the city (Wang 2004). In Shenzhen, applicants enjoy more subsidies if they are in the lower-income group. The subsidy is 70 percent of housing rent if applied household income is more than half of the upper limit of the lower middle- and low-income standard; 80 percent if household income is less than half of the upper limit; 90 percent if applicants enjoy a guaranteed minimum income (Liang 2008).

To ensure that monetary subsidies are used for housing, rent allowances are paid directly to the landlord, rather than to the family itself. This means that a family can get support only when it improves its living conditions by moving to larger accommodations. Households that secure support will have their income and housing situation checked every half year. If a household no longer meets the conditions, the rent allowance will be stopped. In the case of direct housing allocation, the household will be asked to move out of the social housing within six months. If housing and income conditions of the household get worse, there is no automatic increase in the allowance. The family has to apply for an increase and wait in the queue for its turn (Shanghai Property and Land Resource Management Bureau 2002).

Applicants cannot sell, sublease, exchange, or leave idle the dwelling unit for more than six months without warrant. The public housing authorities have the right to cease the contract and recall the unit if the rules are violated. Applicants who falsify their income reports or housing condition will be disqualified from renting low-income housing. Falsifiers could be investigated by the authorities or legal department, and their dwelling unit can be recalled.

Public officials and employees in the housing provision bureaus are supposed to be held accountable for their misconduct. However, there is no specific institute that is charged with auditing their work.

A Comparative Analysis of China-U.S. Public Housing Policy

Much like today's China, the United States embarked on an aggressive low-income housing initiative in the 1950s and 1960s, resulting in the construction of most of the current U.S. public housing stock. While the political, economic, and cultural context of the two countries differs substantially, the U.S. experience with low-income housing (and public housing, in particular) offers a window into the types of implementation issues the Chinese government likely confronts in pursuing its stated low-income (social) housing goals. These implementation issues can be categorized as problems related to intergovernmental relations, the rural-urban migration challenge, and ethnic-regional conflict.

Intergovernmental Relations and Operations

There are abundant references in the literature to the resistance of local decision makers to redistributive policies such as the provision of low-income housing

(Downs 1994; Gramlich 1977; Ladd and Doolittle 1982; Oates 1977; Peterson 1981; Schneider 1989). Much of this literature is rooted in Tiebout's (1956) theory of consumer choice. Tiebout describes municipalities within a region as offering varying baskets of goods (government services) at a variety of prices (tax rates). Given that individuals have differing personal valuations of these services and varying abilities to pay the attendant taxes, individuals will move from one local community to another until they find the one that maximizes their personal utility. Tiebout's theory is used to explain policy choices by local decision makers: They seek to provide the best benefit-cost ratio for public goods and services to retain and attract residents, and their choices are driven by the desire to act in the cities' best economic interests (Bish and Ostrom 1973; Peterson 1981; Schneider 1989). Unlike developmental policies that stimulate the growth of the economy, redistributive policies such as affordable housing programs shift resources from middle- and upper-income to lower-income people and are detrimental to a city. Schneider (1989) argues, therefore, that the federal government should be responsible for redistributive activities such as affordable housing programs. However, housing availability, quality, and cost directly affect localities and are essentially a local concern. What is the best strategy for the operation of public housing?

In the United States, a federal-local partnership governs the construction and management of public housing. The federal government provides resources for construction and maintenance to local public housing authorities (PHAs), which have the responsibility for day-to-day operations, including resident selection, rent collection, and property management. As shown in table 11.3, state and local governments assume only a small portion of the financial expenses related to housing programs. The more than 3,000 local public housing authorities are overseen by a local governing board of housing commissioners. Typically, housing commissioners are volunteer executive officials appointed by the chief executive officer of the municipal government where the public housing is located. Local housing authority boards of directors are frequently governing boards, in that they hire and fire the executive director of the local public housing authority. PHAs have authority over site selection and housing design.

The U.S. Department of Housing and Urban Development is the federal agency responsible for the activities of local PHAs. This federal agency has regional offices around the United States, and each PHA is overseen by a regional federal office. Regional federal offices work in collaboration with locally elected municipal officials and their designees on local housing authority boards (i.e., housing commissioners) to make sure all federal, state, and local laws and regulations are followed.

PHAs collect rent from tenants based on federal regulations, and this revenue is supposed to be sufficient to cover the day-to-day expenses of public housing operations. Funds for new construction and renovation are allocated at the federal level.

The administration of public housing in the United States has been fraught with conflict between various levels of government. Initially, municipal officials fought national involvement in what was viewed as a local affair. They objected to the federal government working through local surrogates (PHAs) in making decisions on where public housing would be located and who would live in it. Many of these objections were rooted in concern that site selection would disrupt existing pat-

TABLE 11.3

U.S. Housing Expenditure (in millions of current dollars)

	Federal Expenditures			State-Local Expenditures		
	FY2002	FY2003	FY2004	FY2002	FY2003	FY2004
Low-income housing aid (Section 8)	18,499	20,950	22,356	–	–	–
Public housing	8,213	4,124	4,584	–	–	–
Rural housing loans (Section 502)	1,540	1,616	1,597	–	–	–
Home investment partnerships	895	992	1,098	–	–	–
Housing for special populations (elderly and disabled)	704.6	721.3	589.6	–	–	–
Interest reduction (Section 236)	579.3	566.1	559.2	–	–	–
Housing opportunities for people with AIDS	314	254	254	–	–	–
Rural rental housing loans (Section 515)	114	115	114.5	–	–	–
Rural housing repair loans and grants (Section 504)	62.4	63.1	63.7	–	–	–
Farm labor housing loans and grants (Sections 514 and 516)	61.8	61.7	53.7	–	–	–
Rent supplements (Section 101)	53.7	55.4	56	–	–	–
Rural self-help technical assistance (Sections 523 and 524)	26.9	42.2	40.9	–	–	–
Indian housing improvement	19.6	19.5	19.4	–	–	–
Home ownership aid (Section 235)	10.8	8.4	4.8	–	–	–
Rural housing preservation grants (Section 533)	8.6	10.1	9.3	–	–	–
Home ownership and opportunity for people everywhere	3	2	2	6.3	5.3	0.8
Housing aid total	34,607	37,449	38,881	6.3	5.3	0.8

SOURCE: Congressional Research Service, 2006.

terns of residential segregation, pushing particular groups and political constituencies to move away from the new public housing developments and into suburban districts outside of a municipal boundary, diluting the political power of local political officials. This led some municipal officials to seek the passage of laws in state legislatures that required the chief municipal official (e.g., the mayor) to approve public housing site selection in a particular municipality.

The tension across levels of government eventually gave way to more local control over public housing programs. This meant that national (and sometimes local) reformers who wanted to use the public housing program as a means of addressing social problems related to racial discrimination and economic marginalization were pushed aside in favor of pursuing local concerns largely focused on maintaining political power and rewarding private real estate interests that played a role in supporting particular parties and candidates. As a result, public housing was used in many cities across the United States to maintain existing patterns of political power (Caro 1974), strengthen existing patterns of residential segregation (Goering, Kamely, and Richardson 1997; Vale 2000; Meyerson and Banfield 1954), and produce what some have called the second ghetto (Hirsch 1998).

In China, the central government determines the framework of low-income housing policy, but the management of the low-rent home programs is decentralized. The construction administrative department of the State Council directs and supervises the work to guarantee the construction of low-rent homes throughout the country. The construction administrative department of the people's government at or above the county level is responsible for the guarantee of low-rent homes within their respective administrative areas. The actual work of guaranteeing low-rent homes may be executed by the institution determined by a city or county government. The development and reform, supervision, civil affairs, treasury, land and resources, financial management, tax, and statistics departments of the people's government at or above the county level are, under their respective functions, responsible for the pertinent tasks related to the guarantee of low-rent homes. This is a very complicated system; the management of public housing easily involves the jurisdiction of more than 15 government offices.

Provincial and local governments have been reluctant to contribute to low-income housing projects. They fear that the price of commercially built private housing will continue to fall if there is a sudden increase of housing stocks built specifically for low-income households. Since the supply of land to be used for low-rent homes is guaranteed by way of allocation, the local government loses potential revenues from land sales for private housing development, which constitutes a significant portion of the local government revenue. Furthermore, the advancement of governmental officials depends, in part, on their region's economic performance rather than distributional equality within their districts. Put together, there are few incentives for local government officials to spend time and resources on the problem of social housing.

However, local governments have traditionally assumed a leading role in innovation and contributed substantially to the success of the Chinese economic reform. The central government publishes the guiding rules for the low-income housing campaign and basically allows provincial and local governments to try out any measures that could work within the set framework. In light of the slowdown of sales of real estate, some municipal governments have proposed to convert part of the vacant jingjishiyongfang to low-income rental housing units, while increasing the number of units constructed at market-rate rents. More important, there has been an upswing in proposals to reintroduce blue-stamp *hukou*. First introduced around 1992 in Beijing, and then in big cities like Shanghai, Shenzhen, Guangzhou, blue-stamp *hukou* differentiates housing benefits based on type of household registration. Under this arrangement temporary city *hukou* could be converted to permanent *hukou* after migrants had lived in the city for a certain number of years (usually five years) and had invested or bought a piece of property whose value exceeded a certain threshold. This policy attracted many migrants and supposedly increased the financial burden of city governments. Thus the practice was stopped in 2000. However, the economic downturn, especially the slowdown in the real estate sector, has prompted local governments to reintroduce blue-stamp *hukou*. Since the beginning of 2009, a number of big cities, such as Tianjin, Chongqing, and Hangzhou, have announced blue-stamp *hukou* policies.

To date, local officials have been immune to political pressure. Low-income people with housing assistance have been relatively unorganized and without much ability to shape the political landscape. However, there have been an increasing number of public demonstrations by laid-off workers, underpaid retirees, and dislocated tenants in urban redevelopment areas, which has been perceived as a sign of social unease by party leaders. The central government has explicitly stressed the importance of social stability along with economic growth as governmental goals in the past few years. With the policy change from the central government to more aggressively address the housing problems faced by low-income households and the passage of the economic stimulus package, it is foreseeable that the attitudes of local governments toward low-rent homes and other social security programs could change greatly.

In sum, the implementation of public housing is frequently a local concern that is initiated and funded at a national level. Conflicts across levels of government typically have profound effects on the ability of public housing programs to achieve social and economic benefits for their residents, as well as their host communities. The success of China's plans to dramatically expand its public (social) housing program will hinge, in part, on the ability of the national government to manage a process that is by default highly decentralized and dependent on the interests of local political officials. Simply giving resources to local officials with a charge of helping low-income segments of the population is likely to exacerbate ongoing social and economic divides.

Rural-Urban Migration

In the United States, much of the public housing stock was built, in part, as a result of overcrowding from rural-urban migration that produced unsafe housing conditions. Many of the migrants were African American and moved from rural southern parts of the United States to urban northern parts. Motivated by economic hardship and the pursuit of economic opportunity, many of these migrants piled into cities looking for work. Private real estate interests responded to the short housing supply relative to the growing demand by increasing rents, dividing houses and apartments into multiple units to expand supply, and converting unconventional structures (such as garages) into permanent living spaces. The result was an explosion of unsafe and unhealthy living conditions for many urban residents from ethnic minority groups.

No compelling evidence suggests that the construction of public housing to serve these rural-urban migrants in the 1950s and 1960s eased their material hardship.

Local municipalities restricted the location of land that could be used for public housing. With limited access to land, local PHAs faced the unpleasant choice of building few units, serving a smaller population, or concentrating large numbers of public housing units on available land and serving more households in substandard housing. Initially, many local housing authorities decided to maximize the number of units built, concentrating large numbers of low-income families in dense high-rise housing developments.

Even though the construction of this housing didn't materially improve housing conditions for the average household, it probably created the perception among rural-urban migrants that safe and decent housing was available. That perception likely fueled additional rural-urban migration. Unfortunately, the continued inflow of rural residents maintained tight housing markets and the type of market conditions that promote overcrowding, doubling-up, and the continued use of unsafe structures for rental housing.

In China, social policies so far are aimed at solving the problems among the official urban residents. Rural migrants are excluded from any of the government support systems. If measured according to the same economic standard, most rural migrants will be eligible to receive housing subsidies. However, the *hukou* system keeps most of them from qualifying. These arrangements are understandable if rural migrants work in cities only temporarily. In reality, most of them stay in cities for many years, however. Demands to respect their citizenship and give them equal rights in cities are getting stronger. There have been recent moves to relax the policy controls imposed on them, especially calls to reform the *hukou* system. However, considering the huge number of rural migrants and the current capacity of city governments, the proposals to provide social housing to rural migrants could take many years to realize. And the perception that public housing expansion is creating new housing opportunities will likely fuel higher rates of rural-urban movement.

Ethnic-Regional Conflict

In the United States, most public housing was officially segregated by race and ethnicity until the 1970s. The large number of African Americans who migrated from rural to urban areas created social instability in urban America. The inflow of new residents seeking employment and housing was frequently perceived as a threat by existing residents. Long-time inhabitants fought to defend their communities from the newcomers. The construction of public housing became one of the primary landscapes where these struggles were fought.

In contemporary China, race and ethnicity are less of a problem than regional conflicts. The most visible distinguisher of the origin of a person is not appearance but speech. There are at least seven language groups within Chinese, and there are a lot more variations within each group. People who speak different dialects often cannot understand each other. Those who do not speak the local dialects are often discriminated against in urban labor and housing markets. This is an especially acute problem for the rural-urban migrants, who often have low educational levels and do not speak Mandarin, let alone the local dialects. The villages within cities are often characterized by the home provinces of the majority of migrants—for example, Zhejiang village, Xinjiang village, Henan village, etc. Because villages within cities are associated with a high concentration of poverty and crime, they are often seen as scars on the face of the beautiful city scenes that need to be demolished. In fact, before the opening ceremony of the 2008 Beijing Olympic Games, the Beijing City government invested 1.5 billion yuan to redevelop the 69 villages within cities within the radian of the third ring (*People Daily* 2005).

Much of the early U.S. experience with public housing construction was embedded in a public struggle over slum clearance and renewal. Frequently, public housing construction was used as an excuse to demolish old units and revitalize parts of central cities. This often resulted in the displacement of existing low-income residents. Since the number of new units almost never equaled the number of demolished housing units, those who were displaced frequently were pushed into nearby neighborhoods. This resulted in community conflict and violence.

The substantial growth of public housing in China will likely be accompanied by similar forms of community conflict. Assuming the number of new units will be less than the number of demolished units, and localities given site-selection discretion, we should expect to see considerable levels of displacement followed by intra-city migration. As displaced residents move to other parts of a city, they may disrupt existing patterns of residential segregation and provoke long-standing residents to defend their communities. Unless managed effectively, this could lead to a substantial social disruption.

Expanding Public Housing Without Social Disruption

Is it possible to dramatically expand public (social) housing, given China's plans, without fostering social disruption? Clearly, the U.S. experience suggests that public housing provision becomes embedded in the ongoing struggles of a society. To the extent that a society suffers from social and economic division, the development and implementation of low-income housing create a platform on which the differences can be fought over. While the same can be said about many spheres of social policy, public housing provision seems especially prone to heightened tensions from preexisting strains in the social structure because of the need to acquire land, combined with the frequent emotional link of individuals and groups to a particular place.

In the United States, the tensions in low-income housing provision are moderated by the nonprofit sector (O'Regan and Quigley 2000). Today, philanthropic grants in low-income housing typically take the form of providing resources to community development corporations (CDCs)[2] and community development

---

[2] While there are many definitions of CDCs, several characteristics distinguish these types of organizations. They are nonprofit 501(c)3 organizations that coordinate and implement strategies for the economic development of a community (typically defined as a discrete physical area or neighborhood). Local residents control the CDC's development strategy by guaranteeing local residents majority control of the board. The mission of these organizations is typically the achievement of social goals that sometimes include the development of business, broadly defined to include commercial facilities and housing development (National Housing and Economic Development Law Project 1974, 9–10). While the total number of CDCs varies, most estimates suggest that there are 2,500–3,500 across the nation (Vidal 1992). Most were created after 1973 and were products of the War on Poverty and the civil

financial institutions (CDFIs)[3] that are in the business of building, managing, and selling affordable housing in poor, distressed areas of the country. Typically, these philanthropic investments are not used to build housing but designed to foster an organizational infrastructure that can take advantage of government housing programs or supplement public funding streams from sources such as the Community Development Block Grant (CDBG) program, HOME grants, and the Low-Income Housing Tax Credit (LIHTC) program.[4] Since these organizations are socially motivated and frequently give substantial voice to low-income groups and communities, they are able to help moderate some of the potentially harmful effects of contending with the profit motives of real estate interests and the power motives of local and regional politicians when dealing with housing policy.

It is worth noting that this philanthropic-sector strategy is very different from earlier U.S. philanthropic efforts designed to address the housing needs of the poor. At the turn of the twentieth century, notable philanthropists such as John D. Rockefeller, Julius Rosenwald, and Marshall Field III invested millions to build housing for the poor. Numerous model tenements were built in New York City, Chicago, Boston, and Cincinnati, among other cities (Lubove 1962).

At the time, many housing activists believed in the utility of private market institutions for the production of housing products, even for the poor, and did not want government policy to crowd out private market activity. To demonstrate that the private sector could help address housing problems without resorting to government-run housing, a variety of settlement houses, wealthy philanthropists, and private investors sponsored model tenements (Dreier 1997).

Model tenements were privately constructed rental housing developments owned by limited dividend corporations that frequently sought to make a profit (but not to maximize profit) by providing rental housing to low-income households. While a small number of model tenements operated on charity alone, many others

---

rights movement. Frequently, such groups started as community action agencies and later became CDCs. Today, the typical CDC operates within a large city, targeting services and strategies to a distressed urban neighborhood. The financial scale of these organizations is modest. Recent studies suggest that the median total budget is about $700,000 (Vidal 1992).

[3] There is also no uniformly accepted definition of CDFIs; however, these are financial organizations—nonprofit or for profit—whose mission is to make loans that conventional institutions would deem unbankable and to link financing to other development activities in communities that are underserved or neglected by mainstream lenders. CDFIs come in a variety of sizes and structures. They may offer loans, subordinated debt, equity, credit enhancement, and basic financial services. Some serve the inner city, while others focus on rural areas, and still others lend to targeted groups such as women, minorities, low-income families, and social service providers. CDFIs may also support specific types of projects, from affordable housing construction and purchase to microenterprise and small business development, job training, and industrial retention (McLenighan and Tholin 1997, 1). As of 1999, there were 334 registered CDFIs (U.S. Department of the Treasury 1999).

[4] A CDBG is an intergovernmental transfer from the federal government to state and local governments to fund community and economic development projects. HOME grants are also intergovernmental transfers, but these monies are more narrowly focused on housing. The LIHTC provides federal tax credits to spur development in affordable low- or moderate-income rental housing (McClure 2000). The LIHTC program is administered by the state, and the tax credits are allocated to nonprofit and for-profit developers through a competitive process. Bidders submit proposals to create affordable housing through new construction or the rehabilitation of existing property. Once the property is occupied, annual tax credits are granted against the tax liability of the property owners over a 10- to 30-year period (O'Regan and Quigley 2000).

sought a limited return on investment (typically 5 percent rather than the 6–18 percent return on residential real estate investment sought by speculators at the time) in exchange for the enjoyment of supporting a social mission. These projects became known as investment philanthropy, or philanthropy and 5 percent, and were an early form of what has since evolved into socially responsible investing.

Some model tenements partnered with religious charity society organizations (CSOs). These tenements would sometimes use charity workers (or volunteers) to manage the housing, collecting rents and visiting residents to council them on appropriate Christian child-rearing methods; proper housekeeping techniques; personal hygiene; and moral teachings on responsibility to work, family, community, and country.

Other model tenements partnered with progressive organizations, including settlement houses, as well as large employers who viewed the housing developments as a natural outgrowth of welfare capitalism. In these cases, the goal was to provide safe and affordable housing that would also have the side benefit of integrating new immigrants into mainstream American institutions and ways of life, while helping to ensure a supply of satisfied and productive workers.

For some investors, the provision of decent and safe housing was seen as the antidote for the problems associated with urban poverty, including disease, delinquency, and social isolation. For others, the design of these model tenements was a blueprint for profit-maximizing housing construction companies, demonstrating that it was feasible and desirable to build high-quality housing for the poor that could produce a profit (hence the term *model*). By providing low-income households with the same physical and social accommodations frequently found in housing for the affluent, investors would be rewarded with well-behaved tenants who would pay the rent on time, resulting in a good return on investment. The concern that model tenements be innovative prompted investors to commission prominent architects to design the homes; one was Frank Lloyd Wright, whose two-story model tenement in Chicago is known as Francisco Terrace.

For those who would occupy these tenement units, the housing was indeed of higher quality than the existing housing stock run by profit-maximizing firms for low-income people. However, critics were quick to point out that the total number of model tenements built was small relative to the number of households in need and lagged far behind the number of units constructed by profit-maximizing companies. For example, it is estimated that between 1870 and 1910 only 25 model tenements were built in New York City, housing approximately 17,940 persons, whereas speculative builders had constructed 27,100 tenements, housing 253,510 families, or over 1 million persons (Dreier 1997).

The perception that the model tenement movement was unable to meet the housing needs of the nation's urban poor undermined enthusiasm for these initiatives. Investors also found that the costs of building good-quality housing and maintaining the property meant that their limited profit expectations could be reached only by charging rents that were beyond the reach of the poorest urban residents. Faced with these constraints, housing activists quickly turned their attention to the passage of municipal laws that would regulate private landlords, requiring them to improve the quality of the existing housing stock or face sanctions. This shift in focus would signal the decline and eventual death of the tenement housing movement, including the use of philanthropic funds to build housing for the poor. Philanthropic efforts eventually gave way to governmental intervention—namely, the creation of the public housing program.

It was not until decades later, after some of the unintended negative consequences of the public housing initiative became apparent, that the U.S. philanthropic sector reengaged with this sphere of social policy. The second wave of activity included the creation of the CDC and CDFI sectors, designed to help make sure the implementation of subsequent low-income housing policy was more effective at helping the disadvantaged. While some have debated the effectiveness of CDCs and CDFIs in achieving this goal, their mediating presence has helped mitigate some of the conflict and potential social disruption frequently observed in the implementation of public (social) housing initiatives.

Efforts to promote a professional nonprofit sector in China dedicated to working on behalf of low-income households may help minimize some of the social disruption inherent in public (social) housing initiatives. While these efforts take time to cultivate, and can sometimes become adversarial, they can play an important role in minimizing some of the anticipated and unanticipated negative effects of low-income housing programs on the households they are designed to help.

Appendix

TABLE 11.A1

Urban Minimum Living Standard, December 2008

	Miminum Living Standard (yuan/month)	# of People Living Under MLS
Beijing	390	7,020
Tianjin	396.67	8,330
Hebei	195.97	37,235
Shanxi	200.2	26,026
Inner Mongolia	195.04	19,699
Liaoning	224.01	23,745
Jilin	161.86	11,330.5
Heilongjiang	200.53	3,6095
Shanghai	400	7,600
Jiangsu	278.19	32,548
Zhejiang	296.61	27,585
Anhui	212.37	24,210
Fujian	211.07	18,363
Jiangxi	193.29	26,867
Shangdong	234.63	38,245
Henan	169.01	28,731.2
Hubei	187.74	19,525
Hunan	180.38	22,908.2
Guangdong	256.07	35,337.5

(continued)

TABLE 11.A1 (continued)

	Miminum Living Standard (yuan/month)	# of People Living Under MLS
Guangxi	178.25	19,608
Hainan	189.29	3,975
Chongqing	231.16	9,940
Sichuan	190.01	35,341
Guizhou	158.25	13,926
Yunnan	197.74	27,880.7
Tiebet	255.75	18,670
Shaanxi	172.31	18,610
Gansu	157.24	13,680
Qinghai	188.15	9,031

REFERENCES

Bish, Robert L., and Vincent Ostrom. 1973. *Understanding urban government.* Washington, DC: American Enterprise Institute.

Cai, Fang. n.d. Invisible hand and visible feet: Internal migration in China. UNDP Working Paper. http://hdr.undp.org/docs/network/hdr_net/China_invisible_hand_visible_feet.pdf.

Caro, Robert. 1974. *The power broker.* New York: Knopf.

Chan, Kam Wing. 1996. Post-Mao China: A two-class urban society in the making. *International Journal of Urban and Regional Research* 20(1):134–150.

China Youth Daily [*Zhongguo qingnian bao*]. 2007. Why Xi'an's low-rental housing was not allocated six years after the construction, February 8.

China News. 2008. China will invest 900 billion yuan to solve the housing problems of low-income households, November 12. http://news.163.com/08/1112/19/4QIRVQ440001124J.html [In Chinese].

Congressional Research Service. 2006. *Cash and noncash benefits for persons with limited income: Eligibility rules, recipient and expenditure data, FY2002–2004.* Report RL33340.

Cook, Sarah, and Susie Jolly. 2000. *Unemployment, poverty and gender in urban China: Perceptions and experiences of laid-off workers in three Chinese cities.* Brighton, U.K.: Institute of Development Studies.

Department of Minimum Living Standards. 2004. Measures for the management of social housing for urban low-income households. http://dbs.mca.gov.cn/article//csdb/zcfg/200711/20071100003525.shtml [in Chinese].

———. 2007. Measures for the guarantee of low-rent homes. http://dbs.mca.gov.cn/article/csdb/zcfg/200712/20071200005662.shtml [in Chinese].

Ding, Chengri, and Yan Song. 2005. *Emerging land and housing markets in China.* Cambridge, MA: Lincoln Institute of Land Policy.

Downs, Anthony. 1994. *New visions for metropolitan America.* Washington, DC: Brookings Institution.

Dreier, Peter. 1997. Philanthropy and the housing crisis: The dilemmas of private charity and public policy. *Housing Policy Debate* 8(1).

Goering, John, Ali Kamely, and Todd Richardson. 1997. Recent research on racial segregation and poverty concentration in public housing in the United States. *Urban Affairs Review* 32(5):723–745.

Goodkind, Daniel, and Loraine A. West. 2002. China's floating population: Definitions, data and recent findings. *Urban Studies* 39(12):2237–2250.

Gramlich, Edward M. 1977. Intergovernmental grants: A review of the empirical literature. In *The political economy of fiscal federalism*, ed. W. E. Oates. Toronto: Lexington Books.

Hirsch, Michael R. 1998. *The making of the second ghetto: Race and housing in Chicago, 1940–1960*. Chicago: University of Chicago Press.

Huang, Youqin, and William A. V. Clark. 2002. Housing tenure choice in transitional urban China: A multilevel analysis. *Urban Studies* 39(1):7–32.

Jiang, Leiwen. 2006. Living conditions of the floating population in urban China. *Housing Studies* 21(5):719–744.

Ladd, Helen F., and Fred C. Doolittle. 1982. Which level of government should assist the poor? *National Tax Journal* 35:323–336.

Li, Bingqin, Mark Duda, and Huaming Peng. 2007. Low-cost urban housing markets: Serving the needs of low-wage, rural-urban migrants? Working Paper. Cambridge, MA: Lincoln Institute of Land Policy.

Li, Si-Ming. 2000. The housing market and tenure decisions in Chinese cities: A multivariate analysis of the case of Guangzhou. *Housing Studies* 15:213–236.

Liang, Ruobing. 2008. Reforming China's urban housing policy: The case of Xiamen. EAI Background Brief No. 365. Singapore: East Asian Institute.

Lubove, Roy. 1962. *The progressives and the slums: Tenement house reform in New York City, 1890–1917*. Pittsburgh, PA: University of Pittsburgh Press.

Ma, Laurence J. C., and Biao Xiang. 1998. Native place, migration and the emergence of peasant enclaves in Beijing. *China Quarterly* 155:546–581.

McClure, Kirk. 2000. The low-income housing tax credit as an aid to housing finance: How well has it worked? *Housing Policy Debate* (11):1.

McLenighan, Valjean, and Kathryn Tholin. 1997. *Partners in community building: Mainstream and community development financial institutions*. Chicago: Woodstock Institute.

Meyerson, Martin, and Edward Banfield. 1954. *Politics, planning and the public interest: The case of public housing in Chicago*. New York: Free Press.

National Bureau of Statistics of China. 1988–2007. *China Statistical Yearbook*. Beijing: China Statistics Press.

National Housing and Economic Development Law Project. 1974. *A lawyers manual on community-based economic development*. Berkeley: University of California Press.

Oates, Wallace E. 1977. An economist's perspective on fiscal federalism. In *The political economy of fiscal federalism*, ed. W. E. Oates. Toronto: Lexington Books.

O'Regan, Katherine, and John M. Quigley. 2000. Federal policy and the rise of nonprofit housing providers. *Journal of Housing Research* 11(2).

People Daily. 2005. "Slums" sting Chinese cities, hamper building of harmonious society. September 9. http://english.peopledaily.com.cn/200509/09/eng20050909_207472.html#.

Peterson, Paul E. 1981. *City limits*. Chicago: University of Chicago Press.

Schneider, Mark. 1989. *The competitive city*. Pittsburgh, PA: University of Pittsburgh Press.

Shanghai Property and Land Resource Management Bureau. 2002. Recommendations for the management of Shanghai low rent housing. http://www.law110.com/law/32/shanghai/223103.htm [in Chinese].

Tiebout, Charles M.. 1956. A pure theory of local expenditures. *Journal of Political Economy* 64:416–424.

U.S. Department of the Treasury. 1999. *Building partnerships: Putting capital to work*. Community Development Financial Institution Fund Annual Report. Washington, DC.

Vale, Lawrence J. 2000. *From puritans to projects: Public housing and public neighbors*. Cambridge, MA: Harvard University Press.

Vidal, Avis C. 1992. *Rebuilding communities: A national study of urban community development corporations*. New York: New School for Social Research, Community Development Research Center.

Wang, Ya Ping. 2000. Housing reform and its impacts on the urban poor in China. *Housing Studies* 15:845–864.

———. 2004. *Urban poverty, housing and social change in China.* Housing and Society Series. New York: Routledge.

Wu, Weiping. 2002. Migrant housing in urban China: Choices and constraints. *Urban Affairs Review* 38(1):90–119.

———. 2004. Sources of migrant housing disadvantage in urban China. *Environment and Planning A* 36:1285–1304.

———. 2006. Migrant intra-urban residential mobility in urban China. *Housing Studies* 21(5):745–765.

Xiao, Jin A. 2006. Lack of rural-urban migrants' participation led to unenthusiastic responses to public housing for rural-urban migrants [*nongmingong gongyu lengchang yuanyu quefa canyu jizhi*]. *New Beijing Daily* [*Xin Jing Bao*], September 13.

Yu, Jun 2005. *Difficulties and suggestions in regenerating urban villages in Beijing, Zhuhai and Guangzhou.* Shenzhen, China: China Development Institute.

Zhang, Heather Xiaoquan, Bin Wu, and Richard Sanders, eds. 2007. *Marginalisation in China: Perspectives on transition and globalisation*, Aldershot, U.K.: Ashgate.

Zhou, Yu, et al. 2005. Villages for workers from the same home villages are destroying the safety of Shenzhen: 643 groups and 2 million people. Guangzhou, China: Southern Metropolitan News.

A Comparative Study of Social Housing in Britain and China

JUAN JING

Cross-national comparison has frequently been used in housing studies in recent years. Many researchers have indicated that the ideas and approaches in housing policy and development in one country could have value in other countries (Dickens et al. 1985; Boelhouwer and van der Heijden 1992; Barlow and Duncan 1994; Doling 1997), especially when economic, political, and cultural globalization is heading toward convergence in social policies and practices, eroding local distinctiveness. By following a cross-national perspective, research findings may facilitate better and more thorough understandings of the strategic and structural issues, and also help to identify knowledge gaps and point to new directions that might be pursued (Øyen 1990; Hantrais and Mangen 1996). In the existing literature, the majority of comparative studies on social housing focus on countries within the European Union. Many studies have offered innovative ideas for policy shifts and program development. However, the findings of the cross-national comparative social housing studies seldom involve developing countries, despite the fact that in recent years the overall social housing stock of developing countries has far more diverse categories than those in developed countries.

Social housing is an important but ambiguous term in housing studies. In different contexts and from different perspectives, definitions may vary (Davis 1998; Bourne 1998; Harloe 1995; Kemeny 1992). In this chapter, it is an umbrella term referring to all housing provision that is not from the free market. This includes low-cost rental housing owned or managed by the state, stock provided by not-for-profit organizations, and other dwellings sold or rented to occupiers with subsidies or allowances. From this perspective, social housing is neither a commodity nor a private asset, but is similar to the public health and education services to a certain extent, as a necessity to guarantee a basic life standard (Torgensen 1987). If it is an objective to improve social justice and harmony, governments should launch a series of policies and practical approaches to deliver a better balance between housing supply and demand and ensure that "people have decent places to live" (ODPM 2004, 12). In many countries, especially the advanced economies, the social housing sector occupies a considerable proportion of the overall housing stock. Social housing policy and development have a significant influence on national economic and social development.

Social housing has a long history in Britain and China. In both countries, social housing policy and practice have experienced many significant reforms. In Britain the earliest social housing policy was developed in the late nineteenth century in response to housing shortages and poor living conditions in industrial cities. In China, after the socialist state was established in 1949, housing provision was predominantly from public agencies. In recent years, Chinese policy makers have adopted many policy changes and approaches from western countries, including Britian.

This chapter contributes to the comparative research of social housing in China and Britain. It provides an overview of the social housing issues in both countries in a parallel structure and analyzes the similarities and differences between them. The findings answer the following questions for both countries: When, why, and how have social housing policies and projects been initiated? What changes have been made in the following years? What are the physical features of social housing? What are the social profiles of the tenants? In answering these questions, the British experience could provide valuable lessons for Chinese social housing development.

Social Housing in Britain

Social Housing Policy and Its Development

The origin of social housing in Britain can be traced back to the late nineteenth century. After the Industrial Revolution, the population of the working class boomed in industrial cities. The majority of that population lived in dwellings provided by private landlords or their employers. The provision of urban dwellings and sewerage could not keep pace with this billowing population, with the result that people were crammed together in poor-quality, unsanitary accommodations (Tarn 1971; Gaudie 1974). In response, the Housing of the Working Classes Act of 1890 permitted local authorities to erect "council housing" to replace demolished slum dwellings deemed unfit for human habitation. The authorities were expected to ask developers to provide more decent houses for the working class, but the commercial return was limited to no more than 5 percent (Morton 1991). In its early years, the development of council housing was on a very limited scale. By 1914 only about 24,000 council dwellings had been built (Merrett 1979), and about 90 percent of households were still renting from private landlords (Lund 2002).

After World War I, the development of social housing in British cities was accelerated. The Housing and Town Planning Act of 1919 made it mandatory for each local authority to create a plan to meet local housing needs and granted subsidies to help local governments finance nonprofit housing development. Large-scale public housing construction projects were initiated, including Homes Fit for

Heroes in the 1920s and booming slum clearance projects in the 1930s (Orbach 1977; Glynn and Oxborrow 1976). Between 1914 and 1939, 1.77 million houses were completed by the public sector or with state aid which comprised 41 percent of overall housing completion during the period (Bowley 1945). Also, substantial progress was made to improve housing conditions; Rowntree (1941) found that overcrowding in York was reduced by two-thirds since 1900, and unfit property had decreased from 26 percent of the housing stock in 1900 to 12 percent in 1936.

Despite significant progress in the interwar years, the serious housing shortage continued in British cities. World War II destroyed or badly damaged approximately 700,000 existing houses (Lund 2006, 28). Meanwhile, Britain experienced rapid population growth driven by the postwar baby boom. Between 1951 and 1961 the population increased by 5.0 percent, with an even higher growth rate of 5.9 percent in the following 10 years (Jefferies 2005). Moreover, the progress of slum clearance created an increasing number of homeless working class people to be re-accommodated. All these factors put greater pressure on public housing development. As a result, the central government offered a higher rate of subsidies to local authorities for public housing development, so the social housing sector kept increasing rapidly in following years. The high-speed drive of the social housing boom finally slowed after the late 1960s, by which time the general housing shortage in Britain had been reduced to a great extent. But public expenditure on housing, which was also used to improve the quality of existing dwellings, remained at a high level until the late 1970s. Though the details of regulations shifted many times, corresponding to shifts of political power, the basic framework of social housing provision remained unchanged (Malpass and Murie 1999).

Public expenditure for social housing was cut off in 1976 because of the financial difficulties of the British government (Lund 2006, 36). When the Conservative Party came to power in 1979, the provision of new council housing significantly declined; meanwhile, the existing stock was privatized through the Right to Buy program (Department of Environment 1987, 3). This program was introduced by the Housing Act of 1980 and Scotland's Tenants' Rights Act of 1980. "Secure" tenants (tenants for over three years originally, later for two years) were allowed to buy the property rights of their homes at discounted prices. Some other council housing stock was transferred to housing associations or similar voluntary organizations. These organizations were partially supported by private capital and also competed to secure public grants or subsidies by meeting the government's social objectives (Lund 2006, 41). Meanwhile, the rents of council housing were pushed up closer to market prices. Some qualified renters who found it difficult to afford the housing cost could receive financial support such as a housing benefit. In all, the social housing supply in Britain has shrunk since the early 1980s, and is now provided and managed in more flexible ways.

The impacts of the privatization process were disproportionate. Most council houses bought by private owners were the better ones—for example, detached houses rather than apartments, or houses in favorable locations rather than those with poor accessibility. The remaining public-owned houses became more "residual" in the housing market with deteriorating reputations (Forrest and Murie 1983). Their tenants had to suffer a much lower level of living conditions than others. Thus, in the following years, the task of improving less desirable housing estates gained a higher priority for the British government. After 1997, when the New Labour government came to power, more public expenditure was invested in the most disadvantaged housing estates. New attempts have been made to reduce the gap between social housing and market properties, including the encouragement of mixed tenure, increased accessibility to decent and affordable social services, and greater tenant participation in neighborhood management. By such means, social housing provision and management have become more diverse and dynamic to better meet long-term housing needs (table 12.1).

Physical Features of Social Housing

In Britain most social housing properties are easy to recognize. The exception is the early council housing projects completed before World War II, which look similar to private properties of the same age. The physical appearance of the majority of postwar social housing schemes was very distinct from other neighborhoods because of several features.

First, many social housing estates were located outside of existing urban areas or far from city centers. Especially for large-scale housing estates, the location choice was typically either the periphery of a town or city, or separated from the city by a "greenfield" or wasteland. In some areas, particularly large industrial cities, social housing demand was extremely high and less land stock was controlled by local authorities. In Britain, every local authority had to meet the social housing demand by developing new construction in their own territory rather than relocating the tenants to surrounding rural areas (Dunleavy 1981). Therefore, many public housing projects had to be constructed on or near derelict land or abandoned industrial land, without easy accessibility to city centers.

The second feature that distinguishes social housing is its high density. The high-rise was very popular in public housing projects in the 1950s and 1960s because of the introduction of new construction technologies and increased state

TABLE 12.1

Housing in the U.K., 2004

	England	Scotland	Wales	N. Ireland
Population (in millions)	49	5	2.9	1.7
Tenure (%)				
Homeowners (%)	71	65	73	70
Private rental (%)	10	6	9	8
Local authority or housing executive (%)	11	20	14	19
Housing association (%)	8	7	4	3
Social housing in total (%)	19	27	18	22
Unfitness (%)	4	1	8.5	4.9
Overcrowding[a] (%)	2	3	3	3.8

SOURCE: Adapted from Office for National Statistics, 2005; Northern Ireland Housing Executive, 2003.
NOTES: Data for Northern Ireland cover up to 2003. [a] Less than one room per capita.

subsidies for high-rises (Zhang 2000; Dunleavy 1981). The peak time of the subsidized high-rise development was the middle years of the 1960s. In every year from 1958 to 1969, over 10 percent of newly completed housing units were in high-rise blocks (defined as six stories and over), and between 1963 and 1967, the proportion was higher than 20 percent. In 1967 the number of completed buildings of high-rise housing reached about 39,300 (in England and Wales), which was 29 percent of all public housing stock, compared with only 3 percent in 1953 (Gittus 1976). In later years, most of the high-rise apartments were not sold to private sectors and occupied a considerable proportion of remaining social housing stock.

The third feature that distinguishes social housing is the wide application of repeated design principles, of both the layout of buildings and the exterior and interior design of the units (Dekker et al. 2005). Most projects were built with wide use of prefabricated components, such as kitchen, toilets, and precast concrete panels produced by "housing factories." Scale merit (economics of scale) was successfully achieved through repeating production of the uniform components. The "international style" of housing design created huge boxes as either slabs or towers, almost always without decoration or amenities (figures 12.1 and 12.2). The launch of a series of minimum standards for public housing conditions—for example, the Parker Morris standard and application of the Housing Cost Yardstick, which specified expenditure ceilings—also contributed to the standardized housing design (Ministry of Housing and Local Government 1961). Malpass and Murie (1999) describe the result: "First, Parker Morris standards soon ceased to be minima but became maxima to be aimed at within limited resources, and second, in order to escape the pincer some most unsatisfactory design solutions were produced to what was a highly artificial problem."

Most infrastructure and neighborhood facilities in social housing projects were allocated by master plans in a rational way. The schools, clinics, pubs, clubs, libraries, retail units, and playgrounds for children, plus the transformer substations, parking spaces, and rubbish collecting points, were almost all constructed with the support of public funds. The initial plans had high standards for allocating such facilities, but in reality the facilities were almost always completed far behind schedule. Also the universal allocations were often out of sync with the real needs of local communities.

Beginning in the late 1970s, the physical condition of most social housing projects declined significantly. Water penetration, poor functioning lighting systems, defective heating systems, leaking roofs, and crumbling plasterwork were the most common problems. Many parts of the collective properties, such as corridors, elevators, stairs, and other infrastructure were more poorly maintained than the dwellings themselves. The poor maintenance might be attributed to a lack of experience of service provision in the early years, but after the 1970s, cuts of public financial support for housing maintenance made the situation worse. Also, as some researchers have argued, the under-monitored collective spaces, dark corners, stairs, and underground garages attracted criminal and antisocial behavior (Newman 1973; Coleman 1985). These poorly maintained properties became residual to the housing market, and the increasing number of empty units provided more neglected spaces and attracted squatters (figure 12.3).

Park Hill Estate at Sheffield: A Typical Example of High-Rise Social Housing in the 1960s

Layout of Park Hill Estate at Sheffield

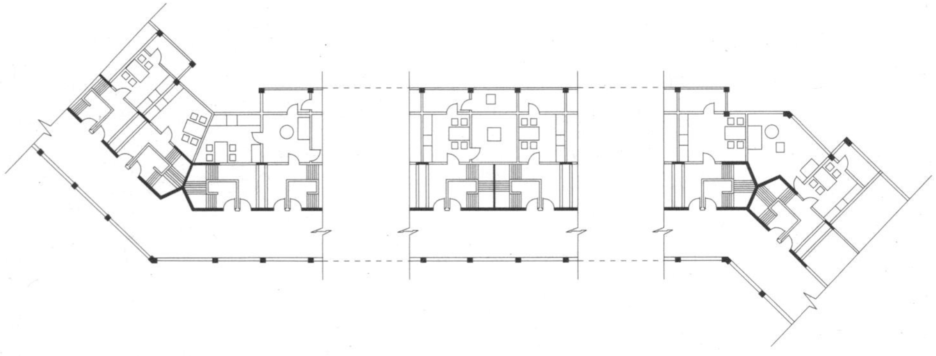

SOURCE: The Courtauld Institute of Art. http://www.artandarchitecture.org.uk.

Social Profiles

Social housing projects were initially conceived as egalitarian shelters to house the homogenous working class and other mainstream social groups. British local authorities owned most social housing stock. At that time, the authorities also held the right to select tenants from the application list. The principles of the selection were to ensure, first, that the public subsidy went to families who really needed the help and were financially excluded by the housing market; and, second, that the tenants be "respectable" and able to pay their rent and look after the property.

FIGURE 12.3

Social Housing with Closed Shops and Damaged Units

Usually, married working-class couples with secure jobs were the first to move in, while single people and recently settled migrant workers received the lowest priority (Turkington 2004). As a result, the social profiles of the initial tenants were homogenous. A large proportion of them were young, married, and employed. In some slum clearance projects, neighbors were rehoused next door to each other so the cohesion of the original community could be preserved.

When the general housing shortage was eased after the mid-1960s, the social profiles of these housing estates began to change. The wealthier tenants purchased homes in better locations and moved out of social housing. The launch of the "Right to Buy" scheme in 1980 accelerated the change. Most buyers were younger, more educated, and had secure incomes. The unsold social housing properties were usually located in less desirable areas, with a higher concentration of vulnerable groups, including the elderly, single parents, and disabled, unemployed, and low-income people (Power 1993; Dunleavy 1981; Forrest and Murie 1983; Murie 1983; Malpass 1990). Figure 12.4 shows that fewer social housing residents were employed and that the change just after the launch of "Right to Buy" is most significant. Figure 12.5 compares the employment status of the tenants in the social rental sector and mortgaged households, which also reveals the gradual downward social restructuring of the tenants.

Social Housing in China

Social Housing and Its Development

The social housing development in China emerged much later than in Britain and other Western countries because of its late industrialization and urbanization. Until the early twentieth century most Chinese cities were still formed of traditional neighborhoods where households lived in their own or private rental dwellings. In the 1920s and 1930s the central and some local governments launched ambitious master plans for some large cities (such as Nanjing, the national capital, and Shanghai, the largest city), which included slum clearance and public housing schemes. However, because of poor public finance and later wars, none of the schemes became a reality.

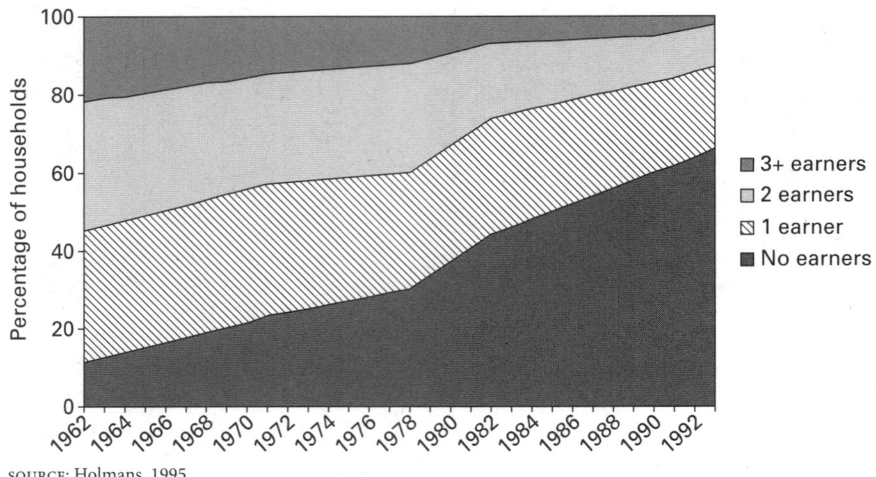

FIGURE 12.4

Council Tenants by Number of Earners in the Household, 1962–1993

SOURCE: Holmans, 1995.

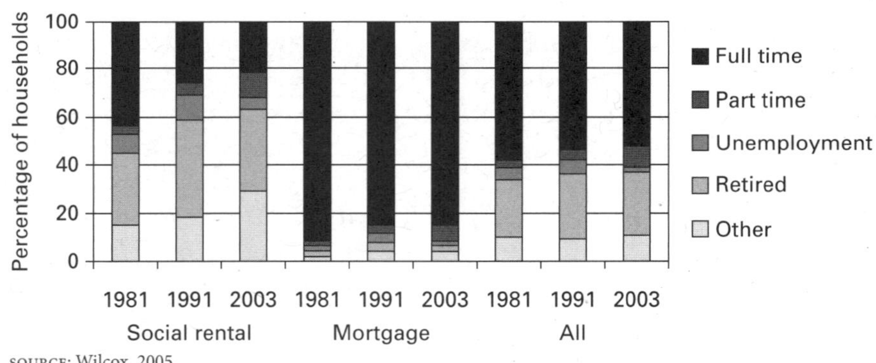

FIGURE 12.5

Employment Status of Household Head by Tenure, 1981–2003

SOURCE: Wilcox, 2005.

Large-scale public housing development started after the Chinese Communist Party established a socialist state in 1949. According to the socialist ideology, housing was not a commodity but a type of social welfare to be provided by the state (Chu and Kwok 1990; Wang and Murie 1999; Zhang and Wang 2001). Thus private developers and a housing market were no longer permitted. The majority of properties owned by big landlords were nationalized, and the disposal and rent setting of the remaining privately owned houses were greatly restricted (Wang 1992). New housing provision was all in the public sector. By the end of the 1970s, private-sector housing had declined to about 10 percent of the total urban housing stock (Chen 1994, 24; Whyte and Parish 1984).

There was no single mechanism for public housing provision in China. Usually, municipal housing authorities and employers (work units or *danwei*) were the two major providers (Wang 1995; Wang and Murie 1999). For municipal housing projects, the cost of housing development and maintenance came directly from state funds. The cost of work-unit housing development also came from public funds, but employers usually had autonomy to decide how to use those funds. In both systems, public funds paid almost all the costs of the process—of land acquisition, housing construction, and maintenance after completion. The tenants had to pay only a nominal rent.

The social housing system in China existed in urban areas only. After the *hukou* system was introduced in 1958, rural populations were restricted from work and life in cities (Chan 1996; Goldstein and Goldstein 1994). Public housing was accessible only to registered urban residents (about 12–18 percent of the national population from the 1950s to the 1970s). Even to registered urban households, however, the inequality of housing provision was apparent (Zhou and Logan 1996; Walder 1986). For municipal housing, the level of funding depended in part on the bargaining ability of regional leaders with the central planning and housing ministries (Struyk 1996). The distribution of public funds for work-unit housing was also not egalitarian; usually, "key" work units—for example, advanced enterprises of favored industries or high-ranked government institutes—received more public funds and additional resources (for example, the use rights of extra land) (Wu 1996, 1607). As a consequence, the better houses were allocated disproportionately to the elite among party leaders, government officials, and managers of state-owned enterprises. The provision to workers or other underclass members was far behind schedule in almost all Chinese cities. Also, the quality of public housing significantly varied according to the level of the tenants.

Although social housing development in Chinese cities was on a limited scale, public finance could not support a sufficient supply to meet housing demands. The first national housing survey, conducted in 1985, revealed that over 28 percent of urban households experienced housing problems: 870,000 were classified as homeless;[1] over 3 million lived in inconvenient conditions with one or two families in one room; and another 3.5 million had less than 4 square meters of average floor space per person (National Bureau of Statistics of China 1989). Facing this almost insurmountable problem, Chinese policy makers began to search for alternative ways to quickly increase the housing supply.

In the late 1980s experimental housing reforms were introduced in several cities. Reform policies included rent increases in the public sector coupled with the sale of public housing (Wang and Murie 1996). The publication of the *Implementation Plan for a Gradual Housing System Reform in Cities and Towns* by the State Council (1988) confirmed the success of those experiments and required the reforms to be carried out in all cities. This led to the large-scale sale of existing public housing at very low prices in a very short time. In 1991, the housing market in Chinese cities was legally reintroduced, and private capital, including foreign investment, was encouraged to contribute to new commercial housing development in order to help tackle the severe housing shortage. In 1994 new policies were issued with the aim

---

[1] Homelessness was defined as no home after marriage, living in nonhousing buildings, or living with relatives.

of establishing a new urban housing system. This led to a unique dual-track housing provision system, in which social housing continued to exist (on a reduced scale) to house middle- and low-income households, while high-income families could purchase commercial housing from private developers (Housing Reform Steering Group of the State Council 1994).

The milestone document of further housing reform was introduced in July 1998, *The Notice of Further Reform of the Urban Housing System and Speeding Up Housing Construction* (State Council 1998). This ended public housing distribution by work units. Instead, all new social housing development was to be handled by local authorities. Approximately 70 percent of urban households were expected to buy economical comfortable housing (ECH; *jingji shiyong fang*), which would be developed with public financial support. Fifteen percent of low-income families could apply for low-rent housing (LRH; *lianzu fang*), which together with ECH formed a new social housing system. The top 15 percent high-income urban households were encouraged to obtain high-standard commercial housing through the market (Wang 2001). In later years, in contrast to the overheating commercial housing market, the establishment of new government-supported social housing was seriously delayed in most cities. The nationwide provision of ECH was always low, and the rate kept dropping (table 12.2). In Shanghai City there was no ECH program at all until 2006, and in Guangdong Province ECH housing was only 0.5 percent of the overall housing supply in the same year (Wang, Shao, and Cheng 2009). In Beijing, the proportion of ECH housing dropped from over 16 percent in 1999 to approximately 6 percent in 2006 (Zhang and Li 2009).

The overmarketized housing system made implementation of the initial target of the 1998 reform unrealistic. By a radical privatization process, the proportion of the social housing stock in the Chinese urban housing system was greatly reduced. In 1981, over 82 percent of urban housing was in public ownership (53.5 percent owned by work units and 28.7 percent by municipal housing authorities); and private housing was only about 17.8 percent (Editors Committee of *Almanac of China's Economy* 1983). By 2003, over 82 percent of urban housing was privately owned (Liu 2003). More urban households are now excluded from the commercial housing supply because of rising housing prices, and few of them get essential help from the insufficient new social housing supply. Housing inequality and affordability have become urgent problems in contemporary Chinese society (Wang 2001; Wang and Murie 2000). As a response, on 20 December 2008, another major housing policy document was published by the General Office of the State Council (2008), *Some Suggestions on Promotion of the Healthy Development of the Housing and Property Market,* which aimed to bolster social housing development with stronger support of public finance.

The central government promised to increase its contributions to social housing and slum redevelopment programs. Local governments were required to increase their social housing supply and ensure a land supply for social housing projects. Commercial banks were encouraged to increase their lending to social housing development projects. A new ambitious plan has been issued to accelerate social housing development in three years (table 12.3). By reemphasizing the role of the social housing sector, a new balanced housing system is expected to be formed.

TABLE 12.2

Housing Units Built in China, 1999–2006

| | | Government-Supported ECH | |
Year	All Housing Units (in thousands)	Units (in thousands)	As Percent of All Housing
1999	1,946.4	485.0	24.9
2000	2,139.7	603.6	28.2
2001	2,414.4	604.8	25.0
2002	2,629.6	538.5	20.5
2003	3,021.1	447.7	14.8
2004	4,042.2	497.5	12.3
2005	3,682.5	287.3	7.8
2006	4,005.3	338.0	8.4

SOURCE: National Bureau of Statistics of China, 2007.

TABLE 12.3

State Council Social Housing Development Plan, 2009–2011

	2009	2010–2011	Total
Low-rent housing (million units)	3.4	6.47	9.87
Economical comfortable housing (million units)	n/a	n/a	1.30
Total households benefited			11.17

SOURCE: General Office of the State Council, 2008.

Physical Features

In China many old social housing estates, in contrast to the British projects, were normally not far from city centers. The majority of work units constructed public housing for their employees near their workplaces. The residential areas, together with the offices and workshops, were usually enclosed by a wall to exclude outsiders and facilitate internal management. Municipal public housing was usually not large in scale, as opposed to the redevelopment projects of some of the worst traditional residential areas. Public housing renewal projects were constructed on site to accommodate original residents. Some residents were relocated, but the new municipal housing estates were usually beside city centers to make access to infrastructure easier. In later years, with the expansion of urban areas, the locations of most old social housing estates became more favorable and allowed better accessibility to city centers. However, after 1998 most new social housing projects developed by local authorities in China began to copy the earlier British practice. To acquire cheaper land, most large-scale social housing projects were located quite a distance from existing urban areas. In many it was also very inconvenient to access an urban public transport system.

From early on, the multistory style was very popular in Chinese social housing construction. Until the 1980s, however, high-rise housing was developed in a very conservative way. *The Technical Provision of Housing Construction* (Ministry of

Construction 1985) clearly stipulated that urban housing should primarily follow the multistory style (no more than six stories and without elevators), and the construction of high-rise housing blocks with more than six stories should be under strict control. The high-rise buildings were permitted only in specially designated sites in cities to save land when adequate technical equipment was provided (Zhang 1990). Thus between the 1950s and 1980s, apartments of three to six stories were the most common social housing products, but after 1998 the density of new social housing increased radically. The housing block with elevators was introduced and widely applied, forming "concrete jungles" to ensure the faster growth in quantity. Further, these large-scale housing estates lacked a mixed land use. In Shenzhen City up to 2004, 98.1 percent of social housing tenants lived in estates with a construction area of over 10,000 square meters, and 67.0 percent lived in estates with a construction area of over 100,000 square meters (Shenzhen Land and Housing Bureau 2005). In Beijing, the largest social housing estate, Huilongguan, was planned to accommodate 230,000 people.

The standardized housing design was also widely applied in Chinese social housing. In the era of the planned economy, public housing distribution was regarded as a kind of welfare for individuals, so the housing standard included several grades for different target groups (table 12.4). The maximum floor space, number of rooms in each unit, and standards of interior facilities were strictly controlled. Although the national standard provided a basic framework to direct public housing design and encouraged diversification, in practice the restrictions of time and cost forced designers to choose the most typical layouts. Thus, thousands of families shared the same layout, no matter what their family structure and lifestyle might be. The housing standard was relatively poor from the 1950s to 1970s; after the 1980s it was improved many times as China entered a period of economic growth. For the new generation of social housing projects after 1998, there was no longer a national standard. Many housing units were constructed according to a high standard. From 1999 to 2007, the average floor space in newly completed social housing in Beijing was approximately 110 square meters, which was very near the figure for commercial housing (Zhang and Li 2009). But in every housing project, one or more "typical" layouts were still frequently repeated. In contrast to the highly diverse commercial housing estates, with many architectural

TABLE 12.4

Floor Space per Household Under National Public Housing Standard, 1981

Targeted Household	Maximum Floor Space (in m²)
Families of employees of factories and mines	42–45
Families of ordinary cadres	45–50
Families of intellectuals with intermediate academic title and of principal heads and deputy heads at county government level	60–70
Families of high-ranking intellectuals and cadres at bureau director level	80–90

SOURCE: State Council, 1981.

innovations, the appearance of social housing was much more monotonous and boring (figure 12.6).

There was also a very detailed national standard for the allocation of neighborhood facilities in Chinese social housing projects since the 1950s. These planned facilities were believed to fully cover all the basic daily needs of local communities and included seven categories: education, health services, economic services, leisure and sports, shopping, community management, and infrastructure. The standardized requirement was presented by the "thousand-person indicator"[2] (table 12.5). After their completion, most social services were managed by public agencies. But after the economic reform of the 1980s, provision of neighborhood services, except education and health care, was commercialized and operated by private agencies. For those housing estates with favorable locations and high population density, the private service provision was adequate. In new social housing estates after 1998, the thousand-person indicator was still a compulsory reference for planning. In practice, however, the completion of many important facilities was seriously delayed—especially the education and health care facilities, which were still supported by insufficient public investment.

Social Profiles

Before the 1998 reform, the tenants of Chinese social housing were selected in the same top-down way the tenants of British social housing had been in the past. But their social profiles were totally different. First, because of the *hukou* system, only

FIGURE 12.6

Huilongguan: A Typical Large-Scale Social Housing Project

---

[2] "Thousand-person indicator" refers to the quantity of public facilities and infrastructures for one thousand people, and is set up by the planning bureaus.

TABLE 12.5

Required Neighborhood Facilities per 1,000 Residents, 1980

Facilities Category	Facility	Number of Facilities	Construction Area (m^2/1,000 people)	Land Use Area (m^2/1,000 people)
Education	Nursery	8–10 seats	32–60	
	Kindergarten	12–15 seats	72–120	144–210
	Primary school	175–270 seats		490–900
	Middle school	80–100 seats	280–400	960–1,500
	Total		559–850	
Health services	Hospital	3–3.5 beds	129–169	240–300
	Clinic	14–15 seats	18–22.5	27–33.8
	Total		147–191.5	267–333.8
Economic services	Bank branch		14–15	
	Post office		25–30	40–50
	Total		39–45	
Leisure and sports	Cinema	36–37.5 seats	56–72	90–114
	Museum	18.5 seats	60–62.5	
	Youth club		20	60
	Athletic field		136–154.5	
	Total		n/a	200–300
Shopping and daily services	Department store		40–50	
	Bookstore		8–10	
	Pharmacy		10	
	Food shop		18	
	Grocery		7–8	27
	Restaurant		15–16	
	Fast-food shop		7.5–14	
	Takeout shop		6.5–12	
	Food open market			22.5–24
	Photo shop	3–3.2 seats	40–45	
	Hair salon	1.9–4.4 seats	4	
	Public bathroom	1.6–3 seats	5	
	Laundry		25	
	Tailor		2–3	
	Appliance fixing		6–8	
	Recycling center		5	10
	Coal shop		2.5–3	20–25
	Total		389–535	
Community management	Management committee		20	
	Housing management office		20–25	
	Total		40–45	
Infrastructure	Transformer substation		12–14	
	Public toilet		3–6	
	Rubbish station			1.5–2
	Total		15–20	

SOURCE: National Construction Committee, 1980.

registered urban households were qualified for social housing. In such a populous and poor country as China, the government used *hukou* as a way to restrain the increase of the urban population and control the public financial burden of housing development. This meant that the rural population, which was over 80 percent from the 1950s to the 1970s, was excluded from the social housing system. Second, the microscale social status in the social housing estates was usually highly homogenous. In municipal or work-unit housing, the employees of the same organization would be neighbors in the same building, or the people living in a particular building could share the same or similar jobs. Some housing estates were even called "professor buildings," "teacher villages," or "doctor mansions." Residents could communicate easily in the neighborhood and in their workplaces. They held similar ideas, and it was often easy to find some common public interests. Many formed gated, specialized communities, which had higher cohesion and fewer troubles in public affairs.

The homogenous social structure began to change after the housing reform moved toward privatization. Many richer households purchased higher-quality commercial properties and moved out. They sold or rented the old properties. Thus, the downward social restructuring that followed was inevitable. However, in individual details, the social profiles of tenants in different housing estates varied greatly. The units of some high-quality estates were still very competitive in the housing market, and many middle-class households chose to reside there and enjoy the good location and sufficient facilities. But in the older estates with lower housing standards, most new tenants were from low-income groups, who could not afford to buy their own homes on the market. Some other tenants were newly arriving migrants, part of the "floating population" in large cities, with temporary jobs or still looking for jobs. The family structures, economic conditions, jobs, lifestyles, and personal preferences of the new migrants differed greatly from those of their neighbors. In many public affairs, they did not trust each other, and it was difficult for them to find a common understanding. Many signs of declining community cohesion and threats of crime and social unrest have since emerged.

The launch of China's new social housing schemes after 1998 initially followed ideas similar to those of British social housing. The government aimed to provide egalitarian houses to not only the low-income but also to the mainstream social groups who could not afford the housing prices on the market. But because it was not clear who qualified to apply for the new kind of social housing, many units were sold to richer people. In Beijing, 49 percent of the buyers of ECH had other private properties, and 26 percent were, in fact, from high-income groups. On the other hand, 52.7 percent of households in Beijing who found it difficult to afford commercial housing were still excluded from the social housing system (Zhang and Li 2009). As a result, the current tenants of the new social housing estates include high proportions of government staff, white-collar workers, doctors, teachers, and other middle-class people. A large percentage of low-income and vulnerable groups are still excluded from the social housing provision and usually have to live in low-quality, private rental houses or informal temporary shelters, suffering below-average living conditions.

Comparison

The history of social housing development in Britain is about one century longer than that in China. However, they both followed a similar trajectory. In both countries, social housing initially emerged as a reflection of a left-wing political ideology, that decent and affordable housing should be seen not as a private asset and commodity but as a basic necessity for all people; therefore, the power of governments should be used to develop nonprofit housing projects. In the early years, public authorities controlled the development process in a top-down way in order that quantitative growth of social housing could be achieved in a short time. After several decades, social housing occupied a high proportion of all housing stock.

In recent years the role of social housing became sidelined in both countries. After a series of reforms, more and more existing public housing stock was transferred to the ownership of private and voluntary organizations, and the provision of new social housing shrunk greatly. The reforms resulted in the significant improvement of living conditions for many well-to-do households, but housing affordability and inequality emerged as new problems at the same time. The crisis has become impossible to ignore and widely regarded as a potential cause of social unrest. Hence, the role of social housing has been reemphasized with the intention of introducing social equity again.

Among the details of this zigzag trajectory are many differences between the experiences of Britain and China. The shifts of social housing policy in China have been more extreme. Over a period of about 50 years (1920s–1970s), social housing in Britain increased from below 10 percent to about 30 percent of total housing stock; after the 1980s the proportion gradually dropped to below 20 percent. In China, the communist authority nationalized private properties for about 30 years, and social housing increased from a small percentage in the 1950s to over 80 percent in the early 1980s. Then after 20 years of privatization since the late 1980s, more than 80 percent of the urban housing stock became privately owned. Such sudden changes may have helped to cover some urgent housing problems in the short term, but they greatly affected the stability of the housing market and the sustainability of the housing system in the long term. As a result, the government has had to re-expand the social housing sector about 10 years after the radical housing reforms initiated in 1998.

In Britain the distribution of social housing was always managed in an egalitarian way. Although regional and demographic inequalities existed, the gaps were never very large. In China, however, the benefits of social housing were seldom equally distributed. For a long period, social housing was accessible only to the urban population, not the whole society. Among social housing tenants, institutional inequality, caused by the fragmented housing provision, was everywhere. In the universal provision of new social housing after 1998, inequality was still significant because of the lack of effective regulations to define qualified beneficiaries. Usually, the elite groups gained more, and the most vulnerable groups were excluded from the social housing distribution. This greatly reduced the contribution of social housing in enhancing social equity. Fortunately, in recent years, the nature of social housing has been rethought in China. After the issue of *Some Suggestions to Solve the Housing Problems of Urban Low-Income Families* (State Council 2007), social housing has been expected to better meet the demand of low-income and vulnerable families.

Physical Features

Many British social housing estates, especially the ones developed in the immediate postwar years, reflect the image of an ideal urban environment proposed by architects and planners at that time. They include spacious apartments in multi-family blocks with large public green spaces around them; wide application of standardized housing designs; residential areas placed far away from workplaces; and service centers and other facilities rationally allocated nearby. These may well have met most requirements of the target households when the estates were completed, but several decades later, these peripheral large-scale housing estates with countless monotonous box-like buildings and without mixed land use fail to attract the new generation of tenants. Those physical features are a significant reason for the residualization of the remaining social housing stock.

In China the standardized housing design was also very popular in most social housing projects. But for the projects developed before the 1990s, there were significant differences compared to British social housing. In China's fragmented housing provision system, there were not as many large-scale projects. There were not many housing estates on the far periphery, and most, especially the ones developed by work units, were very close to the tenants' workplaces. Also, because many of them were developed for elite groups, the infrastructures and neighborhood facilities were installed with high standards. These features kept the previous social housing estates in China from experiencing a radical residualization process after privatization.

Many features of the British social housing were repeated in the new social housing estates developed after 1998 in China: the peripheral locations, the large scale without a mixture of uses, insufficient facilities, and poor accessibility to workplaces and social services. Many surveys in the typical large-scale peripheral estates such as Huilongguan in Beijing have shown that those characteristics have greatly affected the living conditions of local households (Zhang et al. 2006). It is a pity that the British mistakes are being repeated in current Chinese practice under the pressure of achieving quantitative growth of new social housing provision.

Conclusions

Compared with its long history in Britain, the development of social housing policy and practice is still in a very early stage in China. During the socialist planned economy almost all urban housing provision came from public-led nonprofit projects providing decent and affordable housing for a small group of urban elites. Social housing was, in fact, a reward for the elite groups rather than a safety net to ensure decent living conditions for all. In later periods of housing reform, when the majority of public housing was privatized in a radical way, the wealthier households gained more benefits. This led to the rapid polarization of housing distribution in

Chinese cities. Thus after 1998 a new round of social housing development was urgently needed. Just as in Britain several decades ago, quantitative growth was a top priority of the public-funded housing projects. Evidence has shown that the policy framework and the physical features of British social housing has been copied to a great extent in China. The rapid development may therefore lead to many social problems in the future. Most of these challenges are new to Chinese policy makers, but they have existed for years in Britain and have eventually been solved. Hence, the value of international experience through cross-national comparative research is obvious. Such systematic comparative research has produced the following suggestions.

First, China should be careful to avoid the development of large-scale peripheral social housing estates. The wide use of standardized designs should likewise be avoided, and a mixture of land uses is recommended. Currently, in China, a strong desire for quantitative growth could affect the quality of new social housing.

Many middle-class families live in huge peripheral estates because they have not had other choices when general housing affordability has been low, but in the future richer households will likely move and find new homes of higher quality. The concentration of vulnerable groups will then be inevitable, and many social problems will follow, which is the difficulty the managers of British social housing are facing now. Therefore for Chinese policy makers finding the balance between quantitative growth and qualitative improvement should (be) a priority.

Second, more flexibility should be used to develop new social housing projects. Recent British experience revealed that in the current fast-changing society, volunteer groups, local communities, and even private developers should be involved in developing different kinds of social housing projects to meet the requirements of diverse target groups. In China, the development of housing associations or other cooperative organizations should be encouraged. Many young Chinese white-collar workers are finding it difficult to afford market housing, even though they have good incomes, but do not want living conditions that are too low. Thus, the self-help development approach with limited public aid could be a realistic way to tackle housing shortages for this emerging social group.

Third, public participation in decision making in social housing policy and its implementation should be increased. In Chinese cities, the requirements of the target group of social housing will be highly diverse and dynamic. Hearing more voices from the target tenants can effectively avoid a mismatch between public-funded projects and tenants' real needs. Such participation would also enhance community interaction and local cohesion, which are critical in reducing the threats of social problems in the future.

Fourth, more research should be done in the areas of social housing policy and development. Compared with that in Britain, housing development in China is moving much faster, and policy changes are more frequent, while the number of housing researchers is much smaller. To improve its social housing development, China needs to invest more in housing research. Each of the implications and lessons from the British experience could be further studied so that more valuable ideas for practice could be implemented.

ACKNOWLEDGMENTS

The author would like to thank Professor Ya Ping Wang and Dr. Yun Qian from Heriot-Watt University for their insightful and constructive comments on the draft of this chapter.

REFERENCES

Barlow, James, and Simon Duncan. 1994. *Success and failure in housing provision: European states compared.* London: Pergamon.

Beijing Municipal Government. 2006. *Housing construction plan of Beijing (2006–2010).* http://www.bjghw.gov.cn/web/static/articles/catalog_30100/article_ff80808122dedb360 122eea9e5ae0043/ff80808122dedb360122eea9e5ae0043.html [in Chinese].

Boelhouwer, Peter, and Harry van der Heijden. 1992. *Housing SYSTEMS in Europe: Part I. A comparative study of housing policy.* Delft, The Netherlands: Delft University Press.

Bourne, Larry S. 1998. Social housing. In *The encyclopedia of housing,* ed. Willem Van Vliet. Thousand Oaks, CA: Sage.

Bowley, Marian. 1945. *Housing and the state 1919–1944.* London: Allen and Unwin.

Chan, Kam Wing. 1996. Post-Mao China: A two-class urban society in the making. *International Journal of Urban and Regional Research* 20:134–150.

Chen, Guang-Ting. 1994. The housing question of China. In *The challenge of China's urban housing,* eds. Guang-Ting Chen and Marc H. Choko, 9–28. Beijing: Beijing Science and Technology Press [in Chinese].

Chu, David K. Y. and Reginald Yin-Wand Kwok. 1990. China. In *International Handbook of Housing Policies and Practices,* ed. Willen van Vliet. New York: Greenwood Press.

Coleman, Alice. 1985. *Utopia on trial: Vision and reality in planned housing.* London: Shipman.

Davis, John Emmeus. 1998. Housing tenures. In *The encyclopedia of housing,* ed. Willem Van Vliet. Thousand Oaks, CA: Sage.

Dekker, Karien, Stephen Hall, Ronald van Kempen, and Ivan Tosics. 2005. Restructuring large housing estates in European cities: An introduction. In *Restructuring large housing estates in Europe,* eds. Ronald van Kempen, Karien Dekker, Stephen Hall, and Ivan Tosics. Bristol, U.K.: Policy Press.

Department of the Environment. 1987. *Housing: The government's proposals.* London: Her Majesty's Stationery Office (HMSO).

Dickens, Peter, Simon Duncan, Mark Goodwin, and Fred Gray. 1985. *Housing, states and localities.* London: Methuen.

Doling, John. 1997. *Comparative housing policy: Government and housing in advanced industrialized countries.* Basingstoke, U.K.: MacMillan.

Dunleavy, Patrick. 1981. *The politics of mass housing, 1945–1975: A study of corporate power and professional influence in the welfare state.* Oxford: Clarendon Press.

Editors Committee of the Almanac of China's Economy. 1983. *Almanac of China's economy.* Beijing: Beijing Economic Management Publishing House [in Chinese].

Forrest, Ray, and Alan Murie. 1983. Residualization and council housing: Aspects of the changing social relations of housing tenure. *Journal of Social Policy* 12(4):453–468.

Gaudie, Enid. 1974. *Cruel habitations: A history of working class housing 1780–1918.* London: Allen and Unwin.

General Office of the State Council. 2008. *Some suggestions on promotion of the healthy development of housing and property market.* Document No. 131. Beijing [in Chinese].

Gittus, Elizabeth. 1976. *Flats, families and the under fives,* London: Routledge & Kegan Paul.

Glynn, Sean, and John Oxborrow. 1976. *Interwar Britain: A social and economic history.* London: Allen and Unwin.

Goldstein, Alice, and Sidney Goldstein. 1994. Permanent and temporary migration differentials. In *Migration and urbanization in China,* eds. Lincoln H. Day and Ma Xia, 43–88. Armonk, NY: M. E. Sharpe.

Hantrais, Linda, and Stephen Mangen. 1996. Method and management of cross-national social research. In *Cross-national research methods in the social sciences,* eds. Linda Hantrais and Stephen Mangen. London: Pinter.

Harloe, Michael 1995. *The people's home? Social rented housing in Europe and America.* Oxford: Blackwell.

Holmans, Alan. 1995. *Housing demand and need in England, 1991–2011.* York, U.K.: Joseph Rowntree Foundation.

Housing Reform Steering Group of the State Council. 1994. The decision on deepening urban housing reform. In *Urban housing system reform,* eds. Housing Reform Steering Group of the State Council. Beijing: Reform Press [in Chinese].

Jefferies, Julie. 2005. The U.K. population: Past, present and future. London: Office for National Statistics. http://www.statistics.gov.uk/downloads/theme_compendia/fom2005/01_fopm_population.pdf.

Kemeny, Jim. 1992. *Housing and social theory.* London: Routledge.

Liu, Zhifeng. 2003. *Promote healthy and sustained development of housing and real estate.* Speech presented at the 2003 Annual Housing and Property Conference, Wuhan (January 13) [in Chinese].

Lund, Brian. 2002. *Understanding state welfare.* London: Sage.

———. 2006. *Understanding housing policy.* Bristol, U.K.: Policy Press.

Malpass, Peter. 1990. *Reshaping housing policy: Subsidies, rent and residualisation.* London: Routledge.

Malpass, Peter, and Alan Murie. 1999. *Housing policy and practice,* 5th ed. London: MacMillan.

Merrett, Stephen. 1976. *State housing in Britain.* London: Routledge and Kegan Paul.

Ministry of Construction. 1985. *The technical provision of housing construction.* Beijing [in Chinese].

Ministry of Housing and Local Government. 1961. *Homes for today and tomorrow.* Parker Morris Report. London: Her Majesty's Stationery Office (HMSO).

Morton, Jane. 1991. *Cheaper than Peabody: Local authority housing from 1890 to 1919.* York, U.K.: Joseph Rowntree Foundation.

Murie, Alan. 1983. *Housing inequality and deprivation.* London: Heinemann.

National Bureau of Statistics of China. 1989. *China Statistical Yearbook 1989.* Beijing: China Statistics Press [in Chinese].

National Bureau of Statistics of China. 2007. *China Statistical Yearbook,* tables 6–42. www.stats.gov.cn [in Chinese].

National Construction Committee. 1980. *Interim regulation of rational indicators in urban planning.* Beijing [in Chinese].

Newman, Oscar. 1973. *Defensible space: People and design in the violent city.* London: Architectural Press.

Northern Ireland Housing Executive. 2003. *Annual report 2002/03.* Belfast.

Office of the Deputy Prime Minister. 2004. *Annual Report 2004.* London: Stationery Office.

Office for National Statistics. 2005. *Regional trends 38.* London: Stationery Office. http://www.statistics.gov.uk/downloads/theme_compendia/Regional_Trends_38/rt38.pdf.

Orbach, Laurence. 1977. *Homes for heroes.* London: Seely Service.

Øyen, Else. 1990. The imperfections of comparisons. In *Comparative methodology: Theory and practice in international social research,* ed. Else Øyen, 1–18. London: Sage.

Power, Anne. 1993. *Hovels to high rise: State housing in Europe since 1850.* London: Routledge.

Rowntree, Benjamin Seebohm. 1941. *Poverty and progress: A second social survey of York.* London: Longman.

Shenzhen Land and Housing Bureau. 2005. *Shenzhen real estate statistical yearbook.* Shenzhen: Haitian Press [in Chinese].

State Council. 1981. *Regulations on the design standards of workers' housing and supplementary regulations.* Beijing [in Chinese].

———. 1988. *Implementation plan for a gradual housing system reform in cities and towns.* Document No. 11. Beijing [in Chinese].

———. 1998. *The notice of further reform of the urban housing system and speeding up housing development.* Document No. 23, July 3. Beijing [in Chinese].

———. 2007. *Some suggestions to solve the housing problems of urban low-income families.* Beijing [in Chinese].

Struyk, Raymond J. 1996. The long road to the market. In *Economic restructuring of the former Soviet Bloc: The case of housing,* ed. Raymond J. Struyk. Washington, DC: Urban Institute Press.

Tarn, John Nelson. 1971. *Working-class housing in 19th-century Britain.* London: Lund Hampshires.

Turkington, Richard. 2004. Britain: High-rise housing as a "doubtful guest." In *High-rise housing in Europe: Current trends and future prospects,* eds. Richard Turkington, Ronald van Kempen, and Frank Wassenburg, 147–164. Delft, The Netherlands: Delft University Press.

Walder, Andrew G. 1986. *Communist neo-traditionalism: Work and authority in Chinese industry.* Berkeley: University of California Press.

Wang, Ya Ping 1992. Private sector housing in urban China since 1949: The case of Xian. *Housing Studies* 7(2):119–137.

———. 1995. Public sector housing in urban China since 1949: The case of Xian. *Housing Studies* 10(1):57–82.

———. 2001. Urban housing reform and finance in China: A case study of Beijing. *Urban Affairs Review* 36(5):620–645.

Wang, Ya Ping, and Alan Murie. 1996. The process of commercialization of urban housing in China. *Urban Studies* 33(6):971–989.

———. 1999. *Housing policy and practice in China.* London: MacMillan.

———. 2000. Social and spatial implications of housing reform in China. *International Journal of Urban and Regional Research* 24(2):397–417.

Wang, Ya Ping, Lei Shao, and Jianhua Cheng. 2009. Continuing housing reform in China: Managing affordability and market stability. Paper presented at the International Symposium on Housing Affordability and Market Stability, Tsinghua University, Beijing (March 24–27).

Whyte, Martin King, and William L. Parish. 1984. *Urban life in contemporary China.* Chicago: University of Chicago Press.

Wilcox, Steve. 2005. *U.K. housing review 2004/5.* London: Charted Institute of Housing.

Wu, Fulong. 1996. Changes in the structure of public housing provision in urban China. *Urban Studies* 33(9):1601–1627.

Zhang, Jie. 2000. Housing conditions in post-industrial period in Britain. *World Architecture* 5:16–20 [in Chinese].

Zhang, Jie, and Li Li. 2009. Ten-year housing development in Beijing: 1998–2008. Paper presented at the International Symposium on Housing Affordability and Market Stability, Tsinghua University, Beijing (March 24–27).

Zhang, Jie, and Tao Wang. 2001. Housing development in the socialist planned economy from 1949 to 1978. In *Modern urban housing in China, 1840–2000,* eds. Junhua Lv, Peter G. Rowe, and Jie Zhang. Munich: Prestel.

Zhang, Kaiji. 1990. Multiple-floor or high-rise: Controversy on high-density housing construction. *Journal of Architecture* 2:2–5 [in Chinese].

Zhang, Wenzhong, Weihong Yin, Jinqiu Zhang, Bin Meng, and Xiaolu Gao. 2006. *A study of livable cities in China.* Beijing: Social Science Academic Press.

Zhou, Min, and John R. Logan. 1996. Market transition and the commodification of housing in urban China. *International Journal of Urban and Regional Research* 20(3):400–421.

A Systemic View of Housing Policy for China's New Urban Era

13

BERTRAND RENAUD

In its transition from plan to market, the Chinese urban economy has entered a new stage of development, which calls for urban and housing policies adapted to this new environment. During the period from 1979 to 1992, China extricated itself gradually from the grip of administrative-command institutions by relying on a bottom-up, dual-track reform approach (*shuangguizhi*) to benefit all. During a second phase of reforms, from 1993 to the present global financial crisis, China recentralized its public institutions to achieve greater macroeconomic stability, restructuring key sectors such as banking and state-owned enterprises. It invested heavily in infrastructure and opened its cities to export-oriented foreign direct investment activities that rapidly increased China's share of the global economy. In the midst of the Asian financial crisis of 1997–1998, China made the major strategic decision to privatize urban housing, which profoundly stimulated the economy of cities during uncertain times. The very high economic growth and rapid urbanization of this second period greatly reduced absolute poverty, but the high growth unequally benefited regions, cities, and social groups.

Presently, China is going through a major inflection point in its urban trajectory: The country has entered the peak phase of urbanization in its history. Unexpectedly, in the middle of the 11th Economic Plan, the global financial and economic crisis has suddenly intensified the need to rebalance China's economy toward domestic demand and significantly improve both the quality and the equity of urban growth. This need was already well recognized by the current plan before the global shock caused by the financial crisis, but important reforms that affect the dynamics of cities have to be speeded up and successfully coordinated.

There is a close functional relationship between urbanization and economic development that is now widely accepted by economists and policy makers.[1] Rural-urban migration is dominating this era of peak urbanization much more than the redrawing of administrative boundaries, which frequently increased the administrative size of cities during the previous two stages of China's urbanization. The successful integration of migrants into its cities will be central to the positive transformation of Chinese society.

This chapter is written from two related perspectives. First, the pursuit of a sound and successful low-income housing policy cannot be dissociated from the overall performance of the housing system. Second, it is economic growth and not access to housing that is the primary solution to poverty. China has been exceptionally successful in that regard over the past two decades. China's economy has also reached another major transition stage, where it must be rebalanced in favor of domestic demand and endogenous growth. What are the cost-effective housing policies that are consistent with this economic rebalancing? How will this rebalancing work across China's very diverse system of cities?

The degree of success of any national low-income housing program is determined at the local level by demand and supply conditions in each individual city. Local housing demand conditions are shaped by the dynamics of the local economic base. If housing supply conditions are unrestricted, the local housing market will be healthy and the need for costly low-income public housing minimized. International experience clearly shows that in this new phase of urbanization an important factor in modernizing a city's local economic base and attracting new business activities will be whether local housing supply is restricted and distorted by poor land use and zoning regulations.

The ongoing global financial and economic crisis is much worse in scale, intensity, and complexity than was the Asia crisis of 1997–1998. The contraction of the global economy is placing pressure on all governments to stabilize their national economies and prevent the deterioration of living conditions for their low-income groups. The risk is that in the name of short-term stabilization, piecemeal and disconnected policy-making processes may lead governments to adopt policies that are harmful to the long-term soundness and sustainability of their housing system and of the performance of the wider economy.[2] What are the policy actions that China is pursuing under its economic stimulus program? Are they likely to be helpful, harmful, or neutral to China's long-term urbanization?

---

[1] See the conclusions of the International Commission on Growth and Development (SPENCE Commission) in 2008. Even more significant is the 2008 award of the Nobel Prize in Economics to Paul Krugman for his path-breaking theoretical work on a new economic theory that integrates international trade with economic geography, which is concerned with the location of economic activities within and across countries. These two issues are central concerns of China's policy makers in the era of peak urbanization. Yet, as recently as two decades ago, many leading academic economists still dismissed urbanization as a minor field solely because they did not know how to analyze it. Krugman (1991) sharply observed that a shortcoming of the economics profession is that "issues that are awkward to address are generally speaking not addressed" (*Geography and Trade*, x).

[2] Of course, this is not an inevitable outcome. For instance, during its major financial and economic crisis in the early 1980s, Chile did a much better job than most countries of integrating its housing policy choices into a consistent overall macroeconomic policy. As a result, Chile made significant long-term growth gains and also eliminated its long-standing housing shortage (Pardo 2009).

The chapter has two main parts. The first part examines the dynamics of China's uniquely vast system of cities and the relation between economic growth, the location of economic activities, and their impact on rural-urban migration. Income inequality and spatial inequality have increased sharply during the first two periods of the transition to market. Contributing to this is the rapidly widening income gap between rural and urban areas. Will the process continue during this era of peak urbanization, or could a rebalancing of the economy be accompanied by a rebalancing of the system of cities, with more growth in the large and medium-size cities of the hinterland? Rural-urban migration dominates this peak phase of urbanization. What are the constraints and risks facing the supply of affordable housing across China's extremely diverse system of more than 660 statutory cities?

After looking at the future growth of China's cities and their local housing markets, the second part of the chapter examines the internal structure of the housing system itself. What dictates the formulation of housing policies? Housing policy in China is still significantly affected by the legacies of the administrative-command system and the ideological and institutional views that came with it. What are the most important constraints that affect the emergence of integrated housing markets across the Chinese urban system? What components of the housing system create risks for the long-term performance of the sector? This second section draws on the modern economics of housing and maps China's strategic housing constraints and risks according to the core dimensions that together constitute what we call the "seven pillars" of a housing system. The structure of these seven pillars determines the strength and stability of the housing system. Which pillars need to be strengthened the most and where?

What are the conclusions regarding each part of this analysis? First, thanks to the global financial crisis, there is a high probability that the global economy has entered a phase of slower growth for an extended period of time. Will China's urbanization be significantly affected? Current macroeconomic growth projections indicate a lower growth rate than during the global boom years. However, the likelihood of urbanization slowing sharply, as it did during the disorder of the Cultural Revolution, is very low. China's actual level of "secular" growth will depend on the rate of growth of its economic productivity. International experience suggests that urban economic growth during China's era of peak urbanization can reduce income and spatial inequalities, especially if national policy makers are successful in rebalancing the economy toward domestic demand. However, successful growth during the new urban era is not inevitable. Because the housing sector will rapidly gain more weight in the national economy than it has now, its performance will have a major impact on the efficiency of China's long-term growth, as shown by the problems of high-income, highly urbanized countries.

In particular, the performance of China's housing sector will depend on the successful implementation at the local level of well-designed national reforms in four critical and challenging areas: (1) the full integration of property rights across rural and urban land markets; (2) reforms of intergovernmental relations and local finance to correct the heavy dependence of local governments on short-term real estate investments; (3) uniform access to public services by both rural and urban households; and (4) reforms of the financial sector in support of market-based local banking services for small and medium enterprises and households.

Success in these areas will significantly reduce the possibility that low-income housing programs will be taken over by the rapidly growing new middle class and that misinvestment in housing will take place. Beyond these reforms, international experience shows that progress in urban planning and land-use policies will differentiate cities that do well from those that lag behind, as intercity competition and the location of new production will be significantly affected by the elasticity of local housing supplies (Gyourko 2009).

In a policy transition comparable to that experienced earlier in high-income OECD economies as they reached high levels of urbanization, China's scarce central fiscal resources now need to be used to encourage local governments to adopt sound local low-income housing *processes*. As the complexity of cities increases, national policies can no longer attempt to dictate or mandate local quantitative outcomes. Central government officials can not possibly manage these outcomes across China's more than 660 statutory cities.[3]

An important indicator of the likely long-term overall success of urbanization in China will be the policy path chosen toward the "urbanizing villages" (*chengzhongcun*), which we shall call "u-villages." Unexpectedly, u-villages currently play a central role in the supply of market-based, low-income housing in many cities and therefore in the integration of rural migrants into the urban economy.

International experience shows that it would be quite possible to adopt urban planning policies and practices that facilitate the full spatial and socioeconomic integration of u-villages into China's cities. In the spirit of the first stage of transition to markets of 1979–1992, will Chinese policy makers adopt an incremental and organic reform approach that avoids losers and makes everyone better off? Or will they choose forceful physical solutions profitable to higher-income groups that will "modernize" and "eradicate" the chengzhongcun but will also create many losers, raise the overall cost of low-income housing, and raise national labor costs? The challenge for housing policies at the national level is to move away from rigid numerical quotas and physical rules rationalized with broad social principles familiar to urban planners to careful attention to the systems of incentives embedded in laws, regulations, and local practices. Pure physical planning rules are very congenial to central planning, but they have often had unintended negative local social and economic impacts. This is also what OECD countries have found.

China at Its Peak Rate of Urbanization

The percentage of the urban population rises with both industrialization and the level of per capita income, and can be illustrated by a logistic curve. This has been long established and was modeled in the 1970s by Dale Jorgenson and others. The

---

[3] A significant record of this major urban policy transition away from physical planning criteria to a focus on incentive structures in high-income OECD countries can be found in *Managing Urban Change,* a two-volume report of a two-year cross-country project published by OECD in 1983. The first volume is titled "Policies and Finance," and the second volume is "The Role of Governments."

growth rate of an urban system reaches a peak at the inflection point of this logistic curve, around the 50 percent urbanization level, because the growth of the urban population is fueled by the endogenous demographic growth of an already large urban population to which is added a large influx of rural-urban migrants. By 2005, China was 44 percent urban and had entered its zone of historically highest rate of urbanization.

Concurrently, the share of new housing investment tends to peak at around 7–9 percent of GDP—or higher when the growth of the total economy is itself very high. At lower levels of development the share of housing in GDP is lower because much of the construction share of GDP goes to infrastructure investment and not to residential investment.

Comprehensive research projects to measure the total composition of urban assets have been rare.[4] A estimate of the share of housing in the total value of urban assets would tentatively start at 60 percent, with this number rising when the economic base of the city is oriented toward services rather than heavy manufacturing and the spatial structure of the city is more land intensive.

As a result of urbanization, the value of real estate assets of all types grows steadily and becomes an increasingly larger share of total national wealth. This rising share of real estate assets in national wealth at high levels of income explains why the mismanagement of real estate can be very damaging to the national economy. This is demonstrated by the large national problems encountered in the United States, Spain, and Ireland and less acute problems in other countries (see Kim and Renaud 2009). Distorted and wasteful patterns of housing investment have a large and lasting impact on the growth and long-term efficiency of the national economy.

China's level of urbanization had remained at less than 20 percent when Deng Xiao Ping initiated the transition to markets in 1978. Until then, the strong anti-urban policies and widespread disruptions experienced during the Cultural Revolution between 1966 and 1976 had led to an investment freeze in cities.[5] Correspondingly, the urban share of the national population actually fell from 18 percent in 1965 to 17.3 percent in 1975. For lack of significant new investment, the spatial structure of Chinese cities tended to maintain their pre-1949 market shape. Yet the spatial and institutional distortions of the socialist city analyzed by Bertaud and Renaud (1994; 1997) were not entirely avoided during the urban take-off of the first two decades of urban market reforms (1978–1998), a period that ended with the major decision to privatize housing, in 1998. By 2008, the share of urban population had officially reached 45.7 percent.

A strategic opportunity exists today to improve the quality of urban growth and the productivity of Chinese cities during the peak phase of urbanization if urban planning decisions in land use, infrastructure investment, and new housing

---

[4] The most comprehensive analysis of the composition of urban investments was done for Australia during its period of fastest urbanization in the 1970s. See Neutze (1977).

[5] "Level of urbanization" here refers to the "officially registered urban population" and excludes migrants. See www.stats.gov.cn [in Chinese]. The UN Population Division reports slightly different and somewhat higher ratios for China.

production become economically better grounded.[6] The degree of internal efficiency and productivity of individual cities, as well as the overall efficiency of the system of Chinese cities, will continue to grow in importance for the national economy. The percentage of GDP produced in cities can be expected to rise from about 75 percent today to about 95 percent by 2025, when China's urban level will have become close to the saturation levels of high-income economies.

The Magnitude of China's Forthcoming Urbanization

Going much beyond basic demographic projections of urbanization in China, such as those of the UN Population Division, the McKinsey Global Institute (MGI) released in March 2009 a significant study of China's urbanization prospects. This report is based on a two-year project that included the construction of a large-scale econometric model capable of modeling granular city-level options with data based on a significant amount of city-level fieldwork. The historically unprecedented magnitude of China's peak rate of urbanization, which is bound to have large direct and indirect impacts on the rest of the global economy, is detailed in the MGI study:

- By 2025 China's urban population is projected to increase by 350 million, more than the total population of the United States of 306 million in May 2009 (U.S. Census Bureau).
- MGI projects that China's urban population will expand from 572 million in 2005 to 926 million in 2025, with a compounded annual growth rate of 2.4 percent.[7] It will be on track to reach one billion by 2030.
- By 2025, 64 percent of China's population will live in cities, compared to 44 percent in 2005.
- By 2025 China will have over 220 cities of one million or more people. Today Europe, which has a larger population than the United States, has only 35 cities of more than a million. The MGI study also projects that China will have eight megacities of over 10 million that will generate by themselves about 25 percent of China's GDP.
- Migration will be the dominant driver of future urbanization. MGI estimates that urbanization will be fundamentally different from the experience of the past 15 years. More than 240 million new residents will be rural-urban migrants, while 110 million will result from endogenous urban population growth and a

---

[6] In contrast with China, Russia is burdened today by an inefficient urban system that developed under 70 decades of the Soviet administrative-command system that misallocated and mispriced resources because the critical economic concept of "opportunity cost" remained unknown for investment decisions during the entire period. Unfortunately, Russia is now a fully urbanized economy with an urban ratio over 76 percent and limited scope to improve the spatial structure of its now fully built urban system. Absolute demographic decline complicates urban restructuring.

[7] This projected growth rate of the urban system beyond the urban inflection point is considerably lower than previous urban population growth rates when China's system of cities was smaller: 5.04 percent in 1985–1990 with the stock adjustments back from the Cultural Revolution; 3.77 percent in 1990–1995; 3.52 percent in 1995–2000; and 3.08 percent in 2000–2005.

very limited amount of city expansion. Between 1990 and 2005, MGI estimates that 103 million people migrated from rural areas to cities.

The primary objective of the MGI study is to investigate the multidimensional impacts of alternative patterns of urbanization and feasible trade-offs given the serious constraints that China faces in terms of land, financing, and natural and human resources. The study investigates four future urbanization scenarios, each a plausible outcome of urbanization over the next 20 years. MGI concludes that the scenario that would be most likely to mitigate pressures on the environment and raise the productivity of the urban system is the scenario with "a more concentrated pattern of urbanization" (McKinsey Global Institute 2009, 14). The MGI study argues that two forms of land use changes are needed to support the "concentrated pattern of urbanization." The first change, which is related to rural-urban land conversion, is to release the current freeze on rural-urban land conversion and the associated land conversion quota system that distorts land use processes and negatively affects urban spatial land use efficiency.[8] The second change is to improve land use regulations and urban planning practices that control land allocation within cities. Improvements in internal city land use could have a positive impact on the quality of China's growth and could support a more concentrated pattern of urban development.

Geography and Trade: Location of Economic Activities and Labor Migration

Geography and Trade, Paul Krugman's path-breaking work (1991) that unified trade theory and economic geography, provides a framework for understanding China's urban dynamics by modeling the location of economic activities and labor mobility across cities and regions.[9] Krugman's analysis of the historical rise of the manufacturing belt during the industrialization of the U.S. economy finds a direct parallel with the rapid industrial emergence of the coastal regions of China during the past three decades. Highly populated regions are more attractive to migrants because they offer a richer choice of goods and diversified employment opportunities. Companies also have an incentive to move to highly populated regions to keep transportation costs down and benefit from economies of scale. A self-reinforcing process may arise between migration and greater economies of scale that further reinforces the attractiveness of cities.

Krugman's theoretical work helps explain how the coastal urban regions of China have been building a strong comparative advantage and why a similar process may encourage the growth of the larger hinterland cities during the domestic

---

[8] Bertaud (2007) also illustrates how the implementation of rural-urban land conversion quotas assigned from higher levels of government without good knowledge of the urban growth dynamics of a given city leads to significant distortions in local land use.

[9] See Krugman's public lectures on *Geography and Trade* (1991) or the video of his Nobel Prize lecture, "The Increasing Returns Revolution in Trade and Geography," at http://nobelprize.org/nobel_prizes/economics/laureates/2008/krugman-lecture.html. The Nobel Foundation Web site also includes a scientific note from the Nobel Prize Committee, "Trade and Geography—Economies of Scale, Differentiated Products and Transport Costs," that explains Krugman's contributions and his work.

rebalancing of the economy. In *Geography and Trade* (1991, 9), he wrote, "Pervasive increasing returns and imperfect competition; multiple equilibria everywhere; an often decisive role for history, accident, and perhaps sheer self-fulfilling prophecy: these are the kinds of ideas that are now becoming popular."

The preferential fiscal treatment of coastal areas by China's central government, especially during the first stage of transition reforms, together with heavy investments in transport and communication infrastructure has contributed to the primacy of coastal cities in China's urban system. There has been a clear and relatively rapid rise in household-income disparities between coastal provinces and the hinterland.

As China enters its era of peak urbanization there is a rebalancing of the economy toward domestic demand away from exports. The relative growth of different cities and regions is changing. The new view, in which trade may be based on arbitrary specialization based on increasing returns rather than an effort to take advantage of exogenous differences in resources and productivity, seems to apply internally to China, as well. (Regarding the dynamics of urban systems in emerging economies, see, for instance, Duranton 2009 and Venables 2009.)

Income Distribution and Pressures on Low-Income Housing

A dominant factor in China's low-income housing policies is the worsening of the national income distribution. As figure 13.1 shows, income inequalities between rural and urban residents, and between inland and coastal regions, have greatly increased over three decades compared with the low level of income inequality prevailing before the market reforms. At the start of the millennium, China (in 2001) and the United States (in 1999) had the same very large Gini coefficient value of 0.416.[10] Increasing income inequality is a problematic factor for low-income housing policies because it makes the housing stock increasingly unaffordable to a rising percentage of households, and the absolute number of households to be assisted increases more rapidly.

The most important contributor to income inequality in China is the rural-urban divide, but other spatial factors are at work, as well. Luo and Zhu (2008), the authors of figure 13.1, argue that rising income inequality is part of the normal process of development at the present stage of China's urbanization, and that the dynamics of spatial income divergence in the form of a "race to the top" can be desirable, as they unleash competitive pressures and create incentive for investment in skills. This is a variation on the hypothesis made by Kuznets (1955) that rural-urban migration drives income inequality along an inverted U-shaped curve as the economy develops over time. However, Luo and Zhu could well be overoptimistic about the self-correction of income inequality. In the case of China, the institutional dualities left from the central planning era create de facto two classes of economic citizens and rural residents who have reduced opportunities to realize their full economic potential even when they migrate to cities. Bourguignon (2008) provides a more balanced

---

[10] More detailed information on China's income distribution in comparison to the United States is presented in Renaud (2009b).

FIGURE 13.1

Income Inequality, Rural to Urban, Inland to Coastal, 1978–2004

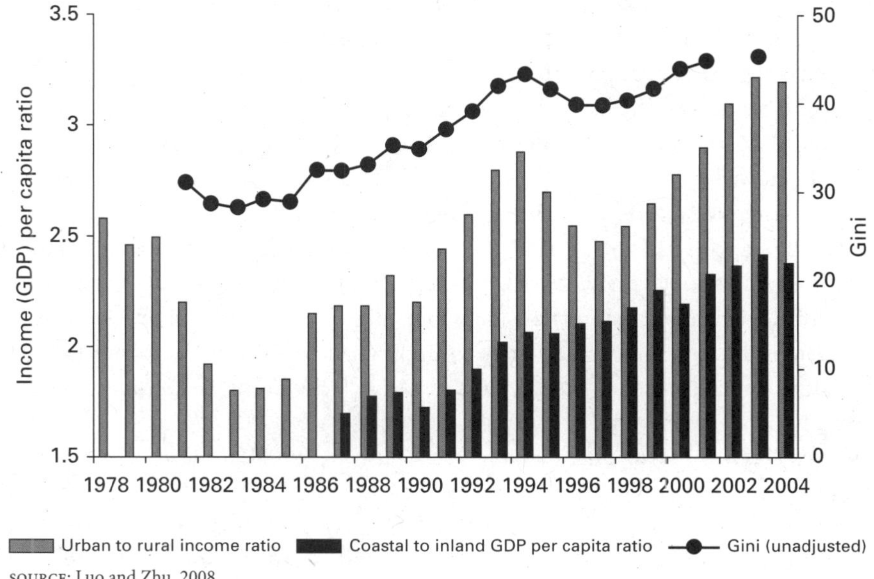

SOURCE: Luo and Zhu, 2008.

view and explores fiscal ways for China to address the widening inequalities through public policies.

The Rural-Urban Divide

Dualities that are legacies from the central planning era are probably the single greatest source of policy risks for the future of Chinese society. Three major dualities have distorted the take-off phase of urbanization:

- *Duality in property rights* between land in rural areas belonging to rural collectives and urban land owned by the state, with discontinuous rights attached across both rural and urban land use, creating important land use discontinuities within cities via the phenomenon of urban villages, which is the Chinese version of the "informal housing" encountered in the cities of market-based emerging economies.
- *Duality in social security systems,* where social security for rural residents is expected to be provided by rural collectives, and social security for urban residents is provided by urban governments, with rights that are not easily portable across employment locations.
- *Duality in socioeconomic status* within urban labor markets associated with the *hukou* registration system, which restricts access to local public services to locally registered urban residents and excludes migrants.

Chinese policy makers have long been concerned by the high risks to social, economic, and political stability that these dualities create. They have made incremental corrections to the *hukou* system and announced potentially significant rural reforms in 2008. The rural reform policy document approved by the Chinese Communist Party (CPC) Central Committee on 12 October 2008 would benefit farmers and also affect China's urbanization in a major positive way if it eventually led to the full integration of rural and urban land markets. However, in its present form the plan proposes only a narrowing of the rural-urban gap and leaves important ambiguities and restrictions. Other causes of rising income inequality today are discussed below.

The exchange rate policy can have a negative impact on rural-urban terms of trade. It is also worth noting that the gradual yuan appreciation that began in July 2005 has distributive effects within China and negatively affects rural-urban terms of trade. China is an international price taker in agricultural products. For a given price in dollars, an exchange rate appreciation will lower the domestic yuan price of local agricultural products and negatively affect rural incomes. See, for instance, Blanchard and Giavazzi (2005).

Additional spatial factors are also increasing income inequality in China. Local protectionism is a legacy of the autarkic policies of the Mao era that also contributes to spatial inequalities today. Recent studies show that the degree of integration of the national spatial economy was low during the decade from 1987 to 1997 and actually even declined during that decade as local governments pursued a double goal of preserving local socioeconomic stability and raising fiscal resources. However, such local policies have been counterproductive by reducing the growth potential of local urban areas; keeping local wages low; and encouraging long-distance migration predominantly to the urban areas, which have better access to the national economy (see Hering and Poncet 2010).

The transition to market in other transition economies has often worsened the income distribution. In a recent paper Milanovic and Ersado (2008) analyze the dynamics of the household income distribution during the transition to market across 26 transition economies of Eastern Europe and the former Soviet Union from 1990 to 2005. They report a prevalent deterioration of the income distribution, but with significant variations across countries. Where there has been deterioration, it usually comes from a fall in the share of the bottom income deciles and a rise in the shares of the top two deciles. Factors worsening the income distribution have been large-scale privatization and infrastructure reforms combining privatization with the raising of fees. Rapid growth has favored high-income groups. Positive factors improving the income distribution have been small-scale privatization that has favored the lower deciles and also low inflation. Milanovic and Ersado also find that democratization has been strongly pro-poor. Interestingly, they find no evidence that a larger government share of Gross Domestic Income has a favorable relation to a better income distribution.

The erosion of social safety nets has increased the level of insecurity among many households. China's extremely high household savings rate, which has risen above 40 percent, is attributed to the weakening of social safety nets in rural areas and the disappearance of the role played by traditional work units for health, housing, pensions, and education. This high precautionary savings rate may have been affected also by rapid housing privatization after 1998.

Highly unusual urban household savings patterns that are different from those of previous periods and inconsistent with the life-cycle hypothesis have recently emerged. The difference between income and consumption does not follow the consumption and savings smoothing that was expected across age cohorts. (See figure 13.2.) Chamon and Prasad (2008) report a U-shaped pattern of urban savings in 2005. Savings rates are currently higher at the start of the life cycle, and a second peak occurs near retirement. Previously, the familiar hump-shaped income and consumption pattern prevailed in 1995, 1990, and 2000.

Chamon and Prasad find that these two local saving peaks reflect very different economic experiences across urban Chinese age cohorts. The high savings of better-educated young cohorts may reflect high and rapidly rising income and a low level of insecurity. In contrast, the high-saving older cohorts are also those that bore the brunt of the market reforms and of the dismantling of the old system of social protection, which have considerably raised the level of uncertainty for them. Overall, the magnitude in yuan terms and the rate of savings have increased dramatically for every cohort between 1995 and 2005. The consumption level declines monotonically from younger- to older-age cohort, which must have an impact on the composition of housing demand.

Plans announced in the spring of 2009 to develop catastrophic health insurance programs for low-income groups in urban and rural areas suggest that long-term safety-net issues are now high on the public agenda. Such policies can and probably will have a positive impact on the necessary rebalancing of China's economy and on improving the income distribution.

How the Economy Affects Urbanization and Housing

Before analyzing the structure of China's housing system, it seems helpful to list briefly the characteristics of the current situation within which local housing policies must operate.[11] These are as follows:

- China is undergoing a major demographic transition. The one-child policy and the aging of the population are increasing the old-age dependency ratio, with projected further increases in the future.
- The extremely rapid rise in per capita income, by any historical world standard, since 1978 is drastically reducing the scale of absolute poverty in China.
- Rapid growth and urbanization are also leading to drastic changes in the physical and the psychological landscapes. Such changes deserve to be compared with those of the high-growth era from 1965 to 1985 in South Korea, the fastest case of economic growth in the world of a significantly large country (of almost 50 million people) until China's own take-off.
- National and local policy makers and private enterprises will have to make more room in their decision-making processes for social changes and the increasing differentiation in values across households with similar incomes in what is becoming a predominantly urban China.

---

[11] More detailed evidence is provided in Renaud (2009b).

Average Urban Disposable Income and Consumption by Age of Household Head

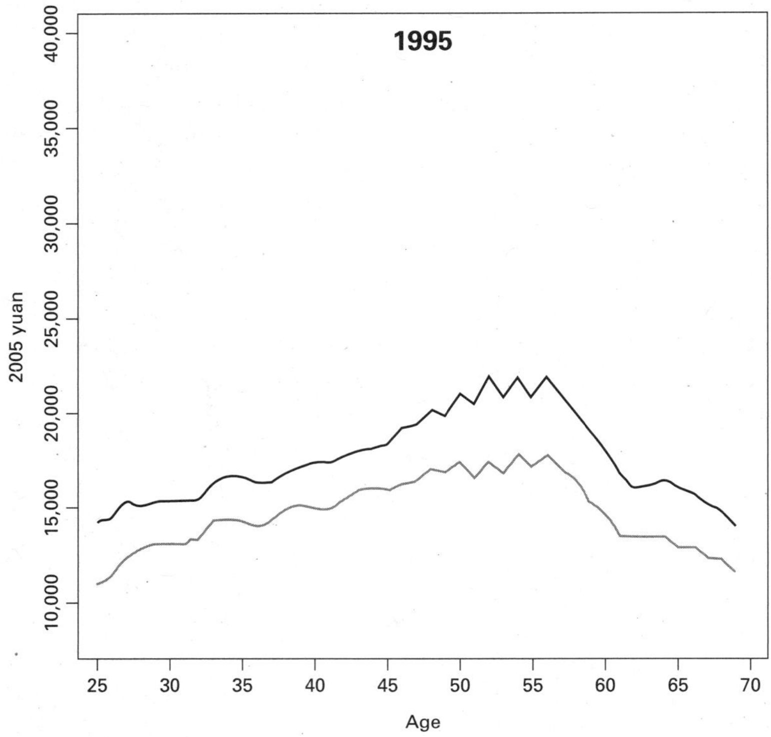

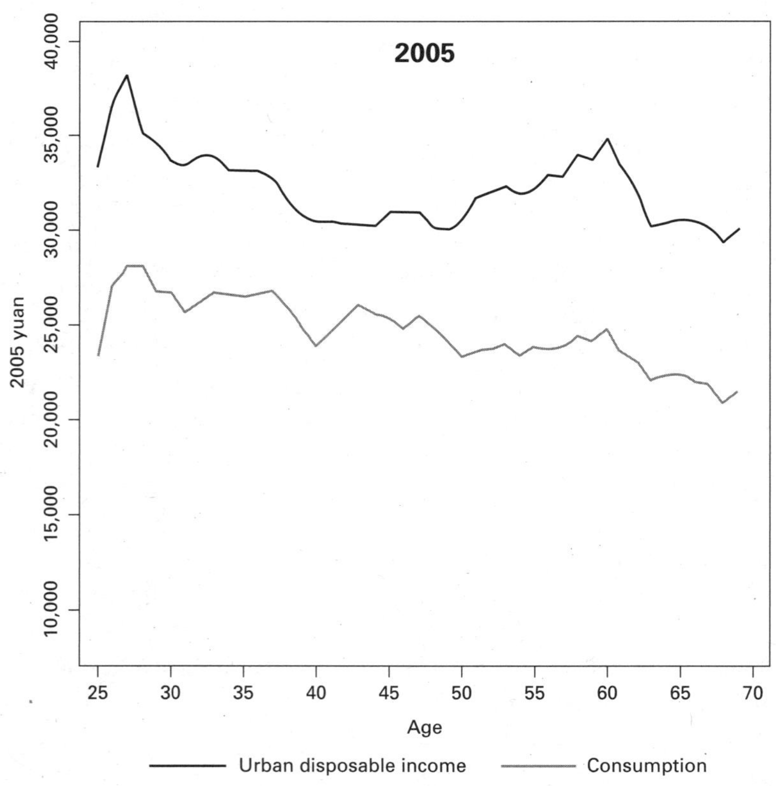

SOURCE: Chamon and Prasad, 2008, figure 3.
NOTE: Usual hump-shaped pattern in 1995; unexpected U-shaped pattern in 2005.

- The rate of urbanization has reached its historical peak, and China's urban population is projected to increase by 350 million, larger than the entire U.S. population today, by 2025.
- China's trade openness after 1978 is high even by East Asian standards. This openness strongly supports technology transfers and learning by doing, which has until recently focused heavily on manufacturing. This trade openness has favored coastal cities that have now built a comparative advantage in many industries over inland cities in line with the Krugman (1991) analytical model of trade and geographic location.
- The high rate of investment remains below the aggregate savings rate and had contributed to global macroeconomic imbalances until the current global crisis.
- There has been uneven growth across sectors, with a relative share of manufacturing that is high and a low share of services, especially of public services.
- Relative overinvestment in manufacturing has favored coastal regions and has had an important impact on the internal spatial growth of cities.[12]
- The financial system remains dominated by state banks whose primary clientele remains the new large corporations and the state-owned enterprises (SOEs), whose relative share has been declining.
- In the absence of local banks and opportunities for private investment into local small and medium enterprises, households have faced negative real deposit rates on their savings at large state-owned banks and cannot easily diversify their savings into alternative local assets.
- The most important driver of income inequality in China is the rural-urban divide, but rising inequality is an intraurban phenomenon that also adds pressure to the demand for low-income housing.

Organization of China's Housing Sector: Constraints and Risks

The best social housing policy is first and foremost the development of sound and responsive housing markets that serve the largest possible share of the population. Otherwise, structural distortions can have large cumulative effects that will make low-income housing policies more costly and less effective.

To identify important systemic risks facing China's housing system, we can use the framework provided by the modern economics of housing.[13] We call this framework "the seven pillars of housing policy" because the structure of a market housing system has seven dimensions related to the demand side, the supply side, and the role of central and local governments in the operation of the system (see box 13.1).

---

[12] See the empirical analyses of land use efficiency in Chinese cities by A. Bertaud, especially Bertaud (2007). See also the fundamental analysis of the spatial dynamics of socialist cities without land markets by Bertaud and Renaud (1995).

[13] This time-tested economic framework is based on extensive empirical research worldwide and was fully developed more than two decades ago. See, for instance, Pozdena (1991), McLennan (1992), or Fallis (1985). A significant use of this framework for emerging markets is the World Bank (1993) report on housing policy. For a recent application to the U.S. case, see Glaeser and Gyourko (2008).

Housing-Demand Side

Pillar 1: Property Rights and Tenure

Duality of land property rights between ownership by the state in cities and ownership by rural collectives. The harmful duality of land property rights between ownership by the state and ownership by rural collectives creates costly discontinuities in land use rights across space and over time between rural and urban areas.[14]

This duality has been widely debated and analyzed in recent years, but it has not yet been resolved. Given the expected massive growth of China's system of cities, no other reform would have a greater impact on the land use efficiency in cities, and therefore on the long-run efficiency of China's national economy. Without the integration of rural and urban property rights into a single set of identical property rights across the national territory, it will be very difficult for China to urbanize along the pattern of urban growth that is considered by the MGI study to be the most desirable among four main scenarios. This is labeled "the more concentrated pattern of urbanization."[15]

This duality of property rights has far-reaching consequences economically, socially, and politically. Among many other problems, it weakens several of the pillars of the Chinese housing system, as follows:

- The current constitution does not permit the use of rural land as collateral for mortgage lending or business or other purposes. This is a serious impediment to the development of local banking and business development.
- The duality of rural and urban land property rights has been exploited by city governments to finance their own activities by taking advantage of the extremely large gap between grossly undervalued rural land and the high value of land reclassified for urban use in high-value real estate projects.
- The discontinuity in property rights between rural and urban areas is the direct cause of the phenomenon of urban villages that are large tracts of land under collective property rights that have become embedded in the spatial structure of cities during the past two decades, which have often been accompanied by the administrative consolidation of rural land into city areas. These u-villages can be considered China's version of the informal housing markets encountered in other developing economies.

The Importance of u-villages in China's current supply of low-cost, low-income housing. It is not fully appreciated that China's u-villages have played a major role in the large supply of low-cost private housing to the low-income migrant labor force that has been a major factor in the successful industrialization of China. Poorly designed urban planning and land use policies that arbitrarily attempt to quickly eradicate this supply of low-cost housing could end up sharply raising the

---

[14] See, for instance, Jiabin Lin (2007) and Chengri Ding (2004; 2007).

[15] For the full description of that scenario, see McKinsey Global Institute (2009), chapter 5.

The Seven Pillars of Housing: Key Questions

In China as in any other country, the economic performance of the housing sector and its impact on the wider economy is determined by institutional arrangements and public policies in seven areas of the system. The overall strengh and stability of a housing system depends on the internal structure and mutual support of each of these "pillars." To understand the organization, structure, and performance of a housing system, key questions in each of these areas need to be answered. This diagnosis framework reflects the cumulative work of several decades of research in the economics of housing. It can be applied nationally or at the level of an individual urban market. It has been validated across a very wide range of housing systems around the world. A notable use of this framework is the influential World Bank report on housing policy, "Housing: Enabling Markets to Work" (1993).

Demand-Side Pillars

1. *Property rights and tenure choice:* Are integrated and enforceable property rights easily tradable? Is there a tenure choice? Do rent controls and other price controls distort property rights?
2. *Housing finance:* Are competitive banking services for housing available? Are there distorting "special circuits" based on a mix of special privileges and government constraints? Is the retail mortgage finance system linked to capital markets through mortgage securities?
3. *Taxation and subsidies:* Is there a system of well-targeted subsidies or are subsidies the cumulative result of piecemeal ad hoc decisions over time? Are target groups the right ones? Are subsidies financed on budget? Are subsidies separated from credit services? Are fiscal resources wasted by subsidizing inefficient, stagnant, and privileged public institutions?

Supply-Side Pillars

4. *Supply of serviced urban land and local infrastructure:* What is the process for rural-urban land conversion? How is local infrastructure planned, financed, and provided? How clear and predictable is the division of labor between public- and private-sector operators in the supply of serviced urban land?
5. *Land use and zoning regulation:* Are local regulatory frameworks for land development and land use raising the price of housing, especially for middle- and low-income families? Are urban planning decisions arbitrary and wasteful, or are they consistent with land use efficiency?
6. *Organization of the real estate industry:* Is there a complete institutional framework to manage risks in the competitive construction and real estate industry? Do timely and reliable housing and real estate information systems exist?

Government Questions

7. *Enabling role of central government and implementing role of local governments:* Is the national government providing a stable legal and regulatory enabling framework? Are autonomous and innovative local governments ensuring a balanced and diversified supply of housing?

To use a medical analogy, a correct housing diagnosis requires both knowing the personal history of patients and measuring correctly their vital signs in each of these seven areas. Policy cures will differ depending on what pillars are weak and how their weaknesses interact. As in medicine, successful treatment requires a combination of quality research and clinical experience, as well as the patient's determination to get better, which is here the government controlling the housing system.

cost of housing for low-income migrant workers at the time China has entered its peak phase of rural-urban migration. Much higher housing costs without commensurate gains in housing welfare for low-income workers would create pressures for much higher wages and a rapid acceleration of labor costs. The net result could be a loss of competitiveness of the national economy without commensurate gains in the social welfare of migrant labor for a significant period of time. This is what happened in South Korea during the peak phase of urbanization in the 1970s and 1980s. Such a costly transition was not inevitable and might have been avoided if more flexible urban planning and land use policies had been adopted.[16]

The legal and administrative legacy from the administrative-command economy in China has affected residency registration, social services entitlements, and land ownership. One spatial legacy of the economic autarky and local self-sufficiency promoted before 1976 is that Chinese municipal administrative boundaries include both rural land that is under "collective" ownership and urban land under "state" ownership. This legacy complicates the task of managing China's growing cities, and the administrative definitions of these government units themselves have been modified repeatedly.[17]

The two main sources of affordable housing, accessible to rural-urban migrants, are the aging and obsolescent *danwei* housing in central locations and the new low-cost housing units produced in the urban villages.

In rapidly growing coastal municipalities, large tracts of rural land have become surrounded by expanding urban districts; these u-villages have been playing a crucial role in providing rental housing at prices that low-income migrants can afford (See Yan Song's case study of Shenzhen in chapter 10). Registered local rural residents build extra rooms on the rural plots they control and provide inexpensive rental housing to migrants attracted by the broader urban labor market that surrounds them. The rental income from housing increases the incomes of these rural landlords significantly, although both they and their renters remain excluded from the urban services provided by the municipality.

Demand driven, characterized by low-cost infrastructure, low construction costs, and ease of entry, these urban villages are under considerable pressure by the urban planning authorities, who complain about unplanned land uses, lower-quality housing conditions, public safety issues, and the erosion of social order. Local authorities would like to transform this type of rental housing to units of much higher cost and higher standards that would no longer be affordable to the low-income sector.

Meanwhile, the official low-income affordable housing is supply-driven and based on the usual characteristics: standardized housing designs, capped developer profits, prices subsidized through the reduction or waiver of a variety of taxes

---

[16] I am grateful to the South Korean participants at the seminar presentation of a version of this chapter at the KDI School on 16 July 2009 for confirming my interpretation of South Korea's housing and labor cost experience during its two decades of peak urbanization. For an overview of the costly remedial land use and housing policies that were then adopted in Korea, see Lee and Kim (1998), especially chapter 4 on housing policies.

[17] In China "municipal" does not refer to a specific level and type of governance, but is a broad administrative label that refers to subprovincial levels of government and covers counties, townships, statutory cities, and towns. "Urban municipalities" include 668 statutory cities (*cheng shi*) and around 19,200 towns (*jian zhi zhen*). Meanwhile "rural municipalities" are counties with constituent townships and no statutory cities or towns. See the joint study *Managing Urban Change* by the Asian Development Bank and the Ministry of Finance (2000).

and fees, donation of public land in less desirable locations, and allocation of these units by the local administration under the requirement that applicants possess the local *hukou*. Predictably, a large percentage of these units end up in the hands of households with incomes much higher than intended. An important disincentive for local governments to supply this housing is the waiver of the land transfer fee, which is a a major source of local revenue.

Demolishing these "urbanizing villages" to make room for more costly housing units has the effect of reducing the supply of housing affordable to low-income migrants precisely when their number is projected to expand. The present policy toward u-villages is rigid and static because it does not ask what flexible local urban planning and land use standards can be used to facilitate the spatial and socioeconomic integration of u-villages into the urban networks of the city while remaining affordable to the migrant population. Urban incomes will continue to rise in Chinese cities and will be able to finance the gradual land recycling and market-based redevelopment that will steadily improve housing standards over time in an affordable and gradual way. This will require not only a combination of more flexible urban planning standards, but also significant local finance reforms to modernize local revenue sources. Reforms in the existing funding of local governments is needed to correct the strong economic and social incentives that local governments have to remove affordable housing in favor of much more expensive housing units for higher income groups, which causes a worrisome wealth redistribution in favor of higher income groups.

An important long-term risk of the policy of demolishing and redeveloping the villages is to repeat the historical regulatory experience of Hong Kong, which became entrapped in a very large program of public housing whose privatization eventually became an important political burden for the SAR. Like the experience of South Korea, Hong Kong's historical experience deserves close examination.[18]

The rural land policy plan of October 2008: A major game-changing plan for urbanization?   On 12 October 2008, when the CPC Central Committee approved the policy document that aims at a more balanced and integrated rural-urban development, it also set the goal of doubling rural per capita incomes by 2020. A major element of the plan is a new land policy that increases the protection of the rural land rights of individual farmers, but at best narrows the gap between the rural and the urban sectors without closing it.

Significant elements of the plan improve the property rights of individual farmers. When the plan is fully implemented, farmers' leases on land will be extended from the current 30-year term to unlimited leases. The rules for the use of "eminent domain" for public land acquisition will be more restrictive. Land transfers between private parties will be permitted. Land acquisition will be permitted only for public purposes, and a compensation mechanism based on market values will be established. This will be a challenge in the absence of markets unless the right of

---

[18] Yue-Chim Richard Wong (1998) takes exception with the frequently repeated misinterpretations of the origins of Hong Kong's public housing program. See, in particular, chapter 3, "Growth of Public Housing from 1954 to 1963: An Alternative View."

land transfer leads to a local market. Plot-level land registration and certification is part of the plan and will be a massive administrative challenge for 250 million farm households with an average of five plots each. However, the present plan does not include the possibility of pledging the land as collateral for credit.

This plan may not successfully eliminate the duality of property rights in China between urban and rural areas. Many ambiguities remain. Under the "household contract responsibility system," rural land is now used by individual families, but land remains "collectively" owned. The October 2008 plan is also vague about the specific process for the transfer of these land use rights. It is not clear whether land use rights could be extended beyond 30 years. Importantly, there is no proposal so far to lift the legal ban on farmers mortgaging their land and their houses, and the collateral power of those assets remains zero.

It is also not clear how the current opaque and questionable practices of control over land use by the local "collectives" will improve the process of creating rural land markets and be replaced by transparent rules.

The October 2008 announcement seems to be another case of gradual reform in China. Gradualism is now an open question. The case for more complete rural property rights reform could prove economically less costly to the national economy and also socially less destabilizing. Gradual reform is not necessarily superior to a big bang. The better choice is shaped by the expectations of potential winners and losers (Wei 1997).

Tenure choice between home ownership and rental housing.   The housing privatization of 1998 gave consumer choices to individual households and freed employers from the burden of directly providing housing to their workers, but it also caused some hardships to specific households during the transition. This policy removed a central constraint on the development of the housing sector. It was preceded by a series of incremental steps in raising the low rents charged for the *danwei* rental stock. The 1998 housing reforms led to the dramatic rise from 17 percent home ownership in 1990 to the very high ratio of 86 percent in 2005. A question is whether China's home ownership ratio will move gradually closer to a long-term housing ownership rate of about 60 percent. A range of home ownership ratios between 55 percent and 65 percent can be observed in countries whose policies are relatively neutral toward the choice of tenure. Home ownership rates outside this 55–65 percent range suggest the presence of fiscal and financial distortions that are affecting access to home ownership.

The global real estate bust since 2006 is leading several countries to revisit the question of what is a sound home ownership rate for the long run. Developed rental markets have important socioeconomic benefits in terms of access to housing and labor mobility and reducing risks for young households. Certainly, the current real estate crisis is leading many in the United States to reconsider the recent policies of boosting the ownership rate above its historical stable level of 64 percent at all costs. The socioeconomic costs of the real estate bust are particularly high in Spain and in Ireland, where ownership rates are also very high (86.3 percent for Spain and 82 percent for Ireland in 2007). The transition economies of Eastern Europe have inherited a legacy of aversion to rental housing from the socialist era. Home ownership rates in 2007 were extremely high in the economies most affected by the crisis: Bulgaria, 96.3 percent; Estonia, 96 percent; Latvia, 86 percent; Lithuania, 97 percent; and Hungary, 92 percent. In contrast, the Czech Republic has a balanced economy not severely disrupted by the global crisis and a home ownership rate of 58.7 percent (European Mortgage Federation 2009).

Very high ownership rates are often a clue to the presence of extensive rent control. A major long-run systemic risk for China's housing system is the political risk of developing rent control. This risk is particularly significant in transition economies because their on-budget fiscal costs are seemingly nonexistent and the policy has considerable short-term populist appeal. The classic quote about this strategic issue is from Assar Lindbeck (1972, 39): "Rent control is the most effective method we know for destroying a city, except for bombing it."[19]

Of particular interest for China are the unintended consequences of rent control in shaping the long-term growth of Hong Kong's housing system: a very large public housing sector whose management and privatization later became a major public policy challenge. (For details, see Wong 1998.)

Exit strategies to phase out rent control as a major constraint to long-run urban growth, efficiency, and fairness are known and have been market-tested for both the private rental sector and the social rental housing stock. Predictably, they focus on strategies to raise rents back to market levels in order to maintain an adequate inflow of resources and expand the housing stock (see Taffin 2007; 2009).

Pillar 2: Housing Finance

The mortgage finance system requires improved regulation.   The long-term performance of the housing finance system is a critical component of China's housing development. Housing finance policies do not exist in isolation; international experience shows that the development of the mortgage finance system is heavily conditioned by the development of the financial system and the financial policy regime. We can make a few strategic points about constraints and long-term risks in this pillar:

- The Chinese housing finance system has developed considerably by international standards since the 1998 privatization reforms, but the legal framework for mortgage lending remains a work in progress as different laws affecting mortgage finance need to be harmonized (see Deng and Fei 2008).
- Similarly, the mortgage finance regulatory framework is also a work in progress. An important driver of such regulatory work has been the priority given to developing

---

[19] Assar Lindbeck, *The Political Economy of the Left* (New York: Harper and Row, 1972). The study by J. R. Kearl, Clayne L. Pope, Gordon C. Whinting, and Larry T. Wimmer, "A Confusion of Economists," *American Economic Review* 69 (May 1979): 28–37, reported that 98 percent of economists surveyed agreed that this form of intervention reduces both the number and quality of available housing units. The results of a similar study by Walter Block and Michael Walker, "Entropy in the Canadian economic profession: Sampling consensus on the major issues," appeared in *Canadian Public Policy,* vol. 14, no. 2, June 1988, pp. 137–150. The authors report that 95 percent of economists surveyed were of the opinion that rent controls are clearly inefficient and in fact harmful. See http://www.iedm.org/main/show_editorials_fr.php?editorials_id=434.

a domestic residential mortgage-backed securities market rather than to strengthening the institutional infrastructure of retail mortgage markets.

- Until now, China's financial authorities have relied heavily on directed credit methods and financial repression, which will soon lead to chronic shortages and pressures to subsidize housing finance. (See Lardy 2007 for China, and Man Cho 2010 regarding the case of South Korea before the financial reforms of 1998.)
- The level of financial education of potential borrowers varies greatly across China and remains low. Borrower behavior remains significantly different from behaviors observed in high-income mortgage markets (see Deng and Fei 2009).
- Important and beneficial regulatory lessons can be drawn by China from the U.S. mortgage subprime disaster in terms of mortgage finance banking regulations, securitization, and in particular consumer protection.[20]

The network of Housing Provident Funds is the most immediate and urgent regulatory challenge.   Immediate challenges arise from the risks embedded in the Housing Provident Funds (HPFs), a type of specialized housing finance institution first established in Shanghai in 1991. HPFs were inspired by the Singapore Housing Provident Fund but operate quite differently.[21] They were promoted out of the need to quickly finance a greater production of housing before the privatization of 1998.

HPFs exhibit most of the well-known shortcomings of "special circuits" for housing and do not amount to a nationally organized system. Rather, they form a nebula of independent local institutions with weak governance and heterogeneous charters. They are subject to some degree of central government pricing control, but they are mostly subject to the operational guidelines and supervision of municipal governments, which in most cases can mean the absence of appropriate financial supervision. Left as they are, these HPFs are a source of problems and could become an obstacle to the development of the mortgage finance system.

Development of local banking institutions: A Chinese policy void that interacts with housing finance.   Housing loans and SME loans usually represent a significant percentage of the loan portfolio of local banks. This matter is gaining increasing attention in emerging economies following findings on the close relationship between local financial development and local growth.[22] Local banking facilitates the expansion of the middle class and, as a result, the improvement of the national income distribution. This issue was raised earlier as an important but not yet addressed policy area for the rebalancing of the economy across regions and cities.

The Housing Provident Funds were created as a means to fill this local banking void at a time when China's banking system was not well developed. A strategic question for China to study is whether the HPFs might now interfere with the

---

[20] For a valuable review of the lessons of the U.S. subprime crisis for emerging mortgage markets, see W. Britt Gwinner and Anthony Sanders (2008).

[21] For an evaluation of the international experience, see Loic Chiquier, "Housing Provident Funds," chapter 11 in Chiquier and Lea (2009).

[22] See Zoellick and Lin (2009) for a policy view of benefits of developing regional and local banking to support SMEs and improve the spatial income distribution in China.

market-based development of local banking and undercut it through underpriced loan subsidies and preferential treatment by national and local authorities.[23]

Pillar 3: Taxation and Subsidies

In times of economic crises, housing subsidies have often been looked at as a mean to keep the housing sector going and to revive the national economy's growth. However, such subsidies can also weaken the stability of the housing sector and cause later crises. Moreover, during the transition to markets the income distribution has deteriorated sharply in China, as in many other transition economies, because risks and vulnerabilities faced by a large segment of the population have increased. With the global crisis, pressures for short-term actions have risen. Yet the goal is to improve the long-term soundness of the housing system, not weaken it.

There are two main dimensions to the taxation and subsidies pillar. The first dimension is the selection and design of subsidies: What types of subsidies? Which problems will they address and for what housing market segments?[24] A second dimension is the rent-seeking behavior of beneficiaries of subsidies that make some subsidies politically difficult to withdraw once they have been created. This is particularly the case for tax subsidies and financial subsidies to the middle class that may not have to be measured and reported properly on national budgets.

The cumulative impact of improperly designed tax and financial subsidies that misallocate scarce national resources to housing on a large scale is a risk that China should avoid. China's massive urbanization has to take place with more limited resources and under much greater environmental constraints than what Western countries faced in the past. The costly experience of the United States is a warning against the long-term impacts and risks of improperly designed housing finance and tax subsidies that can lead a country to overinvest in housing for long periods of time with negative consequences.

Has the United States overinvested in housing? A cautionary tale for China.   Two decades ago, Edwin Mills, who combined depth in macroeconomics with a pioneering role in the development of modern urban economics, started a broad debate in his article "Has the United States Overinvested in Housing?" (1987). The social rate of return to housing describes the total benefit to society from an investment in housing capital. Mills found that the social rate of return to housing was only 20 percent of that to nonhousing fixed capital, on average, over the period from 1929 to 1961. The conclusion of the debate was that indeed the United States had overinvested in housing at the expense of other productive sectors of the economy. United States society could have increased its income and its economic welfare by shifting resources into nonhousing activities with a higher return.

---

[23] See Chiquier and Lea (2009), chapter 10 on state housing banks and chapter 11 on Housing Provident Funds.

[24] For an overview of housing subsidy issues in times of crisis in emerging economies, see the recent presentation made by Marja Hoek-Smit, "Housing Subsidies: Who Gets What and Why it Matters" at the 2009 Urban Forum of the World Bank, March 12 2009. See also Marja Hoek-Smit, "Housing Finance Subsidies," chapter 16 in Chiquier and Lea (2009).

Because the U.S. Tax Reform Act of 1986 significantly reduced the tax benefits of owner-occupied housing and also raised the effective tax rate on rental housing for landlords, Lori Taylor of the Federal Reserve Bank of Dallas revisited the same question for the post-1986 period with her article "Does the U.S. Still Overinvest in Housing?" (1998). She compares the social rate of return to investments in housing, nonhousing fixed capital, and education for the period from 1975 to 1995 (see figure 13.3). Even after adjusting for different degrees of riskiness for different types of investment, she concluded that "despite substantial reforms, the United States continues to overinvest in housing" (Taylor 1998, 14). Taylor found that the U.S. economy could grow faster if society shifted more of its resources away from housing and into high school education and, especially, nonhousing fixed capital. She concluded that "given that the government has other mechanisms through which it can redistribute income a shift would be socially desirable" (Taylor 1998, 14).

High levels of tax and financial subsidies accentuate booms and busts.　Unfortunately, the 2002 U.S. income tax changes went exactly in the opposite direction of what Taylor was hoping for. These changes had the effect of encouraging further investment in housing by lowering the capital gains tax rate, by shifting to the exemption of $500,000 of housing capital gains for a couple for a house held two years, and by permitting the full deductibility of mortgage interest payment for loans of up to $1 million irrespective of household income. These pro-housing tax changes

FIGURE 13.3

U.S. Social Rate of Return to Housing and Nonhousing Fixed Capital, 1975–1995

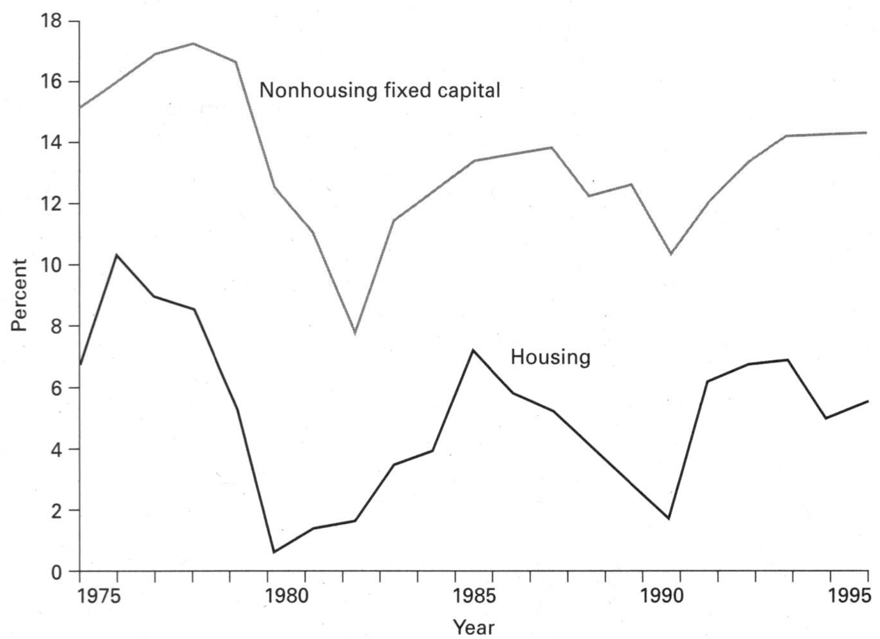

SOURCE: Taylor, 1998, 13.

FIGURE 13.4

Scale of U.S. Housing Boom Stimulated by Tax and Finance Subsidies

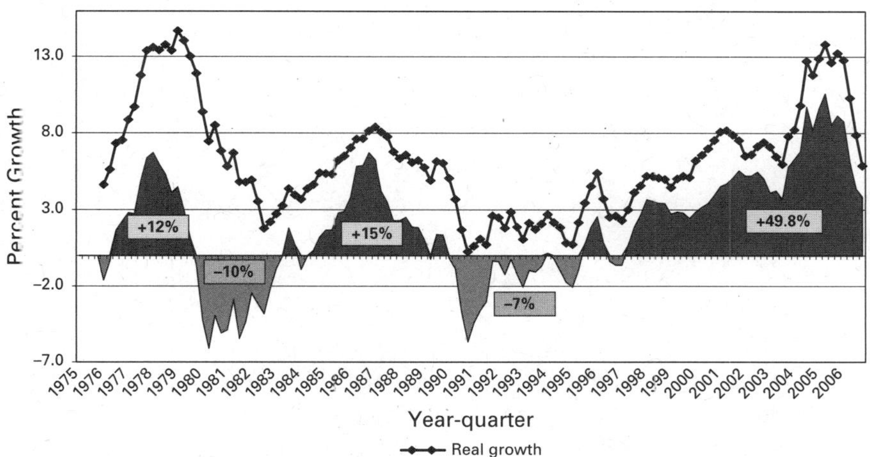

SOURCE: Man Cho, Seminar, Bank of Korea Representative Office, Washington DC, 17 April 2007.

combined with the low U.S. interest policy after 2003 to generate the largest U.S. housing boom on record (see figure 13.4). By the end of 2008, the housing bust had caused the largest loss of household wealth in U.S. history, plus $11.3 trillion loss of financial wealth. In 2009, U.S. housing prices were still falling.

Interestingly, in many other countries housing prices were rising even more rapidly than in the United States. Luci Ellis of the Bank of International Settlements asked why the housing meltdown took place there. Comparing the United States with a peer group consisting of Australia, Canada, Ireland, Spain, and the United Kingdom, Ellis tentatively concluded "that the U.S. mortgage market seems to have been uniquely vulnerable to the prospect of the boom ending badly" (Ellis 2008, ii). Compared with other countries, the United States seems to have built up a larger overhang of housing supply; experienced a greater easing in mortgage lending standards; and ended up with a household sector more vulnerable to falling housing prices. Some of these outcomes seem to have been driven by tax, legal, and regulatory systems that encouraged households to increase their leverage and permitted lenders to enable that development (Ellis 2008).

As a design strategy, tax and financial subsidies should not amplify booms and busts, and redistribute income to higher-income groups. They should improve resource allocation. This means that the income tax deductibility of mortgage interest is generally a low priority. Where it exists, such deductibility should be limited to the initial period of the loan and capped in total amount on a scale consistent with the affordability constraints of a first-time, low-to-middle-income home buyer.

Similarly, capital gains tax exemptions outside the general framework of capital gains taxation should be avoided. The rationale for a capital gains tax exemption is to stimulate investment in a sector where the social rate of return is particularly high. John Muellbauer (2006) has rightly argued that property tax design should have the objectives of improving macroeconomic stability, resource allocation, economic inequality, and the environment. The same design goals apply to other forms of taxation.

Channels used by the United States to subsidize housing and overinvest in the sector.   The structure of U.S. federal housing programs following the housing bubble and the subprime meltdown that began in 2006 has become fluid and uncertain both in scale and targeting because emergency programs aiming to stabilize housing markets have been added to the preexisting federal programs. This preexisting structure itself holds useful lessons for China regarding the channels used to subsidize U.S. housing.

The dominant features of U.S. federal housing policy have been the reliance on "indirect and off-budget activities in direct support of home-ownership—tax expenditure policies and federal credit, insurance, and guarantee programs—rather than the direct provision of housing or the payment of housing allowances to deserving renter households" (Jaffee and Quigley 2009).

U.S. federal housing subsidies are delivered through four main channels: (1) direct fiscal expenditures from the annual budget aimed at low-income renters (Section 8 programs); (2) subsidies through the federal tax code that overwhelmingly benefit homeowners rather than providers of social rental housing, with the ratio of the benefits going to homeowners compared to those reaching renters, estimated at 30 to 1 in 2007; (3) preferential treatment and implicit guarantees to government-sponsored enterprises (GSEs) providing mortgage credit (Fannie Mae, Freddie Mac); and (4) mortgage insurance programs for moderate- and lower-income home buyers (FHA and VA programs).

The current U.S. federal housing programs have conspicuous characteristics. They have a strong bias in favor of home ownership. The largest percentage of these benefits are sensitive to monetary policy and fiscal policy, which made them procyclical, as illustrated by figure 13.5. These federal programs are also regressive in terms of income targeting, due to their predominant reliance on tax and credit channels. However efficient and affordable U.S. housing markets may have become, the income-regressive drift of U.S. housing programs was not corrected by budget appropriations, which grew by only 0.6 percent per year in real terms between 1990 and 2007 (Jaffee and Quigley 2009). During that period the U.S. income distribution deteriorated markedly, and the U.S. population grew at an annual linear rate of 1.24 percent.

The U.S. experience raises several important questions: What is the appropriate role of the federal government in housing? What are appropriate channels of delivery of programs? And what should be their degree of social targeting? Those are also important questions for China, but in a different demographic, social, and economic context: What is the appropriate housing policy framework that is consistent with both the rebalancing of China's economy and the peak rate of urbanization?

Could the politics of housing policy lead China to overinvest in housing?   There are two reasons for worrying that poorly designed housing policies could lead China to overinvest in housing in the sense defined by Lori Taylor for the United States.

First, socialist economies have had a strong systemic tendency to physically overinvest in housing under the "distribution housing" system (Hegedus, Mayo, and Tosics 1996), which is a paradox, because few areas of the socialist economy caused as much universal discontent against the system as housing did.

The second reason is that tax and financial subsidies are particularly attractive in nontransparent, state-controlled financial systems where off-budget large "quasi-subsidies" can be easily delivered to "priority sectors" at the expense of household savers and other depositors, on the funding side, and of alternative borrowers whose projects have a much higher social rate of return, on the lending side.

Given the limited amount of coordination between urban administrations, budget authorities, and financial authorities at the central and local levels, the probability of using tax and financial subsidies is significant. The design of incentive compatible mechanisms (in the sense of Leo Hurwicz) for the selection of financial subsidies that are consistent with the long-run development of the housing system is an open question at this point.

Housing finance subsidies delivered through the financial system can and should be designed in a manner consistent with the long-run efficiency and competitiveness of the housing finance system. These subsidies should have a fixed time frame; their benefits should be capped in terms of incomes. They should not be funded through the implicit taxation of depositors but be explicitly financed on the government budget, which remains a significant policy risk in the directed credit policy environment of China today. They should be portable and delivered competitively across public and private institutions.[25]

Housing-Supply Side

Pillar 4: Supply of Serviced Urban Land and Local Infrastructure

Together with eliminating dual property rights (Pillar 1), improving the process of rural-urban land conversion is the most critical constraint shaping the spatial structure of Chinese cities. However imperfect, incomplete, or ambiguous the October 2008 plan to create rural land markets might be, it could eventually provide the critical missing link in the future development of China.

Developing a full market for rural land would inconspicuously yet drastically change the long-term spatial and economic dynamics of urbanization in China. The absence of rural land markets impairs the goal of market value compensation and precludes any consideration of the market principle of "highest and best use" in land allocation.

Top-down administrative rules from the central government are the present alternative, and they generate problems. For instance, the land use "conversion quotas" intended to protect agricultural land and control the rural-urban conversion process have important indirect negative effects on the spatial structure of cities by triggering the development of large suburban residential districts, which in turn

---

[25] See Marja Hoek-Smit "Housing Finance Subsidies," chapter 16 in Chiquier and Lea (2009).

leads to more traffic problems. Fragmented land use leads to higher costs of infrastructure and of housing for the poor (Bertaud 2007).

Compensation policies on rural land requisition and urban redevelopment and resettlement are a major social issue across the country due to the huge gaps between compensation fees paid to rural collectives and local government transfer prices charged to developers. These huge gaps are prima facie evidence of a dysfunctional process. Local governments face powerful incentives toward excessive development projects (overconstruction). Moreover, some of these local government projects can lead to great injustices, and lower-income groups may also pay more for the construction of public infrastructure.

Corrupt and predatory decisions by local officials have often resulted from ambiguous or missing rules in the Land Administration Law of 1996, which was amended in 1998. Then in 2003, the granting of land use rights between municipalities and developers by "agreement" (private negotiation) was abolished and replaced by "bidding" and "public auction" methods to solve the problem. Yet further improvements of the law and the land allocation process appear inevitable (Cai, Henderson, and Zhang 2009).

Pillar 5: Land Use and Zoning Regulation

In rapidly growing urban economies, real estate prices—not urban planners—are the main mechanism that influences whether firms and individual households will settle in different locations. China needs to make the transition from monopoly pricing by local governments to decentralized and competitive market pricing.

Currently, Chinese local governments act as regulators, partners, and active market players. This combination of conflicting roles has problematic impacts on economic efficiency because of the lack of transparency and heightened risks of wasteful investments in time and space; on governance as existing conflicts of interest need to be replaced by compatible public-private incentives; and on urban development because local governments focus on immediate financial project returns and not on the overall development of metropolitan regions and cities. Spatial efficiency is distorted by high monopoly returns on suburban projects while causing housing and transport problems.

The monopolized government land supply does not have the desired effect on developing real estate markets. Local governments have a strong incentive to adopt a high-land-price policy driven by short-term benefits. Yet the high prices do not have the allocative and space-economizing effects of a fully developed real estate market. The "shortage" of land supply and rapid land price increases associated with this monopoly give local governments weak financial incentives to allocate land for middle- and low-income housing.

Pillar 6: Organization of the Real Estate Industry

Like many other sectors, the real estate industry will be affected by the rebalancing of the economy. One of the legacies of central planning has been a strong pro-manufacturing bias and underrepresented SME and service sectors. The rebalancing of the economy will lead to the rapid rise of a much larger and more diversified

Chinese service economy along several different dimensions. The share of high-quality service inputs into Chinese manufacturing activity will rise. Service inputs are now 77 percent of manufacturing output in the United States and 66 percent in other high-income economies. This share in China is considerably lower. In contrast, consumer-oriented retail services tend to maintain a rather stable percentage of GDP over the long run as the economy keeps growing. The level of national and local public services can also be expected to rise, as their level remains low by international standards.

The central government must provide a more solid legal and regulatory framework in support of a mature and flexible real estate industry across cities through continuous work on real estate codes, regulations, professional training, and practices.

Pillar 7: Performance of Central and Local Governments

Urban development and municipal governance will continue to be at the forefront of public policy. The demand for local public services is likely to continue to grow rapidly, and the range of services to be provided is likely to expand. Local governments face serious operations and maintenance funding gaps. As is often the case in other countries, local finance reforms and housing reforms are interdependent in China.

Four universal public finance issues in emerging economies. In many countries, the central government is still involved in the delivery of local services. Local governments have few sources of local revenues. Local governments have limited access to borrowing for capital projects, and need to be closely monitored. Four universal issues in the design of intergovernmental relations follow:

- Addressing fiscal equity among regions.
- Providing appropriate incentives for fiscal discipline (and improved local regulations).
- Improving performance in the delivery of services.
- Developing local government accountability to citizens.

The case of China is atypical. The case of China is atypical, because the economic reforms that started in 1978 with the dismantling of the central planning system have led to a very strong, bottom-up dynamic of local governments. The 1994 fiscal reforms had an important goal of restoring an adequate level of fiscal resources to the central government, but the evidence 15 years later is that the fiscal position of local governments was weakened in an unintended way that has provided very strong incentives to city governments to misuse their monopoly powers over rural-urban land conversion and land use. Local governments' dependency on real estate transactions and industrialization to finance urban infrastructure is proving increasingly problematic and risky.

A new round of upgrading intergovernmental fiscal relations seems inevitable. Upgrading intergovernmental fiscal relations and local finance systems beyond the reforms of 1994 seems inevitable. To successfully reduce the dependence of local government on real estate activities, the development of better local user fees is needed. Regarding grants and transfers, one important stimulus to the efficient delivery of low-income housing subsidy programs is the reliance on interregional competitive mechanisms for the allocation of incremental central government grants. Competitive grant allocations are used in a number of large countries, such as Brazil and Mexico.

Critical interaction between housing reforms and local government finance. Local Chinese governments are heavily dependent on revenues from land use conversion and allocation to higher-income real estate projects. Further housing reforms to support the supply of housing for lower-income groups are therefore functionally linked to progress in improving the structure of local government funding. Recent press reports about the implementation of the Chinese government stimulus package indicate that many local governments are reluctant to move into low-income housing projects that would have to be funded at the expense of higher-income projects.

Early local government responses to the national stimulus program. The Chinese stimulus package of November 2008, later adjusted in March 2009, includes a significant national budget for low-income housing because of the desirable employment multiplier effects of such programs. The information available suggests that this funding is primarily focused on new construction, and that early local responses have been uneven and tepid. As they are expected to contribute a large proportion of the costs, many local governments are reluctant to initiate programs that negatively affect their finances.

Observed performance of local housing markets across a sample of Chinese cities. What are the factors shaping local housing markets today in China? Research by Fu, Zheng, and Liu (2007) across 90 Chinese cities covering the period from 1998 to 2004 suggests that the supply elasticity of housing (the responsiveness of new housing supply to rising prices) is shaped by several factors.

A major factor that increases the supply elasticity of housing is the ability to expand the supply of serviced urban land through a combination of expansion of the urban area of the city and fixed investment in road and other infrastructure. At given levels of urban area expansion and investment, urban size and population density are two factors that do not appear to directly reduce supply elasticity by themselves. So larger cities do not seem to be more constrained in supplying affordable housing than smaller cities. Provincial capital cities enjoy higher supply elasticities. This is a legacy of the administrative-command system that controlled all forms of investment, including infrastructure investments, and also had a direct impact on local land use regulations and local rural-urban land use conversions.

According to Fu, Zheng, and Liu (2007), the following factors appear to lower the supply elasticity of housing in Chinese cities:

- Cities experiencing *high population growth* and a housing demand shock have lower supply elasticities.
- Cities experiencing *high income growth* have lower housing supply elasticities. The mean nominal income growth across the 90 cities between 1998 and 2004 was 4.9 times. The lowest income growth was 3.3 times, the highest was 7.8 times.
- The larger the *proportion of state-owned enterprises* in the city, the lower the elasticity. One important factor seems to be the excessive percentage of industrial land in the city and its spatial misallocation in high-value locations. Relocation of state enterprises would be very expensive.
- The larger the *proportion of older housing stock,* the lower the supply elasticity. This is due to the higher land redevelopment costs required for new housing.
- A relatively *high initial price of housing* at the start of the period leads to a lower supply elasticity.

Conclusions

Housing policy must consider the future. Short-term concerns with actions to stimulate the economy should not distract from the need to release constraints on the development of the housing and urban system. Short-term actions should be designed to be consistent with desired long-term structural changes.

Thanks to the global financial and economic crisis—which is interacting with China's ongoing transition to market and its peak phase of urbanization—there is a high probability that the global economy has entered a phase of slower growth for a significant but unknown period of time. Will China's urbanization be significantly affected? Macroeconomic growth projections for China do indeed show a lower growth rate than during the global boom years. However, the likelihood of urbanization slowing sharply, as it did four decades ago during the disorders of the Cultural Revolution, is low.

Urban growth during China's era of peak urbanization can also reduce income and spatial inequalities, especially if national policy makers are successful in rebalancing the economy toward domestic demand. However, successful growth during the new urban era is not inevitable. Because the housing sector is certain to gain an increasingly larger weight in the national economy than it has now, the sector's performance will be a major factor in the efficiency of China's long-term economic growth. The U.S. experience is a cautionary tale about the proper design of fiscal and financial incentives to housing.

China's housing-sector performance will depend on the successful implementation at the local level of well-designed national reforms in three critical and challenging areas: (1) the full integration of property rights across rural and urban land markets; (2) reforms of intergovernmental relations and local finance to correct the heavy dependence of local governments on short-term real estate investments and also to ensure uniform access to public services by both rural and urban households; and (3) reforms of the financial sector in support of local banking services for SMEs and households. Success in these three areas will significantly reduce the probabilities that low-income housing programs will be captured by the rapidly growing new middle class and that misinvestment in housing will not take place.

Beyond these three reform areas, international experience shows that the local quality of urban planning and land use policies will differentiate cities that will do well from those that will fall behind. Sound economic theory and international evidence show that intercity competition and the location of new production are significantly affected by the elasticity of the local housing supply (see Gyourko 2009).

A most important—if not the best—indicator of the likely long-term success of urbanization in China will be the policy path chosen toward the "urbanizing villages."

In the spirit of the first stage of transition to markets during the period from 1979 to 1992, will Chinese policy makers be able to adopt an incremental and organic reform approach that avoids losers and makes everyone better off? Or will they choose forceful physical solutions profitable to higher-income groups that will aim to "modernize" and "eradicate" the chengzhongcun, but that will also create many losers and raise the overall cost of low-income policies? As shown by the experience of other East Asian economies, such as South Korea, urban planning and low-income housing policies that restrict the supply of private low-income housing can sharply raise the overall level of housing prices and therefore the level of labor costs in the economy. The result is a weakening of the global competitiveness of the economy, while improving the welfare of only a fraction of low-income families. As was the case in Hong Kong, urban policies that restrict the supply of private housing may lead to a very high share of public housing, which becomes an increasing policy challenge as income levels rise and public expectations change. China's housing policy has reached a new crossroad.

REFERENCES

Asian Development Bank and China Ministry of Finance. 2000. *Managing urban change: Strategic options for municipal governance and finance in China.* Manila and Beijing. www.adb.org/Documents/Reports/Consultant/TA2924_PRC_Final_Report.pdf.

Bernanke, Ben S. 2008. The future of mortgage finance in the United States. Speech at the UC Berkeley/UCLA Symposium, The Mortgage Meltdown, the Economy and Public Policy. Berkeley, CA.

Bertaud, Alain. 2007. Urbanization in China: Land use efficiency issues. Consulting Report to the World Bank and the Chinese government. http://alain-Bertaud.com/ (Asian Cities, study no. 8).

Bertaud, Alain, and Bertrand Renaud. 1994. Cities without land markets: Lessons of the failed socialist experiments. Discussion Paper No. 227. Washington, DC: World Bank.

———. 1997. Socialist cities without land markets. *Journal of Urban Economics* 41(1).

Blanchard, Olivier, and Francesco Giavazzi. 2005. Rebalancing growth in China: A three-handed approach. Working Paper No. 05–32 (November). Cambridge, MA: Massachusetts Institute of Technology, Department of Economics.

Bourguignon, Francois. 2008. Growth, inequality and fiscal policy from a historical perspective: Are there lessons for China? In *Public finance in China: Reform and growth for a harmonious society,* eds. Jiwei Lou and Shuilin Wang, 269. Washington, DC: World Bank.

Brueckner, Jan. 2007. Government land-use interventions: An economic analysis. Keynote paper presented at the World Bank Urban Symposium (February).

Cai, Hongbin, J. Vernon Henderson, and Qinghua Zhang. 2009. China's land market auctions: Evidence of corruption. NBER Working Paper No. W15067 (June). Cambridge, MA: National Bureau of Economic Research.

Chamon, Marcos, and Eswar Prasad. 2008. Why are saving rates of urban households in China rising? Brookings Global Economy & Development. Working Paper No. 31 (December). Washington, DC: Brookings Institute.

Chiquier, Loic, and Michael Lea, eds. 2009. *Housing finance in emerging markets*. Washington, DC: World Bank.

Chiu, Rebecca L. H. 2001. Commodification of housing with Chinese characteristics. *Review of Policy Research* 18(1):75–95.

Cho, Man. 2011 Forthcoming. The mortgage market in Korea: Current state and challenges ahead. In *International Encyclopedia of Housing and Home*. Amsterdam: Elsevier.

Chow, Kenneth K., Matthew S. Yiu, Charles Ka Yui Leung, and Dickson C. Tam. 2008. Does the DiPasquale-Wheaton Model explain the house price dynamics in China cities? HKIMR Working Paper No. 21/2008. Hong Kong: Hong Kong Institute for Monetary Research.

Combes, Pierre-Philippe, Thierry Mayer, and Jacques-Francois Thysse. 2008 *Economic geography*. Princeton, NJ: Princeton University Press.

Commission on Growth and Development (Spence Commission). 2008. The growth report: Strategies for sustained growth and inclusive development. Washington, DC: World Bank.

Deng, Yongheng, and Peng Fei. 2009. The emerging mortgage markets in China. In *Mortgage markets worldwide,* eds. Danny Ben Shahar, Charles Ka Yui Leung, and Seow Eng Ong. London: Blackwell.

Ding, Chengri. 2004. Urban spatial development in the land policy reform era: Evidence from Beijing. *Urban Studies* 41(10):1889–1907.

———. 2007a. Policy and praxis of land acquisition in China. *Land Use Policy* 24:1–13.

———. 2007b. Policy and praxis of land acquisition in China. In *Urbanization in China in an era of rapid growth,* eds. Yan Song and Chengri Ding. Cambridge, MA: Lincoln Institute of Land Policy.

Ding, Chengri, and Gerritt Knapp. 2005. Urban land reform in China's transitional economy. In *Emerging land and housing markets in China,* eds. Chengri Ding and Yan Song. Cambridge, MA: Lincoln Institute of Land Policy.

Ding, Chengri and Yan Song. 2005. *Emerging land and housing markets in China*. Cambridge, MA: Lincoln Institute of Land Policy.

Djankov, Simeon, Edward Glaeser, Rafael La Porta, Florencio Lopez, D. E. Silanes, and Andrei Shleifer. 2003. The new comparative economics. Working Paper No. WPS 3054. Washington, DC: World Bank.

Dong, H. E., Zhiwei Zhang, and Wenlang Zhang. 2009. How large will be the effect of China's fiscal-stimulus package on output and employment? Working Paper No. WP2009–05 (March). Hong Kong: Hong Kong Institute for Monetary Research.

Duranton, Gilles. 2009. Are cities engines of growth and prosperity for developing countries? In *Urbanization and growth,* eds. Michael Spence, Patricia Annez, and Robert Buckley. Washington, DC: World Bank.

Ellickson, Robert. 2008. The mediocrity of U.S. government subsidies to mixed-income housing projects. Paper presented at the Conference on Land Policies and Land Rights. Lincoln Institute of Land Policy, Cambridge, MA (June 2–3).

Ellis, Luci. 2008. The housing meltdown: Why did it happen in the United States? Working Paper No. 259 (September). Monetary and Economic Department, Bank of International Settlements.

Fallis, George. 1985. *Housing economics*. Toronto: Butterworth-Heinemann.

Follain, James R., Patric H. Hendershott, and David C. Ling. 1987. Understanding the real estate provisions of tax reform: Motivation and impact. *National Tax Journal* 40 (September):363–372.

Fu, Yuming, Siqi Zheng, and Hongyu Liu. 2007. Explaining housing supply elasticity across Chinese cities. Working Draft (April).

Fujita, Masahito, Paul Krugman, and Tony Venables. 1999. The spatial economy: Cities, regions, and international trade. Cambridge, MA: MIT Press.

Glaeser, Edward L., and Joseph Gyourko. 2008. *Rethinking federal housing policy: How to make housing plentiful and affordable.* Washington, DC: AEI Press.

Glaeser, Edward L., and John M. Quigley, eds. 2009. *Housing markets and the economy: Risk, regulation, and policy.* Cambridge, MA: Lincoln Institute of Land Policy.

Gyourko, Joseph. 2009. The supply side of housing markets. *NBER Reporter.* Research Summary 2009, No. 2. Cambridge, MA: National Bureau of Economic Research.

Hatzius, Jan, and Michael A. Marschoun. 2009. Home price and credit losses: Projections and policy options. Goldman Sachs Global ECS Research, Global Economics Paper: 177. https://360.gs.com.

Hegedus, Joseph, Stephen K. Mayo, and Ivan K. Tosics. 1996. Transition of the housing sector in the East Central European countries. *Review of Urban and Regional Development Studies* 8:101–136.

Hendershott, Patric H. 1987. Tax changes and capital allocation in the 1980s. In *The effects of taxation on capital accumulation,* ed. Martin Feldstein, 259–294. Chicago: University of Chicago Press.

———. 1989. Comments on "Social Returns to Housing and Other Fixed Capital." *AREUEA Journal* 17 (summer):212–217.

Henderson, J. Vernon. 2003. The urbanization process and economic growth: The so-what question. *Journal of Economic Growth* 8(1):47–71.

———. 2005. Urbanization and growth. In *Handbook of economic growth*, vol. 1B, eds. Philippe Aghion and Steven N. Durlauf, 1543–1591. Amsterdam: North-Holland.

Hering, Laura, and Sandra Poncet. 2010. Market access and individual wages: Evidence from China. *Review of Economics and Statistics* (forthcoming).

Hoek-Smit, Marja. 2009. Housing finance subsidies. In *Housing finance policy in emerging markets,* eds. Loic Chiquier and Michael Lea. Washington, DC: World Bank.

Huang, Yasheng. 2008. *Capitalism with Chinese characteristics: Entrepreneurship and the state.* Cambridge, U.K.: Cambridge University Press.

Inman, Robert. 2004. Financing cities. NBER Working Paper No. 11203. Cambridge, MA: National Bureau of Economic Research.

Jaffee, Dwight M., and John M. Quigley. 2009. Housing policy, subprime mortgage policy and the Federal Housing Administration. In *Measuring and managing federal financial risk,* ed. Deborah Lucas. Cambridge, MA: National Bureau of Economic Research; Chicago: University of Chicago Press.

Jeske, Karsten, and Dirk Krueger. 2005. Housing and the macroeconomy: The role of implicit guarantees for government-sponsored enterprises. Working Paper No. 2005–15 (August). Atlanta, GA: Federal Reserve Bank of Atlanta.

Kim, Kyung-Hwan, and Bertrand Renaud. 2009. The global house price boom and its unwinding: An analysis and a commentary. *Housing Studies* (special issue) 24(1):7–24.

Krugman, Paul. 1991. *Geography and trade.* Cambridge MA: MIT Press.

Kuznets, Simon. 1955. Economic growth and income inequality. *American Economic Review* 49:1–28.

Lardy, Nicholas R. 2007. *China: Rebalancing economic growth.* In *The China balance sheet in 2007 and beyond,* ed. Nicholas R. Lardy. Washington, DC: Center for Strategic and International Studies and Peterson Institute for International Economics.

———. 2008. Financial repression in China. Policy Brief No. PB08–08. Washington, DC: Peterson Institute for International Economics.

Leaf, Michael. 2007. Chengzhongcun: China's urbanizing villages from multiple perspectives. In *Urbanization in China Critical issues in an era of rapid growth,* eds. Yan Song and Chengri Ding. Cambridge, MA: Lincoln Institute of Land Policy.

Lee, Jeong-Sik, and Yong-Woong Kim, eds. 1998. *Shaping the nation toward spatial democracies: Emerging issues and lessons from the past.* Seoul: Korea Research Institute for Human Settlements Press.

Lin, Jiabin. 2007. Characteristics of China's land system and its influence on the housing property market. Paper presented at the Seminar on Land Institutions and Housing Policy, International Experience and China's Reform. Development Research Center of the State Council of the People's Republic of China, Beijing (June 10).

Lin, Justin Yifu. 2008. Impact of the financial crisis on developing countries. KDI Public Lecture, KDI School of Public Policy, Seoul, Korea (October 31).

Lou, Jiwei, and Shuilin Wang, eds. 2008. Public finance in China: Reform and growth for a harmonious society. Washington, DC: World Bank.

Luo, Xubei and Nong Zhu. 2008. Rising income inequality in China: Race to the top. Working Paper No. WPS4700. Washington, DC: World Bank.

Maclennan, Duncan. 1992. *Housing economics.* London: Longman.

McKinsey Global Institute. 2009. *Preparing for China's urban billion.* Washington, DC: (March 1). http://www.mckinsey.com/mgi/publications/china_urban_summary_of_findings.asp.

Milanovic, Branko, and Lire Ersado. 2008. Reform and inequality during the transition, 1990–2005. Working Paper No. WPS4780 (November). Washington, DC: World Bank.

Mills, Edwin S. 1987. Has the United States overinvested in housing? *Areuea Journal* 15 (Spring):601–616.

———. 1989. Social returns to housing and other fixed capital. *Areuea Journal* 17 (Summer): 197–211.

Muellbauer, John. 2006. Property taxation and the economy after the Barker Review. *Economic Journal* 115 (March).

Naughton, Barry. 2007. *The Chinese economy: Transitions and growth.* Cambridge, MA: MIT Press.

Neutze, Max. 1977. *Urban development in Australia: A descriptive analysis.* Sydney: George Allen & Unwin.

OECD. 1983. *Managing urban change.* Paris.

Pardo, Claudio. 2009. *Housing finance mechanisms in Chile.* The Human Settlements Finance Systems Series. Nairobi, Kenya: UN Habitat.

Peterson, George E., and Patricia Clarke Annez. 2007. *Financing cities: Fiscal responsibility and urban infrastructure in Brazil, China, India, Poland and South Africa.* Los Angeles: Sage. http://go.worldbank.org/C1MC7Z5MH0.

Pozdena, Randall J. 1991. *The modern economics of housing.* Westport, CT: Quorum Books.

Quercia, Robert, and Yan Song. 2007. Housing migrants in rural China. In *Urbanization in China: Critical issues in an era of rapid growth,* eds. Yan Song and Chengri Ding. Cambridge, MA: Lincoln Institute of Land Policy.

Ravaillon, Martin, Shaohua Chen, and Youjuan Wang. 2008. Does the *Di Bao* program guarantee a minimum income in China's cities? In *Public finance in China: Reform and growth for a harmonious society,* eds. Jiwei Lou and Shuilin Wang. Washington, DC: World Bank.

Renaud, Bertrand. 1991. Housing reforms in socialist economies. Discussion Paper No. 125. Washington, DC: World Bank.

———. 1992. The housing system of the former Soviet Union: Why do the Soviets need housing markets? *Housing Policy Debate* 3(3):877–899. Reprinted in Russian in a special issue of *Voprosy Economiki* [Economic Issues], Moscow, September 1993.

———. 1995. The real estate economy and the design of Russian housing reforms. *Urban Studies* 32(8–9).

———. 2004. *Permanence and change: East Asian housing policies after 50 years.* Keynote lecture at the International Housing Conference Celebrating the 30th Anniversary of the Hong Kong Housing Authority, Hong Kong. http://www.housingauthority.gov.hk/hdw/ihc/pdf/new_pc50ahp.pdf.

———. 2008. Mortgage finance in emerging markets: Constraints and feasible development paths. In *Mortgage markets worldwide,* eds. Danny Ben Shahar, Charles Ka Yui Leung, and Seow Eng Ong. London: Blackwell.

———. 2009a. China's urbanization: The prism of housing reforms. *Journal of International Property Sciences* (March). http://umrefjournal.um.edu.my/publish/IJPS/.

———. 2009b. Housing policy constraints and risks in China. Paper presented at the Conference on Housing Policy and Housing Markets in China, Lincoln Institute of Land Policy, Cambridge, MA (May 18).

Rodrik, Dani. 2006. Goodbye Washington consensus, Hello Washington confusion? A review of the World Bank's *Economic Growth in the 1990s: Learning from a Decade of Reform. Journal of Economic Literature* 44 (December):973–987.

———. 2007. *One economics, many recipes: Globalization, institutions, and economic growth.* Princeton, NJ: Princeton University Press.

———. 2008. Spence christens a new Washington consensus. *The Economists' Voice* 5(3). http://www.bepress.com/ev/vol5/iss3/art4.

Saich, Tony. 2008. The changing role of urban government. In *China urbanizes: Consequences, strategies and policies,* eds. Shahid Yusuf and Tony Saich. Washington, DC: World Bank.

Shah, Anwar. Fiscal decentralization in developing and transition economies: Progress, problems, and the promise. Working Paper No. WPS 3282. Washington, DC: World Bank.

Song, Yan, Yves Zenou, and Chengri Ding. 2007. *The role of China's urbanizing villages in housing rural migrants.* In *Urbanization in China: Critical issues in an era of rapid growth,* eds. Yan Song and Chengri Ding. Cambridge, MA: Lincoln Institute of Land Policy.

Spence, Michael, Patricia Clarke Annez, and Robert M. Buckley, eds. 2009. Urbanization and growth. Washington, DC: World Bank.

Su, Ming, and Zhao Quanhou. 2006. The fiscal framework and urban infrastructure finance in China. Working Paper No. WPS 4051. Washington, DC: World Bank.

Taffin, Claude. 2007. Private and social rented housing: Basic principles and overview of practices in Europe. Joint State Council DRC–World Bank Workshop on Middle- and Low-Income Housing in China, Beijing (July 19).

———. 2009. The rental sector in housing policy and housing finance. Paper presented at the Shanghai Forum 2009. Fudan University, Shanghai (May 15–17).

Taylor, Lori L. 1998. Does the US still overinvest in housing? *Economic Review* (Federal Reserve Bank of Dallas), 2nd quarter. http://www.dallasfed.org/research/er/1998/er9802b.pdf.

Venables, Anthony J. 2009 Rethinking economic growth in a globalizing world: An economic geography lens. In *Urbanization and growth,* eds. Michael Spence, Patricia Clarke Annez, and Robert M. Buckley, Washington, DC: World Bank.

Wachter, Susan M. 2007. Comment on Jaffee and Quigley, "Housing Policy, Subprime Mortgage Policy, and the Federal Housing Administration." In *Measuring and managing federal financial risk,* ed. Deborah Lucas. Cambridge, MA: National Bureau of Economic Research; Chicago: University of Chicago Press.

Wang, Ya-Ping, and Alan Murie. 1999. *Housing policy and practice in China.* New York: St. Martin's.

Wei, Shang-Jin. 1997. Gradualism versus big bang: Speed and sustainability of reforms. *Canadian Journal of Economics* 30(4b):1234–1247.

Wolf, Martin. 2009a. Choices made in 2009 will shape the globe's destiny. *Financial Times,* January 6.

———. 2009b. What the G2 must discuss now that the G20 is over. *Financial Times,* April 7.

Wong, Christine, and Richard Bird. 2005. China's fiscal system: A work in progress. Working Paper No. 05–20. Atlanta, GA: University of Georgia, Andrew Young School of Policy Studies, International Studies Program. http://isp-aysps.gsu.edu/papers/ispwp0520.pdf.

Wong, Yue-Chim Richard. 1998. *On privatizing public housing.* Hong Kong Economic Policy Studies Series. Hong Kong: City University of Hong Kong Press.

World Bank. 1993. Housing: Enabling markets to work. Policy Report. Washington, DC.

———. 1996. From plan to market. World Development Report No. 241. Washington, DC. See especially chapter 3, "Property Rights, Enterprise Reforms and Privatization."

———. 1999. Urban development in China: An economic assessment. World Bank Policy Note to the Chinese Government (April). Washington, DC.

Yu, Zhou. 2006. Heterogeneity and dynamics in China's emerging urban housing market: Two sides of a success story from the late 1990s. *Habitat International* 30:277–304.

Zheng, Siqi, Matthew E. Kahn, and Hongyu Liu. 2009. Towards a system of open cities in China: Home prices, FDI flows and air quality in 35 major cities. NBER Working Paper No. 14751. Cambridge, MA: National Bureau of Economic Research.

Zoellick, Robert B., and Justin Yifu Lin. 2009. Recovery rides on the G-2. *Washington Post*, March 6.

Contributors

Editor

JOYCE YANYUN MAN
Director
Lincoln Institute of Land Policy
Peking University–Lincoln Institute
 Center for Urban Development and
 Land Policy

Professor of Economics
College of Urban and Environmental
 Sciences
Peking University
Beijing, China

Authors

SHLOMO ANGEL
Adjunct Professor of Urban Planning
Robert F. Wagner Graduate School of
 Public Service
New York University

Lecturer in Public and International
 Affairs
Woodrow Wilson School
Princeton University
Princeton, New Jersey

GREGORY CHOW
Professor
Department of Economics
Princeton University
Princeton, New Jersey

YONGHENG DENG
Professor of Real Estate and
 Finance
School of Design and Environment
National University of Singapore
 Business School

Director
Institute of Real Estate Studies
National University of Singapore

YIPING FANG
Academic Staff
Institute for Housing and Urban
 Development Studies
Erasmus University Rotterdam
The Netherlands

PENG FEI
General Manager
Department of Equity
 Investment
China Foreign Economy and Trade
 Investment Trust Co., Ltd.
Beijing, China

YUMING FU
Associate Professor
Department of Real Estate
School of Design and Environment
National University of Singapore

YOUQIN HUANG
Associate Professor
Department of Geography and
   Planning
Center for Social and Demographic
   Analysis
University at Albany
State University of New York
Albany, New York

JUAN JING
Research Fellow
Peking University–Lincoln Institute
   Center for Urban Development and
   Land Policy

Postdoctoral Fellow
College of Urban and Environmental
   Sciences
Peking University
Beijing, China

JOHN LOGAN
Professor
Department of Sociology
Brown University
Providence, Rhode Island

REBECCA M. LUTZY
Ph.D. Candidate
Woodrow Wilson School of Public and
   International Affairs
Princeton University
Princeton, New Jersey

LINLIN NIU
Assistant Professor
Wang Yanan Institute for Studies in
   Economics
Xiamen University
Fujian, China

DAVID REINGOLD
Professor and Executive Associate Dean
School of Public and Environmental
   Affairs
Indiana University–Bloomington

BERTRAND RENAUD
Principal
Renaud & Associates
McLean, Virginia

RONGRONG REN
Research Fellow
Investment Research Institute
National Development and Reform
   Commission
Beijing, China

YAN SONG
Associate Professor
Department of City and Regional
   Planning
Director
Program on Chinese Cities
The University of North Carolina at
   Chapel Hill

MIDORI VALDIVIA
Senior Financial Analyst
The Port Authority of New York and
   New Jersey
New York City

YAPING WANG
Professor in Urban Studies
Director
Scottish Centre for Chinese Urban and
   Environmental Studies
School of the Built Environment
Heriot-Watt University
Edinburgh, U.K.

LANLAN XU
Ph.D. Candidate in Public Affairs
School of Public and Environmental
   Affairs
Indiana University–Bloomington

CHENGDONG YI
Associate Professor
Department of Urban and Real Estate
   Management
Central University of Finance and
   Economics
Beijing, China

ZHANXIN ZHANG
Associate Professor
Institute of Population and Labor
    Economics
Chinese Academy of Social
    Sciences
Beijing, China

SIQI ZHENG
Associate Professor and Deputy Head
Department of Construction
    Management
Institute of Real Estate Studies
Tsinghua University
Beijing, China

Index

About the Lincoln Institute of Land Policy

The Lincoln Institute of Land Policy is a private operating foundation whose mission is to improve the quality of public debate and decisions in the areas of land policy and land-related taxation in the United States and around the world. The Institute's goals are to integrate theory and practice to better shape land policy and to provide a nonpartisan forum for discussion of the multidisciplinary forces that influence public policy. This focus on land derives from the Institute's founding objective—to address the links between land policy and social and economic progress—that was identified and analyzed by political economist and author Henry George.

The work of the Institute is organized in three departments: Valuation and Taxation, Planning and Urban Form, and International Studies, which includes programs on Latin America and China. We seek to inform decision making through education, research, demonstration projects, and the dissemination of information through publications, our Web site, and other media. Our programs bring together scholars, practitioners, public officials, policy advisers, and involved citizens in a collegial learning environment. The Institute does not take a particular point of view, but rather serves as a catalyst to facilitate analysis and discussion of land use and taxation issues—to make a difference today and to help policy makers plan for tomorrow. The Lincoln Institute of Land Policy is an equal opportunity institution.

113 Brattle Street
Cambridge, MA 02138-3400 USA

Phone: 1-617-661-3016 x127 or 1-800-526-3873
Fax: 1-617-661-7235 or 1-800-526-3944
E-mail: help@lincolninst.edu
Web: www.lincolninst.edu